Little Black Dress

A RADICAL FASHION

National Museums Scotland

Little Black Dress

A RADICAL FASHION

Edited by *Georgina Ripley*

Published in 2023 by
NMS Enterprises Limited – Publishing
a division of NMS Enterprises Limited
National Museums Scotland
Chambers Street, Edinburgh EH1 1JF

www.nms.ac.uk

Text and photographic images © as credited
(and see Acknowledgements, page 154)

British Library Cataloguing in Publication Data
A catalogue record for this book is available from the British
Library.

ISBN: 978-1-910682-27-2

This publication was developed alongside the exhibition *Beyond
the Little Black Dress*, 1 July–29 October 2023 (at National
Museum of Scotland, Chambers Street, Edinburgh EH1 1JF)

Book design and cover by Mark Blackadder.
Printed and bound in Great Britain by Bell & Bain Limited,
    Glasgow.

This product is made of material from well-managed forests
and other sources.

Cover, prelim and end page images
Front cover: © David Eustace: Dress by Gareth Pugh.
    Dress embellished with black bin bags, Autumn/Winter 2013.
Back cover: Dress, by Jean Muir for Jane & Jane, *c.*1964.
    National Museums Scotland K.2012.102. (Image © National
    Museums Scotland)
Page 2: Coco Chanel on the mirrored staircase at 31 Rue Cambon,
    Paris, 1965. Photographer Cecil Beaton. (© The Cecil Beaton
    Studio Archive at Sotheby's)
Page 160: Detail of Fig. 3.7 (page 62) Jean Muir Ltd, British,
    1966–1995. National Museums Scotland K.2005.649.1392.1
    and 2. (Image © National Museums Scotland)

Text credit
Page 70: From *Chroma* by Derek Jarman published by Vintage
    Classics. Copyright © Derek Jarman 1994. Reprinted by
    permission of The Random House Group Limited.

For a full listing of NMS Enterprises Limited – Publishing titles
and related merchandise, visit: **www.nms.ac.uk/books**

CONTENTS

FOREWORD

Dr Christopher Breward

DIRECTOR, NATIONAL MUSEUMS SCOTLAND

As the authors in this timely book demonstrate so clearly, the little black dress has become a constant in modern fashion's complex histories. Its simple form offers a dark mirror in which contemporary debates around beauty, identity and culture find reflection and distortion before the next age wipes the glass and remakes the image anew. I came of age, sartorially speaking, in the 1980s when pop culture was both rediscovering the classic looks of the 1950s and reshaping ideas of sexuality for the MTV and club generation. I remember that in London at least, the little black dress signified the retro-chic of a rediscovered café-culture, embodied by the commodified image of Audrey Hepburn, and a more gutsy reinvention of the torch-singer where, paired with boots, scarlet lipstick and sunglasses, its simplicity suited the style of a new wave of female pop icons from Sade to Madonna. Forty years on, its meanings have shifted once more and, as the following chapters suggest, the LBD (an acronym that suits the politics of now) embraces a new energy, pulling even fewer punches.

These are times, of course, in which pulling no punches has become a shorthand for survival. The book itself is testament to the resilience of its editor and contributors, and National Museums Scotland in which the project was conceived and delivered. All of us were faced with the unprecedented challenges of the global pandemic, and the exhibition plan which has driven the research and approach of the book has had to be postponed several times. We are pleased that it now has a slot in our future programme and our thanks go to Baillie Gifford for their sponsorship of the exhibition. The prescience of the subject matter, however, means that the publication should come first and I am delighted with the originality and range of the book's content. Here we can read about the symbolic meanings of black garments in the past; the appeal of the LBD to 20th-century fashion designers in Paris, Milan, London and New York; its particular history in the evolution of avant-garde fashion in Japan; the sexual connotations which the LBD has always carried; its role as a canvas for technological innovation; and its future as a vessel for revolutionary change, particularly in relation to those questions of equality that frame current thinking around race, gender and the environment.

It is, of course, fitting that a museum should

initiate work on the transformation of the LBD, especially one with a significant fashion collection. For while a key appeal of the LBD and the secret of its longevity is its simple graphic nature, lending its form to striking abstraction and fetishization through advertising, film and photography, its three-dimensional materiality offers it up as the perfect sartorial palimpsest. To arrange one dress form, in one colour, through its iterations over the years, allows the curator to construct a timeline of the utmost purity, reducing dress to an aesthetic algorithm or a sequence of specimens – to be closely examined, admired and compared. The idea is a beautiful one, but real life is messier than that and I am pleased this book, and the exhibition to follow, embrace contradiction and complexity, for the LBD is nothing if not a vital, challenging concept. The task of disrupting its status as a barely changing fashion 'classic' is long overdue and it is time both to appreciate beauty, but also to acknowledge its underlying power.

The final chapter of the book, in drawing on responses from several respected curators, educators, collectors and fashion professionals, shows how the LBD inspires divergent perspectives and opinions.

Georgina, our Principal Curator and editor, set me the same questions asked of our contributors, but of course I have a conflict of interest, both as museum Director and as a historian of masculinities and fashion! Nevertheless, I can't resist the challenge. The essence of the perfect LBD for me lies in its striking, sometimes terrifying simplicity. When I think of it, I think of the sublime images of Princess Diana in Christina Stambolian's dress at the Serpentine Gallery fundraising gala during the very public playing out of her separation from the Prince of Wales in 1994. The press named it the 'Revenge' dress, and it certainly captures the operatic sense of drama that black often evokes for me. It is perhaps that 'statement' quality which lends the LBD to design interpretation again and again. Like a bold signature in black ink, the LBD is a cipher for character and personality: costumed calligraphy. In that sense its formal qualities are not so far removed from my own territory – the masculine suit. The LBD and the suit are almost translations of each other. Yves Saint Laurent's famously bisexual *Le Smoking* tux for women bridges the gap. Both are fashion 'myths' in the true meaning of the word.

Tarana Burke, Michelle Williams, America Ferrera, Jessica Chastain, Amy Poehler, Meryl Streep, Kerry Washington, Natalie Portman, Ai-jen Poo, Saru Jayaraman at the 2018 InStyle and Warner Bros Pictures Golden Globe Awards after party held at The Beverly Hilton Hotel on 7 January 2018 in Los Angeles.

(Image Press Agency / Alamy Stock Photo)

WELL-MANNERED BLACK?
FASHION, FEMININITY AND FEMINISM

Georgina Ripley

In 1926, Gabrielle 'Coco' Chanel designed a simple, short black *crêpe-de-Chine* dress described in American *Vogue* as 'the frock that all the world will wear'.[1] Its origins were radically modern: it disregarded convention as much in its stark design as its sombre shade, previously associated with mourning. Yet the little black dress (or LBD hereafter) subsequently became a wardrobe staple, each morphing silhouette capturing the spirit of its time. It has been both an 'invariable of convention and propriety' and a metaphor for cosmopolitan glamour, but today's avant-garde iterations signal new concepts of modernity.[2] From Dutch designer Iris van Herpen's little black Magma dress (2016 *Lucid* collection), stitched from 5000 3D-printed elements, to CuteCircuit's groundbreaking *Graphene Dress* (2017), incorporating the Nobel Prize-winning material to capture breathing patterns in colour-changing LEDs, the LBD proves to have an infinite capacity for reinvention.

In his 2012 exhibition on the LBD, fashion editor André Leon Talley called it 'undoubtedly the 20th century's greatest fashion phenomenon'; but how will it fare throughout this century as it approaches the centenary of its ahistorical mythic creation?[3] Once a symbol of femininity, how do we now position the LBD in the wake of women's empowerment movements such as 'me too' and Time's Up, which have elevated the global consciousness around women's issues and gender inclusivity and equality? How will the LBD evolve as technological developments and material innovation drive fashion towards a more sustainable future? This future is even more uncertain as the industry attempts to predict what recovery will look like following the destabilizing effects of the Covid-19 pandemic. Aesthetically, the emotive response to the pandemic has manifested on fashion's catwalks in variously apocalyptic and dystopian themes, satirical rejoinders to the imposition of national lockdowns, or colourful kitsch prints, as a desire for escapism and frivolous grandeur coincided with a sombre and reflective mood. As social freedoms began to be restored across parts of Europe in the spring of 2021, Francesco Risso's Autumn/Winter 2021 collection for Italian house Marni notably began with dyeing fabrics black before laying them out in the sun with flowers and other objects laid on top of them; the resulting sun-bleached prints layered with saturated colour engendered the metaphor of light emerging from darkness.[4]

This chapter explores how the blank canvas of the LBD reflects changing ideals of beauty and propriety throughout the last century, and how each permutation redresses gendered constructs to reflect modern issues surrounding femininity. In conjunction with the other chapters in this book, it aims to consider the communicative power of black's many subtle and often contradictory nuances of meaning, as articulated by Amy Holman Edelman:

> … black is the colour most often chosen to cloak the pious and those devoted to spiritual sacrifice. It reflects the humility of a nun's habit and the practical endurance of servants and livery. The flip side of black suggests a darker nature. The black arts, black magic, the blackest night – all calling up references to mystery, magic, and inevitably, a little bit of sin.[5]

Interpretations of black

Black is the 'colour' of fascism, of anarchy, of mourning and of melancholy. It is sinister – associated with night, death and evil.[6] Black is both serious, connoting respect and diligence as in the black worn by religious orders, and rebellious as in the black leather and latex of punk and fetish subcultures. Black is sophisticated yet charged with eroticism. It is both pious and perverse.[7]

Perhaps this is the secret behind its appeal; fashion journalist Marc Bain observed that 'its singular darkness has a unique visual potency, and its adaptability has long made it open to interpretation by the numerous groups that have adopted it'.[8] To that end, we have commissioned essays from acclaimed international scholars, curators and fashion writers, who delve deeper into the multifaceted phenomenon of the little black dress. Iain R Webb takes us on a journey through the salons and ateliers of the 20th century's most innovative and influential designers of the LBD. Makoto Ishizeki considers the unique and cerebral approach taken by Japanese designers to fashion in the 1980s, and how their ubiquitous use of the colour black was received by the Western fashion press – set against the background of dualism between the West and Japan. Fiona Jardine's chapter explores material as a means through which to approach histories of subcultural style – such as eroticised black latex, associated with dissident sexualities and with various subcultural codes, styles and tastes. Pamela Parmal's chapter interrogates the intervention of smart technology in fashion as digital mapping, 3D printing and bio-engineering enable material innovation and customised production, establishing a blueprint for a more sustainable future.

In chapter 2, Lynne Hume reveals the influence of the religious sphere and its multitudinous belief systems on the fashion for black. Much of the controversy surrounding the colour lies in the influence of religious thought on Western society's relationship to black. The Bible links black to sin, death, evil and mourning, yet it is also worn to demonstrate temperance, humility and asceticism. The overwhelming presence of Roman Catholicism in the Middle Ages meant that 'the portrayal of black was greatly contingent upon the religious views of the Church on good and bad, or good and evil, thus the creation of the "devil's colour"'.[9] By the mid-11th century, depictions of the devil were as common in Romanesque art as images of Christ, with one commonality – the devil universally wore a cloak of black. The historic association of black with satanic cults and witchcraft is further rooted in the early Middle Ages, when witches (habitually portrayed as women) were believed to be in league with the devil.[10] Hume's chapter, exploring how 'black as the personification of the dark unknown has morphed into a trope of evil, engendering fear', thus follows on from this one to lay the foundations for modern interpretations of black.

The origin of the little black dress

Beginning in the 19th century, the women's suffrage movement, followed by the First World War, precipitated a new trajectory for women in society. While the extent to which ideologies of domesticity and standards of morality were overthrown during the war has been grossly exaggerated, the inevitable disruption of the existing social and economic hierarchy did come to be reflected in women's wardrobes.[11] The 20th-century fashion revolution had already begun in the first decade of the century, fluctuating in accordance with the whims of social history. The *Belle Époque*'s vision of *froufrou* seductiveness was replaced in two stages: through the *Directoire* period, which developed the old corseted look into a straight but sinuous line, and with the trend for 'Orientalism' led by designer Paul Poiret, concurrent with promotion of a new slender figure. In May 1908, *Vogue* described how the 'long skirt ... reveals plainly every line and curve of the leg from hip to ankle. The petticoat is obsolete, pre-historic. How slim, how graceful, how elegant women look! The leg has suddenly become fashionable.'[12] The shortened hemlines of the 1920s were the next step in the modernisation of women's dress, but, as the fashion historian Valerie Steele noted, they 'bore the symbolic weight of a whole set of social anxieties concerning the war's perceived effects on gender relations'.[13] It was within this context that Chanel revealed her radical, short, black dress, which was to become the defining symbol of modernity.

Chanel's famous LBD appeared in an illustration in American *Vogue* on 1 October 1926 [Fig. 1.1]. A simple long-sleeved day dress, falling below the knee and free from superfluous decoration, it borrowed the concepts of function and comfort from menswear and its durability from service uniforms. It was an example of what Paul Poiret called Chanel's characteristic 'poverty *de luxe*' – an expensive interpretation of a modest design, combining humble origins with couture details. The *Vogue* editorial compared the design of Chanel's model '817' black dress to Ford's mass-produced motor car, emphasising how these designs would become standard wear for the masses. Yet Chanel was not solely responsible for inventing the LBD – plenty had existed before hers, not to mention many of her own designs prior to 1926, which appeared across issues of American and French *Vogue*. While black was 'a central element in her modernist design philosophy', and she often wore black herself – especially following the death of her lover Arthur Boy Capel in 1919 – she did not singlehandedly make black fashionable.[14] In 1918, *Vogue* called black 'at once aloof and alluring, daring and dignified', while Florence Hull Winterburn's *Principles of Correct Dress,* written in 1914, dedicated a chapter to black tailor-made gowns:

> A black silk velvet costume, perfectly tailored, is rich enough for any occasion, and lasts for years. If a woman can have but one very costly toilette, and goes out a good deal, she will not err in owning such a gown. It replaces with the modern women the 'best black silk frock' of our grandmothers, which was worn carefully the first two or three years and for second best thereafter.[15]

Why then did Gabrielle 'Coco' Chanel come to spearhead a radical transformation of fashion and lifestyle that effectively overwrote the existing history of the LBD? 'As Poiret changed the shape of women, Chanel changed the shape of fashion,' Ernestine Carter wrote, remarking upon how Chanel personified 'the essence of the post-First World War mood – independent, arrogant, and a flouter of convention'.[16] As a style icon herself, she embodied a new type of fashion designer, one who Steele has observed 'combined in her person the hitherto masculine role of the fashion "genius" with the feminine role of fashion leader'.[17] Indeed, her attitude to style was arguably more important than the contributions to fashion for which she has now garnered mythic status as sole creator – from the LBD to trousers for women, or the popularisation of costume jewellery. Nevertheless, the enduring legacy of the quintessential Chanel look makes it difficult to conceive just how radical her approach – and that of her peers, male and female – was in its time. Extravagant costume jewellery inverted ideas of luxury by challenging notions of preciousness. She incorporated a practical, masculine-style of pocket into womenswear, formerly functional features of workmen's dress. More than a decade earlier she had elevated the fisherman's jersey, previously used in the manufacture of men's underwear, to the rarefied realm of haute couture,

Fig. 1.1 (overleaf)
Illustration of Chanel's little black dress by Main Rousseau Bocher, *Vogue*, 1 October 1926.

in a similar bid to modernise women's clothing.[18] Chanel's creations were underlined with ideas of practicality and freedom, and nothing was to be superfluous: 'A dress must function; place the pockets accurately for use, never a button without a buttonhole.'[19] The essence of her clothing encapsulated the minimalist, streamlined aesthetic characteristic of the Modernist movement sweeping across decorative arts and architecture, which defined itself in opposition to the past. In short, women throughout the Western world had a new image of themselves that made the ostentatious elegance of the pre-war period look old-fashioned – and Chanel offered a modern alternative of luxury.[20]

Fashion for black

Steele writes that the fashion for black developed in Italy as early as the 14th century before spreading throughout the courts of Europe, from Philip the Good, Duke of Burgundy (1396–1467) in mourning for his murdered father after 1419, to the Spanish Emperor Charles V (1500–1558) and his son, Philip II (1527–1598). Catherine de Medici (1519–1589), queen consort of Henry II of France (1547–1559) and subsequently regent of France (1560–1574), earned the moniker 'The Black Queen', alluding both to her alleged dabbling in black magic and her choice to dress all in black after the death of King Henry II in 1559, despite the traditional custom for French queens to wear white mourning (a custom that continued until the 17th century). In Northern Europe, the Protestant countries of the Netherlands and England encouraged the rise of black clothing in European society. However, it was in the 19th century that the fashionable status of black for both men and women took a decisive turn.

The psychologist John Carl Flügel described a 'great masculine renunciation' of ostentatious dress among men of taste, brought about by the rise of industrialisation and democracy.[21] As Christopher Breward wrote, 'Serious times called for sober dressing' and the rising professional classes are said to have adopted a black uniform.[22] At the same time, the dandy – primarily a social phenomenon of elite men who dressed with good taste – became known as 'the black prince of elegance', lending romantic connotations to black.[23] Social historian David Kuchta, who roots the simplification of the male wardrobe much earlier in the mid-17th century in connection with philosophical and religious debates, nonetheless affirmed the notion that dandyism participated in, rather than resisted, the move towards more sober suiting.[24] Black only became the general custom for mourning in the 19th century. The introduction of synthetic dyes made it cheaper to produce black fabrics and, as Hume writes in the following chapter, Queen Victoria 'turned mourning into an art form'. Yet as black became more prominent, there was an important distinction to be made between the rich black of the ruling classes and the 'respectable' black worn by the lower classes. As artistic depictions of wealthy *Belle Époque* women showed them in fashionable black reception dresses and luxurious evening gowns, the urban working woman was adopting her own simple black dress, in coarse, matte fabrics – a style soon to be appropriated by Chanel.

The fashion historian Valerie Mendes suggested that the little black dress was born sometime in the early 1900s and particularly came under fashion's spotlight following the death of King Edward VII.[25] The ensuing commemorative 'Black Ascot' united London society in mourning – a historic moment that partly informed the cinematic spectacle of Cecil Beaton's black-and-white Ascot costumes for the 1964 musical *My Fair Lady*. Black Ascot marked an occasion where 'the convention of self-effacement in unflattering clothes of undistinguished cut' was all but abandoned and young women were no longer criticised for pursuing fashionable mourning.[26] Shortly after, widespread mourning during the First World War made black ubiquitous. Fashion magazines praised the 'many little models in black', while in 1922 Maison Premet produced 'a plain boyish-looking little slip of a frock, black satin with white collar and cuffs',[27] named *La Garçonne* after the bestselling scandalous novel by Victor Margueritte that told the story of a brazenly independent 'new woman'. According to *Paris on Parade,* Madame Premet's LBD achieved 'probably the most sensational success reached by any individual dress model of recent years' and that 'counting both licensed and illegitimate reproduction, a million *Garçonnes* were sold over the earth'.[28] It is interesting that Madame Premet has not been given more credit in the story-telling surrounding the LBD, but she undoubtedly helped to set the scene for the arrival of Chanel's LBD in 1926.

The cocktail hour

It is likely no coincidence that female designers such as Chanel, Alix (latterly Madame Grès), Jeanne Lanvin, Madeleine Vionnet and Elsa Schiaparelli, among many others, flourished after the war. From a range of social and professional backgrounds, they were themselves representative of the rising number of women entering the workforce and were thus perhaps more in touch with the changing needs of modern women. In Talley's 2012 exhibition catalogue, Robin Givhan wrote:

> In choosing to wear black, women were shunning the fussiness, frills, and constraints imposed upon them by society .... They were no longer forced into the role of the brightly coloured peacock decorating the room .... The black dress redefined femininity and

sexuality, turning both into a force that was controlled – not completely, but more satisfyingly – by the woman herself.[29]

That was until, in 1947, Christian Dior's 'New Look' revived a voluptuous femininity in women's dress. In his autobiography Dior wrote: 'I designed clothes for flower-like women, with rounded shoulders, full feminine busts, and hand-spun waists above enormous spreading skirts' – a look that on the surface of things seemed determined to return women to the domestic sphere.[30] It coincided with a new generation of overwhelmingly male Parisian couturiers, itself emblematic of new social attitudes shaped by the economic environment. Fashion designer Anne Fogarty's etiquette guide of 1959, *The Fine Art of Being a Well-Dressed Wife,* advocated that 'the first principle of wife-dressing is Complete Femininity – the selection of clothes as an *adornment*, not as a mere covering'.[31] In an increasingly consumerist society, clothes were once again eroticised commodities and women sexualised objects.[32] Anne Hollander noted it propelled female sexual fantasy 'back into the vast world of erotic submission and narcissism disguised as modesty, the world of long hair bound up only to be unbound, of tightly girdled waists waiting for male deliverance, of myriad skirts hiding the prizes'.[33] It was the antithesis to everything Chanel's simple little black dress had stood for, representing a time when it was impossible to be both fashionable and comfortable. As Fogarty observed: 'Elegance and queenly bearing go hand in hand with constraint. You're not meant to suffer; but you are supposed to be "aware". After-five wear is not meant for acrobatics.'[34]

Reverting to an old tradition, Dior's creations were often heavily lined with cambric or taffeta, causing Chanel to question, 'Was he mad, this man? Was he making fun of women? How, dressed in "that thing", could they come and go, live or anything?'[35]

Yet it chimed with the tendencies of the times, eliciting a psychological stimulus following 'the *garçonne* of Chanel, the *belle laiderie* of Schiaparelli and the years of wartime restriction and uniforms' which left many yearning to fall back into the ultra-feminine habits associated with happier days.[36] Dior asserted that he 'brought back the neglected art of pleasing',[37] and dreamt of making women more beautiful – a thinly veiled dig, perhaps, at the female-led fashions of the inter-war years and what they had come to represent. However, this was a different time. The Second World War had replaced much of the fuss and frivolity of evening dressing with a little black dress, in part due to fabric shortages; post-war the LBD was to become synonymous with the cocktail hour. By the time Dior wrote *The Little Dictionary of Fashion* in 1954, he described cocktail dresses as 'especially elaborate and dressy afternoon frocks', preferably in black taffeta, satin, chiffon and wool [Fig. 1.2].[38] These dresses became so ubiquitous that Fogarty advised avoiding black, saying 'I hate to wear black for cocktails ... because every other woman seems to be wearing black too'.[39]

In an era of already formalised dressing, the cocktail hour quickly became a prescribed daily ritual for which society women required a new wardrobe. *Vogue* reported in December 1935:

> There is hardly a day when anybody in London society does not have an invitation to cocktails – and they are becoming a very highly specialised form of entertainment .... Just before six o'clock all the smart women return home to change their hats, before starting out for their cocktail rendezvous. Yes, you must now have a hat consecrated to the cocktail hour.[40]

The mid-20th century LBD was not complete without its accoutrements, of which the hat was,

Fig. 1.2
Ligne Longue cocktail dress, by Christian Dior Paris, Haute Couture Autumn/Winter 1951. National Museums Scotland K.2018.3.1 and 2.

(Amelie Blondel / Artdigital Studio / Sotheby's)

Fig. 1.3
Cocktail hat by Christian Dior Paris, 1947–57.
Manchester Art Gallery 2018.153.
(Image courtesy of The Gallery of Costume,
part of Manchester Art Gallery)

according to Dior, considered 'the quintessence of femininity'.[41] Cocktail hats were the fanciest of all, embroidered or bedecked in flowers, feathers or ribbons [Fig. 1.3]. Gloves were equally important, with etiquette guides dedicated to when to wear black or white pairs, wrist-length or elbow-length. Chanel famously flouted convention but thought a suit 'naked' without jewellery. Her return to prominence in the 1950s revived demand for costume jewellery in high fashion, inspired by her collabor-ations with craftsman like Robert Goossens and ornate Renaissance-inspired jewellery supplied by Maison Gripoix, with whom Chanel had worked be-fore the war. The simple silhouettes, plain fabrics and muted colours of Chanel's designs formed the ideal background to offset her costume jewellery, much as Schiaparelli had deemed black to be the perfect ground to the extravagant embellishments created for her by Maison Lesage. This is an un-changing fact of design – the Bluetooth-enabled little black *Nieves Dress* (2018) by Francesca Rosella and Ryan Genz of CuteCircuit combines black silk organza with inserts of laser-cut, colour-changing polyurethane film and their luminous Magic Fabric, embedded with thousands of programmable micro-LEDs [Fig. 6.7]; the play of light effectively mimics

Fig. 1.4
Lily-of-the-Valley brooch by Francis Winter for
Christian Dior, made in France, late 1940s.

(William Wain Collection)

the effect of Chanel's faux jewels, or Schiaparelli's witty embroideries. Unlike Chanel and Schiaparelli, Dior designed much of his own jewellery, but he also collaborated with master jewellers such as Gripoix, Mitchel Maer and Francis Winter, who would re-imagine motifs such as Dior's favourite flower and lucky charm (lily-of-the-valley) in diamanté [Fig. 1.4], or poured glass and gilded metal. Dior advocated women 'use jewellery generously to get the most out of it'; and jewellery sets of matching necklace, bracelet, brooch and earrings became *de rigueur* to complete the evening ensemble.[42]

Royal rebels in black

If the rules of dressing were stringent for the modern middle-class woman, they were – and still are – even more restrictive for the Royal Family. While not strictly prohibited, wearing black has traditionally been reserved for mourning or to denote respect, such as a black ensemble by Norman Hartnell in the Royal Collection designed for Queen Elizabeth II

(1926–2022) for a 1962 State Visit to meet Pope John XXIII in Vatican City. Consisting of a long dress of black lace, with a silk tulle and lace mantilla to cover the head, it respects the convention whereby heads of state wear black when in audience with the Pope.[43] Black was so little a part of the everyday royal wardrobe that it has reportedly been a rule since the mid-20th century that members of the Royal Family must take a black ensemble with them when they travel abroad, so that they might dress appropriately in the event of a family bereavement.[44]

That is not to say Queen Elizabeth II did not wear black purely for fashion's sake: a fashion sketch by Norman Hartnell for the Princess Elizabeth depicts an elegant LBD in the New Look style, accessorised with the requisite strands of pearls and black evening gloves. Presumably there was greater freedom in fashioning a princess than a head of state. Princess Margaret (1930–2002), whose bohemian life was part of a social revolution that would shake both the country and the Royal Family, is often referred to as the 'royal rebel'. She commissioned many a startling couture number in black – such as the black silk and wool faille cocktail dress with sequin and diamanté-embroidered straps by Norman Hartnell in the Victoria and Albert Museum's collection.[45] But she was by no means the only rebellious royal: her uncle, King Edward VIII (1894–1972), famously abdicated the throne in 1936 in order to marry two-times divorcée Wallis Simpson. Sir Roy Strong wrote that 'the world of the Duke and Duchess of Windsor was one of calculated high fashion', and the Duchess was certainly an advocate for the LBD, once saying, 'When the little black dress is right, there is nothing else to wear in its place'.[46]

Preconceptions around the colour black mean that the LBD carries with it a hint of rebelliousness deemed unsuitable for royalty – or, as journalist Chloe Fox described it, 'a flirtatious sartorial call to arms for women unafraid to stand apart from the crowd'.[47] No royal LBD has harnessed that more successfully than Diana, Princess of Wales' (1961–1997) little black 'Revenge' dress. She wore the dress by Christina Stambolian, with the off-the-shoulder sweetheart neckline, ruched body, and daring asymmetric above-the-knee hemline, to attend the Serpentine Gala on the night the former Prince Charles' confession of adultery aired on television. Diana wore black on other occasions – for example, a dynamic fashion sketch by David Sassoon in the Royal Collection indicates a fashionable LBD from 1984 [Fig. 1.5], but none has generated quite so many headlines. More recently, Meghan, Duchess of Sussex's notable fondness for black spawned countless articles analysing the possible reasons for her wardrobe choice. Despite the, at times, scandalous press each royal style icon has attracted, fashion and celebrity are, to quote Fox, 'close bedfellows' and 'for more than almost any equivalent item of clothing, the increase in popularity of the LBD can be directly linked to the profiles of the women who wore it'.[48] There is no such thing as bad press in the ascendance of the LBD.

Popular culture and the little black dress

Fashion does not exist in a vacuum, and a 'classic' cannot be called such until its image reverberates through popular culture.[49] The LBD is one such garment established in the collective imagination. It was, and still is, used as a costume device in Hollywood, an industry which has historically projected new ideas of the female image. In chapter 3, Iain R Webb points to Luis Buñuel's erotically charged *Belle de Jour* (1967) as being a source of inspiration to fashion designers such as Tom Ford. It tells the story of Séverine, a naïve and sexually unfulfilled housewife, who realises her fantasies by taking afternoon work as a high-class prostitute. In her final

scene, her acquired sexual sophistication is implicit in her LBD by Yves Saint Laurent [Fig. 1.6]; its contrasting white silk collar and cuffs are curiously prim and schoolgirlish – hinting at both her former buttoned-up life and the film's reproachful denouement. Historically, getting one's first black dress was considered a rite of passage, and as black denoted maturity, and thus the association of sexual experience, it often signified immorality in popular literature. In Edith Wharton's *Age of Innocence* (1920), Mrs Archer questions the moral character of the scandalous Countess Ellen Olenska, asking, 'What

Fig. 1.5 (above)
Fashion sketch by David Sassoon for Princess Diana, 1984.
(© Historic Royal Palaces)

Fig. 1.6 (right)
Actress Catherine Deneuve as Séverine Serizy and Jean Sorel as Pierre Serizy in the film *Belle de Jour* (1967, Luis Buñuel).
(John Springer Collection / Getty Images)

can you expect of a girl who was allowed to wear black satin at her coming-out ball?'[50] In *Anna Karenina* (1877), when the protagonist appears at the Moscow ball where Count Vronsky falls in love with her, she is wearing a 'low-necked black velvet gown which exposed her full shoulder and bosom that seemed carved out of old ivory'.[51] While the reader is to understand her appearance to be charming on the surface, it is Leo Tolstoy's intention to present Karenina as a sexual being and thus a doomed figure, '[invoking] the power of the black dress to signal both acute sexual readiness and tragic distinction'.[52]

This description of the black gown against ivory skin is telling: Steele calls black 'the fetishist colour *par excellence* because of its cultural associations with sin and evil, and because of the way it contrasts with white skin'.[53] John Singer Sargent's portrait *Madame X,* depicting socialite Madame Gautreau in a décolleté black satin evening gown with barely there jewelled straps, exposing her unnaturally pale aristocratic skin, scandalised Paris society in 1884.[54] There are many theories as to why: that Madame Gautreau had a reputation for promiscuity, her make-up was too obvious, her pose suggestive, or because, as originally exhibited, her dress strap was painted slipping from her right shoulder (and was latterly painted over). Yet Edouard Manet had already exhibited *Olympia* in 1865, a painting of a nude woman assumed to be a prostitute, causing *The Guardian* art critic Jonathan Jones to conclude that in the case of *Madame X* 'it was the dress that caused distress', for 'money and sex are both flaunted by a fashion utterly incompatible with bourgeois life'.[55] While Jones' opinions are often divisive, his question of why Sargent's painting should prove more controversial than Manet's is pertinent, for it speaks to the deep-rooted erotic associations of black that sit uncomfortably alongside its connotations of piety, virtue and mourning. As black mourning garb was once intended to publicly signal social and sexual

unavailability, perhaps it was this very marking out of a woman as forbidden fruit that inspired a seductive allure to black.[56]

Women's Liberation

Following almost a decade of Dior's sculptural feats of sartorial engineering, Cristóbal Balenciaga's refreshingly simple chemise dresses, achieved with a singularity of line, were arguably the equivalent of Chanel's LBD from three decades before. Iain R Webb's chapter notes how Balenciaga's customers all attested how comfortable and easy his clothes were to wear, no matter 'how simple or startling' the design. In 1955, *Vogue* reported:

> A significant struggle is taking place in Paris. On the one side there are designers whose achievement is to create clothes of so strong a shape that they look as if they could walk across the room alone ... on the other side there are designers whose clothes are not superimposed on a body: they have no existence apart from it.[57]

A new chapter was dawning in fashion. Mirroring the socio-political upheaval that was leading a sexual and sartorial revolution, not only was the reign of Dior's New Look in decline, but the rising tide of ready-to-wear was about to upend the couture industry.

The beginning of second-wave feminism was credited to the publication of Betty Friedan's *The Feminine Mystique* in the USA in 1963. Friedan challenged the widely shared belief that 'fulfilment as a woman had only one definition for American women after 1949 – the housewife-mother'[58] – and women's dress responded accordingly to this quest for sexual and social emancipation. Where the constricting and concealing nature of 1950s' fashions had formerly been considered 'aesthetically, socially, and above all sexually satisfying', Hollander noted how they became 'really insupportable only as the social agreement and sexual fantasies of men and women changed their terms'.[59] The counterculture of the 1960s and ensuing revolution in social norms – in dress, music, drugs and sexuality – caused some to lament the decay of social order. The Women's Liberation movement of the late 1960s was implicit in this, as historian Susan Glenn wrote:

> Unlike the suffragist who tried to convince the public that the typical activist was as pretty and charming as an actress, many ... 1960s feminists made a spectacle of abandoning the trappings of middle-class white feminine beauty (high heels, make up, coiffed hair, girdles, bras and high fashion) and flaunting a range of counter-cultural looks and images.[60]

It is worth cautioning against crediting the 'Swinging Sixties' too heavily with the single sartorial liberation of women, much as we must exercise the same caution with the 'Roaring Twenties'. The regressive decade of the 1950s had overshadowed the important inroads already made by women in education, employment and winning the vote. This led to the assumption that there was no freedom in female clothing before the 1960s, dismissing the impact of Chanel's LBD on fashion entirely.[61] But fashion of the 1960s and '70s did reflect anti-establishment feeling and political disillusionment, much as it later retaliated against the fitness-crazed, skimpy, padded, corseted and sculpted creations of the '80s, which amounted once again to a 'travesty' of womanhood. This retaliation was led in part by the weaving of Japanese philosophy into Western design, as outlined in Makoto Ishizeki's chapter

exploring the legacy of Japanese designers Rei Kawakubo, founder of Comme des Garçons, and Yohji Yamamoto. Kawakubo's first Paris catwalk in 1981 interrupted fashion's *Dynasty*-style glamour with a collection of black shapeless garments with asymmetric hems and distressed fabrics, and was attacked by critics on a political level, labelled as 'Hiroshima chic' or 'post atomic'. Yet Kawakubo, alongside Yohji Yamamoto and Issey Miyake, elevated the fashionable status of black once again, and collectively their work challenged contemporary notions of femininity shaped by the overtly sexual, high glamour of leading labels like Versace.

The little black dress and sexual politics

Hallmarks of subcultural style have been steadily assimilated into mainstream fashion and inevitably reflected in the design of the little black dress, from the anti-establishment ethos of the Beatnik generation and the rebellion of punk, to the darkness of gothic fashion as explored in Lynne Hume's chapter, or the sex appeal of fetishwear as discussed by Fiona Jardine (chapter 5). Fetishism's influence on fashion catwalks is clear – from thigh-high 'kinky boots' and corset lacing, to *The Avengers*-inspired leather catsuits, or Madonna's conspicuously erotic S/M imagery realised by Jean Paul Gaultier. In 1992, *Vogue* wrote: 'Today bondage, leather, rubber, "second skins", long, tight skirts, split dresses, zipped *boutines* – everything from a fetishist's dream – is available directly from Alaïa, Gaultier, Montana, Versace ...'.[62] Versace's famous dress for Liz Hurley in 1994, sutured with silver and gold-toned safety pins, took on the effects of punk fabrication and body apertures. Richard Martin, formerly Curator at The Costume Institute, wrote, 'We had been accustomed for more than 60 years to see the little black dress as an etiquette covering, sublimating and all but eliminating the body. Versace instead gives primacy to the body in deep décolletage and the bare expanses threatening to disprove the partial closure of the safety-pins.'[63] It was audaciously erotic, a gesture which, to quote Martin, 'was to throw the little black dress into the fray and furore over propriety from which it stemmed'.[64]

Scottish designer Christopher Kane stood out for his Autumn/Winter 2018 collection redressing the notion of propriety in the little black dress [Fig. 1.7]. With explicit references to *The Joy of Sex* by Alex Comfort (1972), it fearlessly tackled 'the troubled relationship with sex embodied by this moment in time'.[65] That moment was mere months after Jodi Kantor and Meghan Twohey broke the story of sexual harassment allegations against film producer Harvey Weinstein in *The New York Times* on 5 October 2017. It was just one month on from the 75th Golden Globe awards, when Hollywood's most high-profile stars turned the red carpet into a sea of black in support of the Time's Up campaign that aims to end sexual harassment and gender disparity across the USA [pp 8–9]. It was just weeks after a group of women in the US congress followed their lead, donning black for the first state of the union address by President Trump, who had himself been accused of sexual misconduct. Anders Christian Madsen's show report described how Kane's garments 'responded with a *déshabillé* panache: erotic lace slips, bat-winged dominatrix leather dresses, and nipped-in power tailoring with cut-outs galore'.[66] The lace – which both reveals and conceals in the manner of fetishwear – and the frequent use of zips recalled both fetishist and punk signifiers. Like both these subcultures, Kane's collection designated an overriding message of empowerment – the notion that women can reclaim both their sensuality and their sexuality in the wake of the 'me too' movement. While each look felt sexually suggestive, Madsen argued that 'this sexually volatile time has made us

Fig. 1.7
Christopher Kane, Look 31 Ready-to-Wear
Autumn/Winter 2018.
(© Chris Moore Catwalking)

all so aware of our own gaze that [we are] looking at old signals with new eyes'.[67] Though other collections that season alluded to the sex-centric zeitgeist, Kane's broke the silence on harassment culture. As Madsen questioned: 'What constitutes sexy clothes in a world where Time's Up? And are we even supposed to call them "sexy" anymore?'

Designers have returned time and again to the cocktail dress, reworking it with concepts that highlight the complexity of contemporary femininity. Moschino's teddy bear-embellished LBD of 1988 poked fun at 1980s' excess. Gareth Pugh famously turned bin bags into ball gowns for his Autumn/Winter 2013 collection [Fig. 1.8]: specifically chosen for their very cheapness, it could be argued this recalls a hint of Chanel's ethos in turning a typical maid's dress into a symbol of upper middle-class elegance. Woven into extraordinary forms, their texture was almost raffia-like, literally transforming trash into treasure. For Autumn/Winter 2015, Pugh's dresses hand-embroidered with black plastic drinking straws created thorny, intimidating exoskeletons in a macabre reimagining of the little black cocktail dress.[68] Fashion, so intricately meshed with society, is invested with political meaning. The season in which Kane addressed harassment culture, Nicole Phelps reported that Marc Jacobs' high-impact, 1980s-inspired glamour aligned the period to the times we are living in, 'with the tax cut for the ultrarich and the rolling back of everything from reproductive rights to environmental regulations'.[69] While Jacobs called attention to the regressive nature of global politics through his retro clothing, Angelo Flaccavento's round-up of the Paris Spring/Summer 2020 couture week – notably the last before the Covid-19 pandemic temporarily shuttered the industry – concluded that 'the best collections were a homage to tradition, reverting back to shapes and ideas from the "Golden Age" of the 1950s and 1960s'.[70] He saw this collective return to

couture's roots as a love letter to the 'last bastion of the old-world order',[71] a time when Balenciaga and his peers dressed women with restraint and sophistication. Showing on the eve of Britain's troubled exit from the European Union, in a world fractured by war, refugee crises, the fear of far-right political ascendancy, increasing threat to LGBTQIA+ rights, and the climate crisis, was fashion in fact seeking solace in anachronism?

The LBD, for its very purity of expression, carries more onus than any other garment to encapsulate the zeitgeist. Designer Muiccia Prada once said that 'designing a little black dress is trying to express in a simple, banal object, a great complexity about women, aesthetics, and current times'.[72] The retro style of Prada's LBD from Spring/Summer 2009 [Fig. 1.9], considered in juxtaposition with a silk taffeta haute couture cocktail dress from Dior's Autumn/Winter 1951 collection [Fig. 1.2], recalls the overt femininity of the post-war period with its ruched brassiere, boned bodice and below-the-knee pencil skirt. The period of the 2008 Great Recession, declared the worst recession since the Great Depression of the 1930s, thus mirrored the post-war economic upheaval that resulted in Dior's reinstatement of femininity in dress.[73] Prada's spring collection concept was 'going back to what counts'. Sarah Mower's show report asked:

> And what counts most in a back-to-basics time, when most of us will need truly visceral temptation to get us out and shopping? Why, glamour and eroticism, of course. When the chips are down, there is no one who can turn up the thermostat of subversive sexual provocation quite as high as Mrs Prada.[74]

It is no coincidence then that, amid a pandemic, the Spring/Summer 2021 catwalks reflected a renewed optimism in disco-inspired glamour, as sequin, lamé

and lurex looks appeared at high-profile houses such as Louis Vuitton, Balmain and Chanel. Fashion trends for 2021 have been rooted in the risqué, with seductive cut-out detailing, crop-tops and body-conscious dressing marketed as the antidote to the booming athleisure and loungewear industries that profited during long periods of at-home isolation.

Towards a sustainable future

If modern fashion acts, to quote Hollander, 'as the illustration of modern civilization's discontents', it follows that it must address consumers' urgent concerns over sustainability to secure its future.[75] More broadly, the far-reaching effects of the Covid-19 pandemic and the international Black Lives Matter protests in response to the murder of George Floyd in 2020 have amplified ongoing conversations around diversity, inclusivity and systemic racism in the fashion industry, as well as issues of social responsibility and cultural appropriation, ethical production and environmental impact. Prior to the pandemic and the ensuing disruption to supply chains, sales and consumer habits, the narrative backdrop to the fashion catwalks was the climate crisis, and the industry's impact on people and the planet were arguably 'all the more keenly felt during such a catastrophic year for human life'.[76] The global fashion industry is one of the most energy-consuming, polluting and wasteful of modern industries. The material innovation of designers like Iris van Herpen, whose interdisciplinary collections incorporate inventive sourcing and ingenious manipulation of high-tech materials, or Yuima Nakazato's biocouture, introducing fermented microbes and digital fabrication into the hallowed halls of haute couture, is therefore not a gimmick of technology but rather a call to arms to rethink the status quo. Pamela Parmal, in chapter 6, thus builds on earlier

Fig. 1.9 (above)
Prada, Look 22 Ready-to-Wear Spring/Summer 2009.
(© Chris Moore Catwalking)

Fig. 1.8 (opposite)
Gareth Pugh, Look 47 Ready-to-Wear Autumn/Winter 2013.
(© Chris Moore Catwalking)

research for the exhibition *#techstyle* at the Museum of Fine Arts, Boston, which considered how the art of innovation – from clothes that respond to the environment, fabrics patterned by lasers and ready-to-wear garments produced by a 3D printer – are poised to have a profound impact on the future of fashion. Within this future, the LBD perhaps has potential to be a vehicle for change: just as the fashionable black dress became a practical and versatile option for women in wartime, doubling up as mourning wear and a formal afternoon dress, today it is still considered an essential of the aspirational capsule wardrobe. A versatile garment suited to all occasions – Dior once famously declared, 'You can wear black at any time. You can wear black at any age. You may wear it for almost any occasion. A "little black frock" is an essential to a woman's wardrobe'[77] – is the LBD the secret to slow fashion? And what then is the male equivalent?

These questions are considered in the final chapter that acts as a companion piece to this one, tracing the significance of black across cultures, geographies, genders and identities to confront history's Eurocentric vision of the LBD. Global case studies are interwoven with anecdotes from collectors, designers and scholars to consider what is behind the enduring appeal of the LBD, and what lies in its future. After all, the success of the little black dress is in part its combination of timeless chic with current fashion, and in today's fast-paced fashion world it has achieved the status of being above the fray.[78] The reign of the LBD over fashion has waxed and waned – in July 1995, *W* magazine asked, 'Aren't you *really* ready to tear off the basic blacks that have been shrouding your body basically practically since the dawn of time?'[79] Yet Karl Lagerfeld's Autumn/ Winter 1995 collection marked its re-emergence, with a modern, timeless silhouette in black, which was not black for black's sake but, according to Lagerfeld, 'black as in chic' – associations it has held ever since the image of Audrey Hepburn wearing Givenchy's LBD in *Breakfast at Tiffany's* became the ultimate symbol of inestimable style in 1961 [Fig. 1.10].[80] Over the last century, the LBD has, to take Amy Holman Edelman's view,

… become a uniform that expresses a modern woman's contradictions and celebrates her independence. It is emblematic of a woman's freedom of choice, her equal participation in the world, and her declaration that, this time, she is dressing for herself. The little black dress is an indication … of how far a woman has come from being merely a prettily dressed object.[81]

Acknowledgement

I am indebted to Carys Wilkins for her advice on the sections relating to jewellery.

Fig. 1.10 (opposite)
Breakfast at Tiffany's (1961, Blake Edwards), Paramount film with Audrey Hepburn.
(Pictorial Press Ltd / Alamy Stock Photo)

Notes

1   Anon., 'Vogue introduces Coco Chanel's LBD', Vogue (1926), p. 69.
2   André Leon Talley, Little Black Dress (2012), p. 11.
3   Ibid.
4   Osman Ahmed, 'Marni AW21 appears via a fashion show on Zoom', i-D (2021): <https://i-d.vice.com/en_uk/article/k7avqm/marni-aw21-appears-via-a-fashion-show-on-zoom>
5   Amy Holman Edelman, The Little Black Dress (1998), p. 30.
6   Lynne Hume, in chapter 2, highlights that black is not technically a colour; rather it represents the absence, or complete absorption of visible light, thus lending itself to binary meanings in relation to white, and taking on negative connotations accordingly.
7   Valerie Steele, The Black Dress (2007).
8   Marc Bain, 'Only black is the new black: a cultural history of fashion's favourite shade', Quartz (2018): <https://qz.com/quartzy/1194798/only-black-is-the-new-black-a-cultural-history-of-fashions-favorite-shade/>
9   Michel Pastoureau, Black: The History of a Color (2008), p. 46.
10 Leah M Provo, 'The Little Black Dress: The Essence of Femininity' (2013), p. 10.
11 Valerie Steele, Fashion and Eroticism: Ideals of Feminine Beauty from the Victorian Era to the Jazz Age (1985), p. 234.
12 In Vogue (May 1908), quoted in Steele, Fashion and Eroticism (1985), p. 227.
13 Steele, The Black Dress (2007).
14 Mary Louise Roberts, 'Samson and Delilah Revisited: The Politics of Women's Fashion in 1920s France', in The American Historical Review 98:3 (1993), p. 661.
15 Florence Hull Winterburn, Principles of Correct Dress (1914), p. 199.
16 Ernestine Carter, The Changing World of Fashion, 1900 to the Present (1977), p. 37.
17 Valerie Steele, 'Chanel in Context', in Juliet Ash and Elizabeth Wilson (eds), Chic Thrills: A Fashion Reader (1992), p. 123.
18 Two years after she began making jersey sweaters, Chanel produced the Biarritz collection, a groundbreaking line of jersey tailoring, made from a batch of machine-made jersey purchased at a substantial discount from textile manufacturer Jean Rodier. In August 1916, British Vogue wrote: 'Paris can think of but two things – war and jersey; for jersey is no longer a fabric, it is an obsession.' In October, Vogue proclaimed that in Chanel's hands, jersey had attained the 'distinction of being a classic tissue'. See Bronwyn Cosgrave, Vogue on Coco Chanel (2012).
19 Ann Montgomery, Another Me: A Memoir (2008), p. 157.
20 Steele, Fashion and Eroticism (1985), pp. 216–17.
21 Christopher Breward, The Suit: Form, Function & Style (2016), p. 15.
22 Ibid., pp. 15, 27.
23 For further reading on the dandy, see Valerie Steele, Paris Fashion: A Cultural History (2017 [orig. 1998]), pp. 79–93.
24 David Kuchta, The Three-Piece Suit and Modern Masculinity: England, 1550–1850 (2002), p. 252.
25 Valerie Mendes, Black in Fashion (1999), p. 9.
26 Ibid.
27 Robert Forrest Wilson, Paris on Parade (1926 [1925]), p. 53.
28 Ibid.
29 Quoted in Talley, Little Black Dress (2012), p. 17.
30 Christian Dior, Dior by Dior (2007 [1956]), pp. 22–23.
31 Anne Fogarty, Wife Dressing: The Art of Being a Well-Dressed Wife (2011 [1959]), p. 6.
32 Susan Glenn discusses the relationship between clothes as eroticised commodities and women as sexualised objects in her book Female Spectacle: The Theatrical Roots of Modern Feminism (2000), p. 165.
33 Anne Hollander, Sex & Suits: The Evolution of Modern Dress (2016 [1994]), p. 126.
34 Fogarty, Wife Dressing (2011 [1959]), p. 117.
35 Valerie Steele, Women of Fashion: Twentieth Century Designers (1991), p. 49.
36 Carter, The Changing World of Fashion (1977), p. 38.
37 Dior, Dior by Dior (2007 [1956]), pp. 27, 36.
38 Christian Dior, The Little Dictionary of Fashion: A Guide to Dress Sense for Every Woman (2008 [1954]), p. 24.
39 Fogarty, Wife Dressing (2011 [1959]), p. 118.
40 Josephine Ross, Society in Vogue: The International Set between the Wars (1992), p. 57.
41 Dior, The Little Dictionary of Fashion (2008 [1954]), p. 54.
42 Ibid., p. 64.
43 Royal Collection Trust, RCIN 250458.
44 The Netflix original series The Crown, which follows the reign of Queen Elizabeth II, dramatised the occasion that prompted the regulation. In 1952 her father, King George VI, unexpectedly passed away while Elizabeth was visiting Kenya and she was unable to disembark the aeroplane on returning to the United Kingdom until suitable clothing could be brought to her.
45 Victoria and Albert Museum (V&A), T.238-1986.
46 Roy Strong, Cecil Beaton: The Royal Portraits (1988); Chloe Fox, Vogue Essentials: Little Black Dress (2018), p. 6. Manchester Art Gallery collection, 2007.23: a narrowly corded, black silk-faille ensemble, comprising bodice and two separate skirts, one narrow and one wide, commissioned by Wallis Simpson from Christian Dior, Paris, in 1949. Two sketches and one model photograph from the Dior Archives identify a very similar outfit from spring/summer 1949, Ligne Trompe L'oeil.
47 Fox, Vogue Essentials (2018), p. 83.
48 Ibid., p. 10.

49   Edelman, *The Little Black Dress* (1998), p. 96.

50   Edith Wharton, *The Age of Innocence* (2008 [orig. 1920]), p. 34.

51   Leo Tolstoy, *Anna Karenina* (1999 [orig. 1877]) (translated by Louise and Aylmer Maude), p. 77.

52   Anne Hollander, 'The Little Black Dress' (1984), p. 86: <http://www.anne-hollander.com/wp-content/uploads/2015/02/The-Little-Black-Dress-Connoisseur-1984.pdf>

53   Steele, *The Black Dress* (2007).

54   *Madame X (Madame Pierre Gautreau),* by John Singer Sargent, 1883–1884, oil on canvas, The Metropolitan Museum of Art, New York, Arthur Hoppock Hearn Fund, 1916 (16.53).

55   Jonathan Jones, 'Madame XXX', *The Guardian* (2006): <https://www.theguardian.com/culture/2006/feb/01/3>

56   Provo, 'The Little Black Dress' (2013), p. 22.

57   Georgina Howell, *In Vogue: Six Decades of Fashion* (1975), p. 288.

58   Betty Friedan, *The Feminine Mystique* (2013 [1963]), pp. xi–xx. In 1957, Friedan was asked to conduct a survey of her former Smith College classmates for their 15th anniversary reunion. The results, in which she found that many were unhappy with their lives as housewives, prompted her to begin research for *The Feminine Mystique*, conducting interviews with other suburban housewives, as well as researching psychology, media, and advertising.

59   Hollander, *Sex & Suits* (2016 [1994]), p. 103.

60   Glenn, *Female Spectacle* (2000), p. 221.

61   Hollander, *Sex & Suits* (2016 [1994]), p. 110.

62   Quoted in Valerie Steele, *Fetish: Fashion, Sex & Power* (1995), p. 33.

63   Richard Martin, 'A Note: Gianni Versace's Anti-Bourgeois Little Black Dress (1994)', in *Fashion Theory: The Journal of Dress, Body & Culture* 2:1 (1998), pp. 95–100.

64   *Ibid.*

65   Anders Christian Madsen, 'Christopher Kane Autumn/Winter 2018 Ready-to-Wear', *Vogue* (2018): <https://www.vogue.co.uk/shows/autumn-winter-2018-ready-to-wear/christopher-kane>

66   *Ibid.*

67   *Ibid.*

68   Tim Blanks, 'Gareth Pugh Fall 2015 Ready-to-Wear', *Vogue* (2015): <https://www.vogue.com/fashion-shows/fall-2015-ready-to-wear/gareth-pugh>

69   Nicole Phelps, 'Marc Jacobs Fall 2018 Ready-to-Wear', *Vogue* (2018): <https://www.vogue.com/fashion-shows/fall-2018-ready-to-wear/marc-jacobs>

70   Angelo Flaccavento, 'At Paris Couture, History Over Hype', *Business of Fashion* (2020): <https://www.businessoffashion.com/reviews/fashion-week/at-paris-couture-history-over-hype/>

71   *Ibid.*

72   Quoted in Talley, *Little Black Dress* (2012), p. 69.

73   National Museums Scotland, K.2018.3.1-2.

74   Sarah Mower, 'Prada Spring 2009 Ready-to-Wear', *Vogue* (2008): <https://www.vogue.com/fashion-shows/spring-2009-ready-to-wear/prada>

75   Hollander, *Sex & Suits* (2016 [1994]), p. 19.

76   Hayley Spencer, 'Dressing after times of crisis: What can we learn about post-pandemic fashion from the 1920s', *Independent* (2021): <https://www.independent.co.uk/life-style/fashion/pandemic-fashion-roaring-twenties-trends-b1819559.html>

77   Dior, *The Little Dictionary of Fashion* (2008 [1954]), p. 14.

78   Edelman, *The Little Black Dress* (1998), p. 140.

79   Quoted *ibid.*, p. 88.

80   *Ibid.*, p. 41.

81   *Ibid.*, p. 149.

2

SPIRITUAL BLACK

Lynne Hume

When Coco Chanel introduced the little black dress as a fashion item in 1926, she may not have foreseen the longevity of its potency. Not only was its tenacity maintained throughout the 20th century but it has continued into this century, changing and adapting according to the ingenuity of contemporary designers. One of the myriad sources designers have at their disposal to draw upon for inspiration is the religious sphere with its multitudinous belief systems stretching from monotheism to polytheism, offering a wellspring of inspiration.

However, religious dress is principally a symbol of religious affiliation, an outward representation of inner beliefs, one that often incorporates long-term commitment to certain wearing apparel. It has been suggested that fashion is 'the art of borrowing creatively transformed'.[1] So, when designers turn to religious clothing as a possible spark for creative innovation, where do they search and what happens to religious garb in the transition from sacred to secular? What are the religious meanings behind clothing that is subsequently selected by designers to create the 'look' that finally appears on the catwalk?

The religious focus here is Roman Catholic Christianity on the one hand, and Western occultism and modern Paganism on the other, and how certain fashion designers have creatively borrowed from the distinctive clothing and accoutrements of these disparate groups to shape innovative designs that bridge the sacred and the secular. Before focusing on the fashion design aspect of religious garb, its underlying sacred meanings will be discussed, along with their significance to the wearers.

The 'colour' black

Strictly speaking, black is not a colour – it is the absence of colour. Binary opposites such as good/ bad, purity/evil, are symbolically and pictorially symbolised by white/black. Black clothing has been linked variously with death, mystery, sensuality, evil and the occult, yet also with secular notions such as sophistication, 'power dressing', and professionalism. In Buddhism, black signifies the primordial darkness. For Christians, black is closely linked to death, grief and mourning; it is the liturgical colour for Good Friday which commemorates the death of Christ, whereas white originally signalled purity and virginity. However, some cultures employ white for funeral wear (China). The popularity of black in fashion is therefore somewhat of a mystery itself.

Black for mourning

In the Christian religion, black as a signifier of death and grieving reached its fashion peak in 19th-century Britain, during the reign of Queen Victoria (1837–1901). This was a time of significant social, economic and technological change, characterised by changes in fashion, the arts and literature; it was also the nascence of the science and art of photography. The death of Queen Victoria's beloved husband Albert, in 1861, turned mourning into an art form [Fig. 2.1], and funerals were sombre occasions that displayed death in all its macabre glory.

The public, outward sign of a widow's bereavement took on the shape of the infamous 'widow's weeds'. No matter which period of the Victorian fashion era, a woman in mourning wore a full floor-length dress with long sleeves, appropriate head-covering, and black shoes and gloves. Friends, relatives and domestic staff of the newly deceased were expected to be covered entirely in heavy black garments in respect for the deceased and to avoid bad luck. Bespoke boutiques specialising in fashion for funerals were at their height. Modesty was prescribed during the whole Victorian era, with ladies'

arms and legs being covered and skirts reaching to the ankles; any deviation from this and a woman was branded as 'loose' and subjected to social ostracism.[2] Often this led to women being encased in punitive corsets and weighed down under the heavy burden of copious layers of fabric, a look that has often inspired contemporary fashion. The designer Olivier Theyskens' black silk taffeta moiré, full-length, gothic-inspired gown from the Autumn/Winter 2019 ready-to-wear collection [Fig. 2.2], is reminiscent of this Victorian style of full mourning. A black silk coat-style evening dress by Karl Lagerfeld for Chanel's Autumn/Winter 2003 haute couture collection [Fig. 2.3] similarly portrays a streamlined version of the total body coverage in women's black mourning garb, softened by a waterfall of white chiffon ruffles at neck, cuffs and front of hem.[3] Religious themes ran throughout this show in other ways too: set in a 17th-century convent, the backdrop added narrative emphasis to the medieval-inspired lace skull caps and legion of black floor-length coats that evoked the priest's cassock.[4]

Black was *de rigueur* in the Victorian era even for decorative additions such as ribbons and accoutrements such as umbrellas, fans and purses. A wide variety of fabrics was available for different occasions: crêpe, silk, linen, satin, twilled and plain cotton, worsted and cotton hose, grosgrain, and gloves made of lace and silk, but crêpe surpassed all others as the favoured fabric for deep mourning.[5] Yards and yards of this material, its crinkled lustreless surface imitating the lifelessness of a corpse, filled the drapery shops for the entire period of Queen Victoria's reign after the death of Prince Albert. A full mourning bonnet in the 1890s might consist of bands of black crêpe placed over a stiffened foundation or bonnet, a knot and a semi-circular black tulle veil to hide the mourner's face. Thus dressed, the woman was completely hidden from view: a figure in black, gliding along with not a flash of flesh.

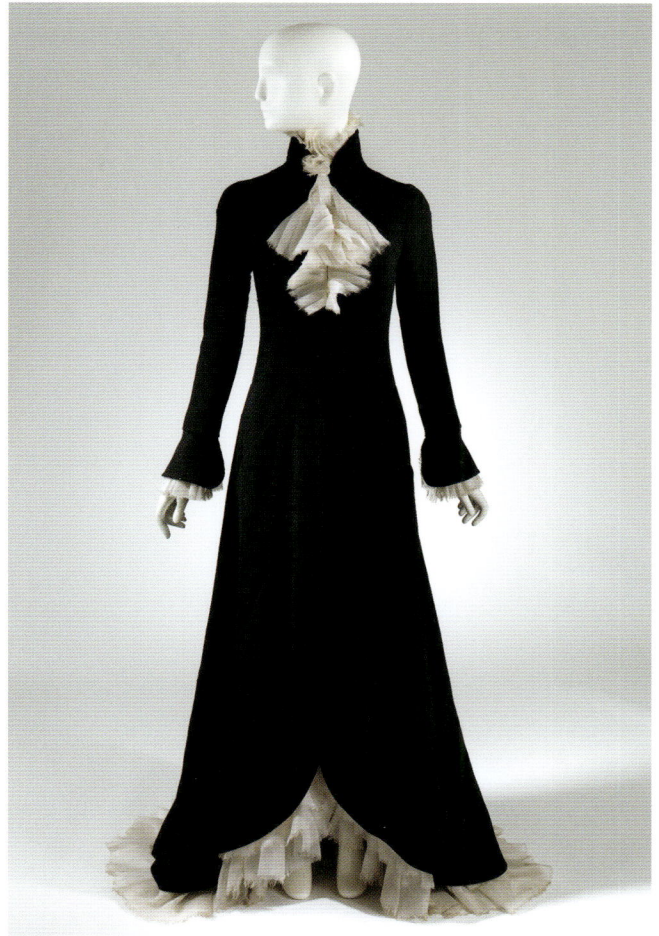

Fig. 2.3 (above)
Karl Lagerfeld for Chanel, Haute Couture Autumn/Winter 2003.
(Image copyright The Metropolitan Museum of Art / Art Resource / Scala, Florence)

Fig. 2.1 (opposite)
The Hessian children with their grandmother Queen Victoria.
(Royal Collection Trust / © His Majesty King Charles III 2023)

Fig. 2.2 (overleaf)
Olivier Theyskens, Look 38 Ready-to-Wear Autumn/Winter 2019.
(On loan from Olivier Theyskens.
Image © National Museums Scotland)

Men's mourning dress was not nearly as demonstrative as that of women, even that of a widower. Mourning suits of black frock coats with matching trousers and waistcoats were usual, worn with gloves, black cravats, and the black top hat, often with the addition of a fashionable walking cane. The onus of responsibility for the upholding of the moral order in relation to mourning garb thus fell on women's shoulders, particularly those of the widow.

Christianity and the Roman Catholic Church

In the early years before Christianity became a full-fledged religion, followers of Jesus Christ wore clothes that were simple and practical. Some of the garments still worn today, such as the alb (a simple, full-length white robe), were traditionally made of linen, wool or a cotton blend and can be traced directly to ancient Roman clothing. Throughout Christianity's history there have been overt displays of rich vestments, expensive fabrics such as silk, furs such as ermine, precious gems and gold thread, all in stark contrast to those early humble beginnings. However, such wealth of garments has uniquely graced the male body, articulating not only hierarchy but male focus and power. Today, each rank is made vividly apparent by the use of specific colours for vestments: black for seminarians, deacons, priests and chaplains; purple for bishops, prelates and promontories; crimson for cardinals; and white for the supreme representative and head of the Roman Catholic Church, the Pope. A collection of cardinals provides onlookers with a splendid sea of red and white vestments.[6]

A distinction is made between non-liturgical and liturgical clothing. The latter are sacramental vestments, which are set apart and blessed by the Church, allowing the wearer to perform sacred duties associated with their rank. By the act of attentive dressing in vestments, the wearer is reminded of the sacred nature of his position, and the sacred powers received; to the Roman Catholic lay person, seeing such dress is believed to emote good thoughts and increase devotion. In addition to the colours associated specifically with hierarchical ranks are those which pertain to specific celebrations in the Catholic liturgical year: purple or violet during Advent and Lent and, along with white and black, they may also be used for the funeral Mass; white and gold at Christmas and Easter; red for feasts of the Passion of Jesus and for the Holy Spirit, representing red tongues of fire, and for the feasts of martyred saints who shed their blood for Christ; rose pink at the Third Sunday of Advent and the Fourth Sunday of Lent, worn as a sign of anticipated joy.

A complete account of the history and significance of clothing items worn by all sections of the Roman Catholic Church is too extensive to describe here, so in this instance the focus is on items which fall under the rubric of 'spiritual black', and which have inspired fashion designers. Catholicism's attention to black, principally in the form of those at the base of the pyramid of importance, is evident in the priest's cassock, and that of the women religious, the nun's habit.

The cassock

Also known as a *soutane*, worn by the clergy as early as the 5th century, the cassock became the standard daywear outside church ceremonies for prelates and priests. Hierarchy was again indicated by colour: the pope, white; cardinals, red; bishops, archbishops and other prelates, purple; ordinary clergy, black. The cassock comes in many styles or cuts, though no particular symbolism attaches to these variations. At its most simple, worn outside church ceremonies, the cassock consists of a long-sleeved, ankle-length robe with a trim black collar and 33 buttons from neck to hem representing the number of Christ's earthly years.

When engaged in religious ceremonies an officiant wears the liturgical vestments of his rank, and any appropriate additions. In the case of priests the stole is added, which symbolises the bonds and fetters with which Jesus was bound during his Passion (Christ's final day of suffering prior to the crucifixion). Although the stole may be embroidered at each end, often with a cross, the cross is prescribed for the centre of the stole and is ceremonially kissed before it is carefully added to his cassock. There are no extra precepts concerning the material of the stole, but silk, or at least a half-silk fabric, is most appropriate. Black shoes complete the ensemble which is topped with a *biretta* (clerical cap).

In many countries the black cassock was the normal everyday wear of the clergy until the 1950s. The Second Vatican Council (1962–1965) – commonly referred to as Vatican II – brought about changes in virtually all aspects of Catholic life. The main goals of the Council were to bring the Church in line with the modern world, to attempt to create a new vision of ecumenism and to reinterpret the liturgy in order to encourage participation of all members of the true Catholic Church.[7] Among the sweeping reforms that ensued were those that pertained to ecclesiastical dress, creating what William J F Keenan called a 'seismic shift'.[8] In many cases in the West, the cassock was replaced by clothes that are indistinguishable from the lay population. Church expectations were only that priestly clothing be characterised by simplicity and modesty, avoiding worldly vanity. Some still prefer dress that is generally black, such as a black shirt incorporating a clerical collar. Today, the cassock is less used in the West except for religious services, with the exception of clergy in traditionalist Catholic Orders.

The habit of Roman Catholic women religious

In contrast to religious vestments of men, the dress of the Roman Catholic religious woman today is devoid of colour, being almost always wholly black or black and white, articulating her lowly status and her deep commitment to holy and modest clothing. In the early 8th century, however, there was relatively little difference between the dress of the clergy and that of the laity; many of the female religious Orders were composed of ladies of rank, used to dressing for life in the world rather than in cloistered confines, a world that would have included the wearing of fine clothes. In the 8th century this became a subject of concern to St Aldhelm (*c.*639–709), who wrote disparagingly of such grandeur:

> Silk underclothing ... scarlet tunics and hoods, sleeves with silk stripes, shoes edged with fur; hair carefully arranged on forehead and temples with the curling iron – this is the modern habit. Dark veils yield to headdresses white and coloured, sewn with long ribbons and hanging to the ground, fingernails are sharpened like the talons of hawks or owls seeking their prey.[9]

St Aldhelm declared that such luxury was excessive and 'hateful to God'. Particular condemnation was given to dresses whose colours were scarlet or purple, as these colours were considered to lead to 'lust, unholy intercourse, indifference to reading and prayer, and the ruin of souls'.[10] By the 12th and 13th centuries in Europe, chastity and virginity were expected of women, and became highly desirable qualities. The chaste and enclosed woman was personified in the figure of the nun, sleeping alone in a small, sparse cell, with only thoughts of her bridegroom, Christ.

'Habit' refers to the ensemble of black and white clothing and accessories worn by women who have taken the three perpetual vows of poverty, chastity and obedience within an institute approved by the Church. Though the habit can vary from one Order of Roman Catholic women religious to another, there is a classic image of the habit that is universal: starched white linen headbands and wimples, floor-length heavy woollen or heavy cotton dresses, and flowing black veils. To those donning the habit, it is an outward visible sign of a sacred life devoted to God and Jesus. While outsiders may regard the habit as a symbol of patriarchal domination, those wearing it invariably see it as a wearable sacramental linking them to the subject of their devotion, and silently conveying a link from past to present. They are wearing clothes that are imbued with significance, are deeply meaningful, and they wear them with respect and honour. Wearing the habit is accompanied by a sense of dignity and of belonging to a religious community.[11]

The headpiece is made up of three parts: a white coif (form-fitting skull cap) and bandeau (band across the forehead), and the black veil that drapes from the coif to flow down the nun's back. The wimple is the small white piece that covers the neck and upper chest. The long-sleeved black tunic, long enough to reach the ground, is secured with a woollen belt which holds a set of rosary beads. Worn over the belted tunic is the scapular, an apron that covers both the back and front of the tunic and falls free. The nun usually wears a cross around her neck and a silver ring on her left hand to indicate that she has taken perpetual vows and is a bride of Christ. Practical, common-sense black shoes complete the outfit. Nuns' habits vary slightly depending on the religious Order, with the most striking variations seen in the headgear (for example, the unusual white-winged cornet of the Daughters of Charity).

The items that make up this modest, austere apparel are meaningful symbols of their spiritual commitment. The belt is a reminder that Christ wore chains; the scapular represents commitment to take on the 'yoke of the Lord'; the veil is the sign of the nun's consecration. The veil and coif cover the nun's hair to protect her from vanity and to remind her that she is given fully to God.

Vatican II relaxed some of the clothing restrictions that were formerly fixed for women religious. However, it was not always an easy transition for the women themselves. For some it was a liberating experience which made easier their practical work in the modern world; others did not want to discard this ultimate symbol of their lives. For the latter it was confusing and emotionally draining.[12] Since Vatican II, Catholic nuns in some Orders place less emphasis on the importance of wearing a habit but still maintain clothing that is simple and non-ostentatious.

The habit revisited and reinvented

Monastic black-and-white clad nuns have long been alluring subjects for writers and film-makers, variously portraying them as figures of fun, authoritarian, or close to angelic. They have also sparked the creative impulse of fashion designers. Under the label Cimone, designer Carli Pearson's contribution to the Metropolitan Museum of Art's 2018 exhibition *Heavenly Bodies: Fashion and the Catholic Imagination* signals a visual connection to the black-and-white nun's habit, incorporating as it does a black wool hood after the style of the black veil lined in white that flows down a nun's back [Fig. 2.4]. Pearson's headgear, however, stops short at the mid upper arm. The dress itself is black, sleeveless, fitted at the waist and falling to the ankles, over which is added a short, flared, ivory peplum skirt lined in black, emanating from a fitted waist. Plain black leather shoes finish the outfit.[13] While the entire

outfit elegantly and demurely covers the body, the fitted waist brings the sensual body back into shape. Thus, Pearson has emphasised the woman concealed, the hidden body underneath the masses of fabric that make up the traditional nun's garb. Of this piece Pearson is reported as saying:

> I wasn't raised around nuns [or with] any particular religious beliefs [but] I find there is something innately appealing about the blasphemous concept of religious garments being seen as sexy – very much the opposite of their intended purpose. In my work, I love to play with these notions of power, and the provocative nature of the untouchable.[14]

It seems Pearson is not the only one. When designers start to use their creative genius with religious apparel, there is often an implicit irreverence and subversion inherent in their designs. Not only does the most reverent become sensual, but male power often becomes relayed through female bodies, made manifest by tall slim models with pinched-in waists. Indeed, the pinched-in waist is probably one of the most distinguishing fashion features displayed in the transition from liturgical to fashion wear shown in the *Heavenly Bodies* exhibition.

As irreverence, even blasphemy, is a recurring issue, the question is how to resolve the perplexing matter of creative fashion appropriating religious garments. When couturier Jean Paul Gaultier presented his 1993 collection *Chic Rabbis*, based on Hasidic religious attire, Jewish critics disapproved of the use of ritual clothing as costumes on a catwalk. They were particularly offended by the presentation of women in rabbinical clothing.[15] Undeterred by such criticism, Gaultier was invited to contribute several Roman Catholic-themed designs from his archives to *Heavenly Bodies*. His spectacular halo-like head adornments atop faces painted with tears evoke in the viewer strong sentiments of the Madonna's grief without any sense of sacrilege. In Gaultier's Spring/Summer 2007 collection he sought inspiration from devotional church art and stained glass icons [Fig. 2.5], resulting in other images of the Madonna and Child. Gaultier expressed his own relationship to Catholicism as, 'It's part of my education. I am born Catholic.' After viewing the delicate gold filigree on a cape of Pius IX, he added, 'It is beautiful to see this thing that is such a part of our lives'.[16]

The Metropolitan Museum of Art's exhibition team for *Heavenly Bodies*, principally Andrew Bolton (Wendy Yu Curator in Charge of The Costume Institute), with strong support from Anna Wintour (Global Editorial Director of *Vogue* and a Museum trustee), spent years in careful and lengthy negotiations with Vatican officials before the exhibition was finally approved and given the endorsement of Cardinal Gianfranco Ravasi, President of the Pontifical Council for Culture. Not only did Rome give its blessing, but the Vatican sent over more than 50 vestments borrowed from the Sistine Chapel collection, many of which had never previously left the Vatican. These included the golden cope of Pope Benedict XV; the chasuble and mitre of Pius XI; the dalmatic of Pius IX, which features a scene from the crucifixion, and his heavily jewelled tiara. All contributed to make the 2018 exhibition the outstanding success it proved to be. Attracting over 1.6 million visitors, it became the most-visited exhibition

Fig. 2.4 (opposite)
Florence hood and *Spray* dress by Cimone, Autumn/Winter 2017.
(© Cimone Ltd / Photo © Rhiannon Adam)

Fig. 2.5 (overleaf)
Jean Paul Gaultier, Look 19 Haute Couture Spring/Summer 2007.
(Photo Patrice Stable)

in the history of The Metropolitan Museum of Art.

Pre-empting those who may consider the accessorising of papal vestments with modern fashion a blasphemous exploitation, both Cardinal Ravasi and Cardinal Dolan, Archbishop of New York, took a supportive stance towards the exhibition. Their response to anticipated criticism was that the fashion interpretations of the vestments were 'a thing of beauty' and for 'art, poetry, music, liturgy, and yes, even fashion' [we] 'thank God for the gift of beauty'.[17] We can only marvel at the various hermeneutics and ponder on what 8th-century St Aldhelm might have said about it all. The *Heavenly Bodies* exhibition was, indisputably, a thing of beauty: all the garments were exquisitely displayed in such a divinely perfect location as to engender awe in the most vociferous critics and non-believers alike.[18]

Modern Paganism, the occult, and the esoteric

Christianity, with its 2000-year history, is a relative newcomer in the history of humanity. Evidence clearly indicates that early humans believed in spirits and an afterlife and these beliefs have persisted for millennia, taking shape and diversifying as humans populated and spread to different parts of the world. The diverse environments in which humans found themselves over thousands of years shaped their beliefs, changing according to geography, cultural diversity and idiosyncratic zeitgeists.

Modern Paganism (neo-Paganism) is based on the concept that pre-Christian Pagan beliefs and practices held a spiritual reality and worthwhile values that were suppressed and replaced by monotheistic religions like Christianity. Pagans talk about the Old Religion in a generic sense as a collective body of knowledge that contained enduring wisdom regardless of the passage of time. There is no particular doctrine, nor even a founding figure such as Jesus Christ. Rather, the ideas contained among the different sub-groups today reflect influences from many sources. Polytheism, animism, the Kabbalah, magic, Hermeticism, Freemasonry, Theosophy, folklore, ancient myths, the natural environment, and the notion that ritual acts performed with intention can alter consciousness. Any, or all, of these aspects can be woven together with current concerns, such as climate change and gender issues, sometimes turning into impassioned activism.

On the whole Pagan groups are inclusive, having no restrictions or injunctions against homosexuality, or any gender identity. To speak of Roman Catholicism as embracing all denominations of Christianity would be misleading. Similarly, in Paganism's diversity, any discussions of Pagan apparel are conditional on a specific sub-group, among which can be found Wiccans, witches, Druids, magicians, Asatru, Heathens, eco-Pagans, and goddess-focused groups.[19] Pagans can vary enormously in their ideologies – from 'green' eco-Pagans (with elements of eco-philosophy, deep ecology and eco-feminism) to politically right-wing Slavic Paganism.[20] In short, while there are Pagans scattered throughout the Western world, there is no worldwide structure with a presiding figure such as the pope and therefore no abiding central organisation to exert control.

Paganism is a religion of enchantment and magic. Indeed, the origin of the word 'glamour' is to bewitch or enchant through magical means such as spells. Pagan bodily adornment is colourful, splendidly imaginative and enormously varied: through the nude, painted, or tattooed body, to highly elaborate ritual costumes made of anything from modern fabrics to materials taken from the natural environment (stag horns, animal skins, flora, bones, teeth, fur and feathers). At times, so covered with elaborate headgear and costumed from head to toe, a Pagan body can give the appearance of being other than human. This type of costume has been used by Indigenous people for centuries. No matter that audiences know there is a human underneath, such total coverage never fails to awe spectators, especially when appearing at night around a flickering fire, in a highly charged atmosphere where all the senses are engaged.

Pagan dress and colour

Despite public misconceptions that Pagans all wear black, colourful dress is prolific in both everyday wear (non-liturgical) and ritual (liturgical) dress. Celebrations of the seasons (called the Wheel of the Year) follow a mythological story that anthropomorphises the annual cycle. Colours can be incorporated into ritual dress as the Wheel turns to reflect spring, summer, autumn and winter, the phases of the moon, and the four elements of earth, air, fire and water. Pagan ritual performances are many and varied, displaying a rich repertoire of colourful, mystical, magical dress that symbolises both the natural world and the spirit world.

Some of the highly evocative and dramatic designs of the late Alexander McQueen have a noticeably Pagan element. His use of items from the natural environment – such as peacock and pheasant feathers, antlers, and allusion to inter-species hybrids, were particularly relevant. The exhibition *Alexander McQueen: Savage Beauty* (The Metropolitan Museum of Art, 4 May–7 August 2011; and Victoria and Albert Museum, 14 March–2 August 2015) featured a long-sleeved, figure-hugging ivory dress with spectacular veiled antler headdress (*Widows of Culloden*, Autumn/Winter 2006), which conveyed Pagan notions of nature and mystery without resorting to black – it could well be a design that a Wiccan might wear to a handfasting.[21] McQueen is reported as saying: 'Life to me is a bit of

a Brothers Grimm fairy tale', and some of his designs bore the undercurrent of 'grim' in the Grimm fairy tales.[22] McQueen also made reference to the darker aspect of some of his creations, saying, 'There's something kind of Edgar Allan Poe, kind of deep and kind of melancholic about my collections'.[23] His inspirations appear to have ranged from the Salem witch trials to the melancholia and darkness of the Victorian era; he even used pieces of human hair in linings, reflecting the 19th-century's preoccupation with death and *memento mori*. Some of McQueen's theatrical runway shows were reminiscent of earlier Pagan practitioners, such as the infamous Aleister Crowley who used dramatic clothing and jewellery to communicate his magical presence and prowess.

Designer Sarah Burton, who replaced Alexander McQueen upon his untimely death, has taken the 'darkness' out of Alexander McQueen fashions and introduced a lighter, 'greener' Paganism. In her Autumn/Winter 2017 collection she selected a more nature-oriented Pagan direction with its focus on the natural environment and magical folkways. Her personal abiding interest in history and nature has taken her to remote corners of Britain to explore ancient stone circles, medieval churches, Paganism and witchcraft. She is quoted as saying: 'I felt this sense of groundedness, of needing to feel the land, and tradition.'[24] Some of Burton's fashion pieces in the 2017 collection incorporated multiple coloured ribbons floating from ensembles. These were inspired by the trees around clootiewells and springs, places of pilgrimage in Celtic areas where people tie strips of cloth or rags as part of a healing ritual. Burton's designs also reflect a more down-to-earth

Fig. 2.6 (opposite)
Sarah Burton for Alexander McQueen,
Look 43 Ready-to-Wear Autumn/Winter 2017.
(Sipa US / Alamy Stock Photo)

sense of young womanhood, yet without departing from the Alexander McQueen magic. Other dresses in the same collection included dresses beaded with silvery trees, medieval tapestries of flora and fauna, and symbols of stars and suns traced in jet [Fig. 2.6].[25]

The body in all shapes and sizes is viewed as something to be honoured within Paganism, and sexuality is celebrated. Some rituals are performed sky-clad (naked) honouring the sacredness of each and every body and casting aside the inhibitions and prohibitions of everyday life. However, the Pagan desire to act out their 'magical selves' overrides nudity in most cases.

The purpose of ritual is not merely to 'dress up' and celebrate. Rather, the goal is transformation from the mundane to the extraordinary. Creating an aura of mystery and magic is important as it contributes to a change in consciousness. Dress aids in that transformation, but it is only one aspect. Ritual participation involves all the senses: the sound of drums, the smells of incense, smoke curling up from a fire, the excitement of dance and ritual enactment, all within a highly charged atmosphere. The combination of these things contributes to bringing about a change in consciousness in participants. Clothes worn only during rituals are said to build up their own special energies and contain their own magical properties. Pagan dress assemblages have a generative power that includes the notion of magical energy.[26]

Black robes

The hooded robe could be said to be the most basic item of ritual dress. In its most simple form, the shape of the robe resembles an 'ankh', the ancient symbol of life, with the flared sleeves forming the horizontal bar of a 'T'-shape and the hood the rounded loop of the cross.

Many Pagan rituals are performed in natural environments such as forests and woods, or near a body of water. Some say the traditional black robe enables the wearer to 'disappear' into the night if disturbed by non-Pagan voyeurs. The black robe can be worn to any ritual at any time of the year. It is often accompanied by a sleeveless full-length cape, frequently made of velvet, satin, cotton or hemp, that is tied at the neck and open in front with two slits so that the arms may go through to enable movement. The cape's hood is usually large, so that it drapes slightly onto the neck, giving it a medieval appearance. Some sew mystical symbols onto the fabric, or display them via face paint, tattoos and jewellery such as pendants, earrings and rings. The five-pointed star, or pentagram, is particularly but not exclusively relevant to Wiccans. Pagan ritual places importance on connecting with the energy of the earth, so footwear is usually discarded before entering the ritual space.

The occult

While the belief in magic and astrology is ancient, the occult practices of today most likely stem from the 16th and 17th centuries. Astrology and alchemy were considered science in those times, not separated from religion until much later. Occultism can be understood as seeking that which is beyond the range of ordinary knowledge. Practitioners were, and are, supposed to have some knowledge of, or have the power to activate, the secret and mysterious forces of nature that are beyond current scientific explanation. Esotericism, another term which is paired with occultism, basically refers to that which is hidden, such as the knowledge offered to initiates after proper preparation. The basis of this secrecy is that, without appropriate instruction, such knowledge can be dangerous or used improperly. Occultists seek to probe the sub-conscious mind into action using symbols that might aid in this. How the mind is probed, and the techniques used to attain spiritual and metaphysical awareness and access other realities, becomes of prime importance. The magical quest is self-transformation, an ongoing process of self-discovery.

Both anthropologists and occultists have referred to magic as being either 'black' or 'white', with black referring to practices with the intent to harm (such as sorcery) and white to practices with benign intent (such as spiritual healing). Nevill Drury suggests that contemporary magical practitioners are more likely to use the terms Left-Hand Path and Right-Hand Path when talking about their beliefs and practices because of outsiders associating magic with evil.[27] However, so entrenched in the Western psyche are dichotomies of 'black = evil' and 'white = good', played out in folk stories, fairy stories and mythologies, that black as the personification of the dark unknown has morphed into a trope of evil, engendering fear.

Gothic fashion highlights the associations of black and death. Fashion historian Valerie Steele has written extensively on all aspects of fashion, including gothic.[28] As dissolution of the body at death seems to evoke fear in people everywhere, it is associated with darkness and the unknown. Vampires and clothes reminiscent of Victorian mourning outfits, black clothes, lipstick, fingernails, eye make-up, hair, and symbols on jewellery – such as skulls, reverse pentagrams, safety pins and chains – are a feature in gothic subculture.

Accompanying this style is an overt rebelliousness against contemporary mores. The designer Vivienne Westwood's introduction of punk seemed to be the harbinger of 'going against the grain' through fashion, and her 1983 collection devoted to witchcraft took that idea even further.

Elsa Schiaparelli had already introduced occult themes as early as the mid-1930s; her attraction to Theosophy was a natural evolution from her childhood interest in the lore of ancient cultures and religious rites, and which translated into a natural affinity with the Dada and Surrealist movements. Many of her contemporaries were shocked at her 1938 black skeleton evening dress [Fig. 2.7], thinking it an offence against good taste. Made in silk crêpe, trapunto quilting and cotton wadding, it outlined a human skeleton on a dress so figure-hugging that it gave the appearance of a second skin.[29] In contemplating what constitutes magic(k)al clothing in 2020, Charlotte Rodgers comments that Pagan motifs have a 'small degree of edgy currency' in the fashion world at the moment, and somewhat wistfully adds that Pagan ritual apparel has evolved to become 'a costume that defines one's whole approach to living, rather than something worn in order to enter a different reality'.[30]

Conclusion

As we have seen, depending on the time and context, 'spiritual black' conveys different messages to different people. In Roman Catholicism, black indicates those members of the hierarchy's most humble ranks on the one hand, and death and mourning on the other. The black habit and symbol of the cross of a nun or priest may not evoke the fear that the black robe and pentagram of a Pagan emotes to those unfamiliar with their deeper meanings, but holds the same potency.

Fashion is about creating an original piece of wearable art, a thing of beauty, or creating an original look that will bring international acclaim and financial benefit to the designer. This might include some visible sign of the zeitgeist of a historical period, act as a sign of rebellion or anarchy, or say something about gender in relation to power. Whether parading a high fashion item on a catwalk, or 'dressing up' as

a witch for a Halloween party, the wearer *is gazing outward*. In contrast, the occult practitioner dons ritual attire with the intention of altering their consciousness and attaining a desired spiritual goal: the wearer *is gazing inward*.

Black apparel has intrigue. We have seen that black, to the Western mind, is indicative of many things: humility, death, mourning, sexuality, mystery, fear/evil, as well as professionalism. In January 2020, a photo of four women in the most powerful government positions in Finland, including Sanna Martin (at age 34 the youngest sitting prime minister in the world), showed them all wearing their versions of the little black dress, conveying strong powerful young women.[31] The little black dress has proven to have perennial appeal. There seems to be no end to what the innovative designer has made of it – it is a fashion diamond of many facets.

Fig. 2.7

The *Skeleton Dress*, by Elsa Schiaparelli, Paris, 1938.
Victoria and Albert Museum T.394&A-1974.

(© Schiaparelli / Victoria and Albert Museum, London)

Notes

1   Adam Anczyk, 'The Art of Borrowing: Interpreting contemporary Pagans' ritual fashion', in Adam Anczyk and Joanna Malita-Król (eds), *Walking the Old Ways in a New World: Contemporary Paganism as Lived Religion* (2017), pp. 183–207.

2   Margaret Beetham, *A Magazine of Her Own? Domesticity and Desire in the Woman's Magazine, 1800–1914* (1996), p. 85.

3   The Metropolitan Museum of Art, 2016.757.1a-d.

4   Anon., 'Autumn Winter 2003 couture: Chanel', British *Vogue* online (2003): <https://www.vogue.co.uk/shows/autumn-winter-2003-couture/chanel>

5   Robert Nicol, *The Ritual of Death in Colonial South Australia* (1992), pp. 16–28.

6   Lynne Hume, *The Religious Life of Dress: Global Fashion and Faith* (2013).

7   Ecumenism: promoting unity between all Christian denominations.

8   William J F Keenan, 'Clothed with Authority: The Rationalization of Marist Dress Culture', in Linda B Arthur (ed.), *Undressing Religion: Commitment and Conversion from a Cross-Cultural Perspective* (2000), p. 86.

9   Quoted in Aileen Ribeiro, *Dress and Morality* (2003 [1986]), p. 32.

10   *Ibid.*

11   Elizabeth Kuhns, *The Habit: A History of the Clothing of Catholic Nuns* (2003).

12   Hume, *The Religious Life of Dress* (2013), pp. 26–28.

13   Emily Farra, 'This Under-the-Radar Designer in the New Met Exhibition Takes "Fashion Nun" to New Heights', May 2018, *Vogue* (2018): <https://www.vogue.com/article/met-gala-2018-exhibit-designer-cimone>

14   *Ibid.*

15   Aaron Ealy, 'The Five Most Scandalous Fashion Shows in Recent History', *Paper* (2015) [accessed Jan. 2020]: <https://www.papermag.com/the-5-most-scandalous-fashion-shows-in-recent-history-1427643470.html>

16   H W Vail, 'Inside the Met's *Heavenly Bodies* Exhibit', *Vanity Fair* (2018): <https://www.vanityfair.com/style/2018/05/met-exhibit-heavenly-bodies>

17   Timothy Cardinal Dolan, *Heavenly Bodies: Fashion and the Catholic Imagination,* comments from the press conference (2019): <http://cardinaldolan.org/index.php/heavenly-bodies-fashion-and-the-catholic-imagination/>

18   See 'Gallery views of The Costume Institute's spring 2018 exhibition, Heavenly Bodies: Fashion and the Catholic Imagination, narrated by exhibition curator Andrew Bolton': <https://www.youtube.com/watch?v=sXGN7XfhNmI> [accessed 26/1/2020]

19   *The Pomegranate: The International Journal of Pagan Studies,* published by Equinox Publishing, covers the field of Pagan studies dealing with contemporary Paganism and other forms of Pagan religion. Editor-in-chief: Chas S Clifton.

20   Mariusz Filip, 'Wolves Amongst the Sheep: Looking Beyond the Aesthetics of Polish National Socialism', in *The Pomegranate* 21:2 (2019), pp. 210–36.

21   Handfasting: Pagan equivalent of a wedding ceremony where the couple is bound to one another ('tying the knot').

22   Lindsay Baker, 'Alexander McQueen: Fashion's dark fairytale', BBC (2015): <http://www.bbc.com/culture/story/20150313-fashions-dark-fairytale>

23   Anon., 'Alexander McQueen: Savage Beauty – About the Exhibition' (2015), V&A Museum: <http://www.vam.ac.uk/content/exhibitions/exhibition-alexander-mcqueen-savage-beauty/about-the-exhibition/>

24   Sarah Mower, 'Alexander McQueen Fall 2017 Ready-to-Wear', *Vogue* online (2017): <https://www.vogue.com/fashion-shows/fall-2017-ready-to-wear/alexander-mcqueen>

25   Vivian Chen, 'Alexander McQueen brings pagan legends to Paris Fashion Week', *South China Morning Post* online (2017): <https://www.scmp.com/magazines/style/fashion-beauty/article/2077158/alexander-mcqueen-brings-pagan-legends-paris-fashion>

26   Lynne Hume, 'Religious Dress', in *International Encyclopedia of Anthropology* (2019) [entry: wbiea2406].

27   Lynne Hume and Nevill Drury, *The Varieties of Magical Experience: Indigenous, Medieval, and Modern Magic* (2013), pp. 131–57.

28   See especially Valerie Steele and Jennifer Park (eds), *Gothic: Dark Glamour* (2008).

29   V&A Museum, T.394&A-1974.

30   Charlotte Rodgers, 'High Glamour: Magical Clothing and Talismanic Fashion', in *The Pomegranate* 21:2 (2019), pp. 172–85.

31   Photograph in *The Australian Women's Weekly*, January 2020.

SUBLIME BLACK
PERFECTION OF LINE
AND TECHNICAL WIZARDRY

Iain R Webb

'A woman can't really go wrong with a Little Black Dress.'

These pearls of wisdom are not the words of an esoteric couturier expounding upon his latest collection of sleek cocktail ensembles, or the mantra of a fashion maven informing her readers of a well-worn wardrobe staple. No, this slick one-liner was proffered to me by the driver of a London cab while on my way to the airport to catch a plane to Milan for the unveiling of the Autumn/Winter 1995 collections.

The little black dress is so ubiquitous, so familiar, part of fashion's furniture if you like, that it is now common parlance. I was so taken by his bravado that I used the statement to begin my review in *The Times* newspaper, adding, 'It's true, and that goes for designers too'. That season there were LBDs on every catwalk. Some, it had to be said, better than others. During my career as a fashion editor I have seen legions of LBDs stroll down the catwalk in every possible manifestation. I have also been witness to racks of them on offer by every high-street brand, at every price point. Since the early 20th century the LBD has been part of fashion's vocabulary. They are the stuff of a designer's arsenal, the nice little earners for designers and retailers alike. Yet, not everyone gets it right. Despite their appearance, LBDs are not as simple as they first seem. The purity of the LBD offers the designer nowhere to hide. For this reason, the masterful designers are something of illusionists – the trick being to have the confidence to know when to hold back, to strip away, underplay and leave well alone. To construct a thing of such sublime sophistication that it will transcend time. Lucinda Alford runs a London-based vintage fashion resource with an international clientele and sells a lot of LBDs:

> From a design point of view, the LBD is quite architectural, quite structural. The starkness of the black is not distracting. I have a whole rack of black cocktail dresses and the black allows you to see the cut, see the ruffle and appreciate the detail. The sparseness of the silhouette breaks down to the bare bones. Colour can date a garment. Colours are fashionable, with specific colours for specific times.[1]

Cristóbal Balenciaga

In a previous life as Fashion Editor of *The Observer* newspaper, Alford styled a fashion story called 'Frock of Ages', featuring three generations of women (27–82 years old) all wearing LBDs.[2] For another LBD story she dressed drag queens, musing 'I guess I was being inclusive even then'. 'Now,' she says, 'everybody always asks for Balenciaga references. All the time.' 'Black is dramatic and plays to the gallery,' wrote Elizabeth Wilson, and if there is one word that encapsulates Spanish-born Cristóbal Balenciaga's *raison d'être* it is drama.[3] This materialised as sculptural silhouettes – minimal for day, voluminous for night – and what better means of showcasing this than with black. Balenciaga's designs drew heavily upon his heritage. His vision veered between extremes: from the flamboyance of flamenco dancers, ostentatious costumes of toreadors, royal Infantas and decorative statues of the Madonna, to the dramatic, pared-down purity of the religious paintings of Diego Velázquez, Francisco Goya, Francisco de Zurbarán and 'El Greco'. His more austere attitude mirrored the mood of monastic calm that prevailed in his fashion house and all-white studio.

Often described as using 'a deep thick black' as if pitch or paint, at his core Balenciaga was a purist; his designs were a tension between volume and tailoring. The use of black fabrics allowed him to realise these ideas and his appreciation and understanding of his materials. He relished black lace (not surprisingly given his Spanish heritage), heavy silks, taffeta, *cloqué*, gazar and grosgrain; his innate appreciation and understanding of these fabrics emphasised his extraordinary silhouettes. He utilised a fabric's specific properties rather than forcing or cajoling it with complicated underpinnings. It is a given that the ultimate LBD must never look tortured at the hands of the designer. Balenciaga's forte was his attention to detail and his determination to push fashion design forward. There were the balloon-hemlines, the semi-fit silhouettes, the babydolls and the extraordinary four-point envelope dress, which underline his move in later life into more abstract ideas. He would go on to create dresses with just one seam.

Balenciaga is rightfully acknowledged as one of the most innovative and influential designers of the 20th century. He and his work have been revered by designers throughout the decades, including the late Azzedine Alaïa, a celebrated creator himself of some of fashion's most fabulous LBDs. The latter's laser-cut, fit-and-flare, stretch knit and leather dresses are extraordinary feats of technical wizardry. It has been reported that Alaïa, described as 'couture's rebellious outsider', collected dresses designed by Balenciaga and held 500 in his personal archive.[4]

For all his experimentation Balenciaga did not believe that the designer should overshadow the client. For this reason, he became popular with an American clientele including Pauline de Rothschild, Jackie Kennedy, Gloria Guinness and Wallis, Duchess of Windsor, and film stars such as Grace Kelly and Ava Gardner. 'Balenciaga's seemingly unassuming clothes, none of which shout out with fancy ornamentation and decoration, matched the wearers,' says Rosemary Harden, Curator of Fashion Museum, Bath, which boasts a black silk taffeta balloon-hem dress dating from 1950 among its world-class collection.[5] 'They were women and clothes of presence. All achieved through genius cut and an assured choice of fabric. Put them on and they became walking sculptures.' The women who wore Balenciaga's designs, no matter how simple or startling, all attested how comfortable and easy his clothes were to wear; they were constructed to follow the shape of a woman's body, so they never felt trapped or confined. Balenciaga was at odds with the concept of fashion and saw no merit in change for change's sake, instead refining ideas and looks from one season to the next. In her book *20th Century Fashion*, Linda Watson noted how, 'In 1962 *Vogue* observed that Balenciaga was "an implicit believer … that the essence of chic is elimination".'[6] When Balenciaga closed his house in 1968, it is reported that he recommended his clients take their business to Givenchy.

Hubert de Givenchy

Hubert de Givenchy – the man in the white laboratory coat – is probably the designer most instantly and inextricably linked with one particular LBD. Hailed as the most famous little black dress in the history of the cinema, the sinuous black satin sheath (technically a *long* black dress) created by Givenchy in 1961 and worn by Audrey Hepburn as Holly Golightly in the opening scene of *Breakfast at Tiffany's* is the stuff of fashion legend [Fig. 1. 10]. When the dress featured in a sale at Christie's in London in 2006, it is reported to have sold for £467,200 – at the time setting a new world record for a garment featured in a film. When Givenchy redesigned the *Breakfast at Tiffany's* dress in 1993 for Barney's department store in New York, they apparently flew off the rack.

Givenchy originally met Hepburn in 1953 when

Fig. 3.1
Julien Macdonald for Givenchy, Look 17
Haute Couture Autumn/Winter 2003.
(Photographer: Iain R Webb)

Givenchy endowed her [the Golightly character] with a blend of restrained power and urbane sensuality' and dubbed it the 'most versatile of chic party outfits'.[7] Of course, throughout his career Givenchy designed many more exquisite LBDs – Hepburn also wore knee-length versions during the film – yet none quite gained the traction of the unforgettable *Breakfast at Tiffany's* LBD, etched forever into the collective public consciousness. Hepburn has continued to inspire subsequent designers for the house of Givenchy, including John Galliano, Alexander McQueen and Julien Macdonald [Fig. 3.1].

The British designers

'Brit boy' John Galliano was appointed creative director at Givenchy when Hubert retired in 1995. The appointment of the flamboyant genius from South London, with a pencil-thin parody of an Errol Flynn moustache and a penchant for dressing as a pirate, certainly caused a stir. Not only was Galliano the first British designer to run a French couture house, but his 'bad boy' repute for sartorial high jinks went before him. Galliano had a fondness for the experimental and excessive, dating from the wild antics of his early eponymous catwalk shows that featured fantastical tableaux vivant and clothes worn every which way. This became something of a default setting for the designer, culminating in the massive theatrical productions staged during his time as creative director at Dior, in which models wore show-stopping dresses that reached gargantuan proportions. However, in an interview

she was filming *Sabrina* in Paris, and he went on to design for her in films such as *Love in the Afternoon* (1957), *Charade* (1963) and *How to Steal a Million* (1966). However, it is the *Breakfast at Tiffany's* LBD that has achieved iconic status, embodying a mood of understated glamour and charming sophistication. When the Design Museum published a book called *Fifty Dresses that Changed the World,* it chose to feature Hepburn wearing Givenchy's *Breakfast at Tiffany's* dress on the cover. Inside it noted that 'with this simple dress

following the debut of Galliano's Autumn/Winter 1996 Givenchy ready-to-wear collection, shrewdly unveiled to a soundtrack featuring *My Fair Lady* (another of Audrey Hepburn's iconic roles in 1964), he described how taking couture into the 21st century was about making clothes that are both 'desirable and wearable'.[8] The article was illustrated with a black organza coat-dress edged with ruffle upon ruffle. Hinting at the 1950s, in Galliano's hands this ensemble oozed modern glamour, the perfect cocktail party look for the 1990s. Perhaps not surprisingly, during his short tenure at Givenchy it was reported in the press that sales at the house had risen by 80 per cent. His long-time collaborator, milliner Stephen Jones, confirmed: 'People thought that John could only do crazy extravagant haute couture ... [they] only tend to think of the big ballgowns but there were also the things that were much lower key, they also have a life.'[9]

A closer study of Galliano's archive reveals that it has often been in those quieter moments where the designer has showcased his true bravura. In earlier eponymous shows, Galliano offered some extremely understated LBDs among his more challenging designs. A single black square neck, cropped sleeve, sack dress from Spring/Summer 1987 was photographed in a fashion story for *BLITZ* magazine [Fig. 3.2], while the *Evening Standard* noted that Galliano's Autumn/Winter 1988 collection ended with a selection of 'the longest, simplest bias-cut evening dresses in a clever, simple, timeless collection worthy of the Designer of the Year' (his first win).[10] This was John Galliano's first foray into bias-cutting (borrowed from his great inspiration,

designer Madeleine Vionnet), and the finale to his follow-up collection featured a handful of technically complex gowns in black bias-cut satin.[11] For Spring/Summer 1990, fashion editor Kim Bowen wrote: 'One high spot was a bevy of barefoot maidens – all lissom limbs, huge lips and hair-a-tumble – in dramatically simple black dresses.'[12]

In fashion circles, Galliano is most revered for a collection known as *The Black Collection* that eschewed showboating shenanigans. In the spring of 1994, only a year before his ascent to Givenchy, Galliano was without financial backing. With the help of a handful of high-profile fashion friends including American *Vogue's* Anna Wintour and André Leon Talley, the designer created a collection of fewer than 20 ensembles from a few rolls of black satin-backed crêpe and organza, and presented it in an empty, ramshackle, borrowed Parisian townhouse belonging to socialite Sao Schlumberger. Supermodels including Linda Evangelista, Christy Turlington, Nadja Auermann, Naomi Campbell, Shalom Harlow and Kate Moss walked free of charge. Galliano's designs cleverly melded Japanese kimonos with 1940s tailoring for an irresistible collection that was to become influential far beyond its scale. He once again showcased his love of the bias cut in slender black gowns, their seams hidden within the black on black patterning. One of these dresses earned the accolade of Dress of the Year 1994 at Fashion Museum, Bath.[13]

Around this time another British designer, Rifat Ozbek, was also garnering accolades from the press. Ozbek offered themed collections in the style of his hero Yves Saint Laurent, looking to far-flung destinations as inspiration – one season Mexico, the next Turkey (his homeland). He audaciously clashed colour and loaded his designs with luxurious embroidery and glittering embellishment, but his team boasted savvy Marketing and Development Director Robert Forrest, who cleverly cajoled the

Fig. 3.2 (opposite)
Dresses by Rifat Ozbek (left) and John Galliano (right), *BLITZ* magazine, 1987.
(Photographer: Mark Lewis)

Fig. 3.3 (above)
Antony Price corset dress for Philip Treacy, February 1998.
(Trinity Mirror / Mirrorpix / Alamy Stock Photo)

Fig. 3.4 (opposite)
Fiona Dealey dress worn by Sade. Photography by Mike Laye,
The Face, February 1983.
(© 2019 – Mike Laye / image-access.net)

designer each season to add a plain LBD to his collection. The resulting dresses featured achingly spare, thoughtfully-considered structural seaming and graphic necklines, reflecting Ozbek's earlier training as an architect. These dresses proved immensely popular with his clientele.

Like Galliano, Antony Price has always been viewed as a rock-'n'-roll designer, not least because musicians (most notably Roxy Music and Duran Duran) and their girlfriends have been drawn to his design ethic – exaggerated glamour, cleverly constructed to streamline the body to cartoon-like proportions. Price has always been captivated by the black-and-white Hollywood of yesteryear, which promoted an idealised form of men with broad shoulders and women with hourglass curves. In 1971 the forward-thinking *Nova* magazine ran a feature titled 'How To Undress In Front of Your Husband'. The accompanying photo spread by Brian Duffy featured Amanda Lear, stylishly extricating herself from one of Price's black clingy ciré dresses that has a zipper spiralling diagonally around it. The dress was another feat of imagination and construction. Sadly, Price has often been overlooked by the mainstream fashion industry, although he is afforded cult-like status by fashion aficionados who liken his talent for construction to couturiers Charles James and Christian Dior. Like Dior, Price often used black to accentuate the fiercely carved silhouette, especially of the female form.

When milliner Philip Treacy decided to show a couture collection of hats as part of London Fashion Week in February 1998, he commissioned Price to make him a series of second-skin black corset dresses [Fig. 3.3]. 'He's the master of cutting and illusion. In an age when everybody and anybody is a designer, Antony is a true fashion designer,' opined Treacy. 'Those dresses he created for me looked sprayed on.'[14] Throughout his career, Price has continued to sharpen his cutting skills and has now by the sultry singer/songwriter Sade in the 1980s. The dramatic V-backed, black jersey dress [Fig. 3.4] was designed by Fiona Dealey, a St Martin's School of Art graduate and habitué of the New Romantic Blitz Club. 'It was important,' Dealey says, 'that the dress looked like it was defying gravity, that with just a little shrug of the shoulders it would fall to the floor.'[16] 'The whole point of my design was to look effortless.' The dress was realised with the pattern-cutting skills of her then partner, Gioia Meller Marcovicz, who has since gone on to design sculptural furniture. This dress defined Sade's image as much as her music defined an era, both perfectly echoing the mood of sensual, pared-down elegance.

Italian sexuality

A kind of subversive sexuality betrays the heritage of Italian design duo, Domenico Dolce and Stefano Gabbana. Though they hail from the extreme north and south of the country – Gabbana was born in Milan, Dolce in a small town near Palermo – the roots of their brand lay in the culture of old world Sicily. Black-and-white promotional photographs taken in the late 1980s by Ferdinando Scianna, picture model Marpessa Hennink among the locals: a romantic snapshot of widows sunning themselves on their doorsteps, the rugged menfolk in tweed cloth caps and white cotton vests smoking in a nearby bar. With Marpessa bathed in black through-out, the images evoke Sophia Loren in *Two Women* (1960) or Anna Magnani in *The Rose Tattoo* (1955). 'Our fashion is undoubtedly rooted into the great Italian and Mediterranean tradition, so it's natural that the icons of Neo-realistic cinema are always present in our collections,' said Dolce.[17]

Another campaign featured Monica Bellucci in a wildly passionate homage to Federico Fellini's cult movie *La Dolce Vita*, the film that immortalised Anita

morphed into a couturier of sorts, creating one-off outfits for an international clientele that includes Camilla, Queen Consort. 'I think that best defines his brilliance,' said Treacy. 'He has an obsession that ensures a more than happy clientele. He never fails [them]. Antony knows all the tricks. He makes a person look the best they've ever looked.' Paul Gorman, author of *The Look*, observed how Price's 'technical skills and ability to create a total look makes him one of rock's most influential stylists'.[15]

Image has always been a crucial tool for pop performers. There are few dresses that capture a mood or a moment in time as distinctively as the LBD worn

Ekberg romping in Rome's Trevi Fountain, clad in a strapless, form-fitting corseted black velvet dress created by the costume designer Piero Gherardi. '[Cinema] has always been one of our most important sources of inspiration,' agreed Gabbana. In 2018 the designers closed their Spring/Summer catwalk show with an army of models squeezed into a variety of hourglass black dresses, cut in sheer organza, lace and satin. These dresses evoked the original underwear-as-outerwear looks that defined their earliest collections and were testament to the pair's undeniably skilful technique and craft.

Mary Quant and the Swinging Sixties

It was a new generation of young women who demanded to be freed from the corsets of the 1950s, and fashion designer Mary Quant spoke to and for that generation when she opened her boutique, *Bazaar*, on London's King's Road. The Swinging Sixties British poster-girl of *Youthquake*, Quant dressed women who were intent on living their own lives, not those imposed by their parents. Her clothes represented all that was new and exciting, from attitudes about sexuality, identity and liberation to new movements of art and design. 'There were a lot of ideas spilling out in every direction,' remembered Quant, 'not just fashion design, but music, writers, film and everything .... Art schools really forged a whole new attitude to things. They were very important, brewing all sorts of talent.'[18]

In 1964, when a young Terence Conran opened *Habitat*, offering sleek, modern interior design influenced by a European aesthetic, he chose to dress the staff of his Fulham Road store in dresses from Quant's *Bazaar*. A photograph promoting the *Habitat* store shows a female sales assistant wearing a design called 'Miss Muffet', an LBD edged with white wavy collar and cuffs [see Fig. 3.5]. A paper pattern of this dress was also created for the New York-based company Butterick – it was shown on the packet with hemlines illustrated in mini, or midi (calf length). In her autobiography, Quant stated that several of these dress patterns sold over 70,000 copies.[19] The younger generation yearned for a simpler life, freed from the shackles of the traditional work ethic and the complexities of the establishment. Her designs 'were perfectly suited to the realities of young working women around the world,' acknowledged Jenny Lister, author of *Mary Quant*.[20] 'I did not want to grow up and thought it was wonderful to be young. It turned out a lot of other people thought so too,' said Quant. 'Before the Sixties fashion was designed for grown-ups and young people tried to look grown-up. During the Sixties the young took control.'[21]

Quant's cartoon cut-outs and graphic styles, that appeared as though her felt-pen sketches had become real, suited block primary colour but looked best in black. They were dynamic, minimalistic and carefree. They also tapped into a new youth movement: the Existentialists, known more commonly as Beatniks, were emerging simultaneously in New York's Greenwich Village and the Left Bank in Paris. Beatniks questioned establishment and authority. Initially, they wore black because it was a cheap option and presented a dark, edgy mood. Brooding Beatnik pin-ups included Françoise Hardy, who sat front row at Yves Saint Laurent shows in black leather and dark glasses, and Juliette Gréco, who eventually bought her little black dresses from Balenciaga. This was the moment head-to-toe black became the uniform of the cool kids. Quant took inspiration and interpreted this look, as did Yves Saint Laurent, offering London's Chelsea girls little black shift dresses and matching headscarf, black kinky boots, black stockings and, later, lace tights and black patent shoes. Quant's *Wet Look* collection even featured 'liquorice black' PVC raincoats.

Fig. 3.5
Mary Quant *Miss Muffet* dress, Terence Conran (standing, right) and Habitat staff, 1964.
(Photograph by Terence Donovan, Camera Press, London)

In *Colour by Quant,* the designer observed:

> Black is the most chameleon in its sex appeal. It can be all things to all women – and men. It can be demure as in the ubiquitous little black dress that clings with subtle suggestiveness to otherwise unsuspected curves. It can hit the heights of drama in black satin. Black is romantic in lace, voluptuous in velvet.[22]

Quant's mini-dresses referenced the flapper dresses of the 1920s, another era when young women wished to be in the driving seat and live a fast-lane lifestyle. Speed, modernity, ease and simplicity were all attributes that also echoed Quant's own 'wash 'n' go', deceptively simple, five-point bob championed by Vidal Sassoon. Together Sassoon and Quant launched the insouciant King's Road look. Fashion designer Jasper Conran, the son of Terence, said, 'I walk along the King's Road everyday on the way to my studio and 99.9 per cent of the people I see are dressed in black'.[23] '[Black is] the basis of my business,' he continued. 'People buy black because they don't get sick of it the same way they get sick of that fuchsia-striped whatever .... More importantly, it makes them look slim and it doesn't get dirty in two minutes flat.' There appears to be an affinity between certain fashion designers who share a disregard for fashion trends, and a desire to design for the realities of life. From the start of his career, Conran built a loyal clientele eager to buy into his pared-down pragmatism:

> There is a strong difference between what I do and fashion. I've never said that I make fashion ... I feel that I am more dressmaker than showman. I like making the much quieter things that are craft and skill based, that's my love. For me making quite simple dresses is a pleasure.

Jean Muir and the Modernists

Alongside Mary Quant emerged Jean Muir, another designer whose career is inextricably linked with the LBD. Miss Muir (as she was courteously addressed) was responsible for some of fashion's most timeless black dresses [Fig. 3.6]. Showing the same unpretentiousness as Jasper Conran (a huge fan of Muir), throughout her glorious career Miss Muir invariably referred to herself as a 'dressmaker'. '[She worked in] an evolutionary way, one collection coming out of the other,' explained her husband Harry Leuckert, following her death in 1995.[24] 'Jean was never hung up on silly fads, she was not distracted by *fashion*, she disliked that word and always thought it should be used as a verb, as "to fashion something".' Moreover, Miss Muir was enamoured by the mathematics of design. Described by Linda Watson in *20th Century Fashion* as having 'the hands of a craftswoman, the mind of an engineer and the sensibility of a Scot', she was also another 'perfectionist without compare'.[25] 'My style has developed through an adherence to anatomy and technique of dressmaking. It's structure and balance,' Miss Muir once said.[26] 'One diverts, exaggerates and pares down the line to make the kind of shape and movement one wants .... You can be irreverent and way-out but structure and order are the basics on which clothes must stand.'

Historian Sir Roy Strong noted that, 'People do not attend Jean Muir's shows expecting to be shocked by the new, they expect to see what is new for Jean Muir'.[27] A constant was the designer's elegant, languid LBDs that became favoured attire for an artistic clientele including Bridget Riley, Elizabeth Frink, Dame Maggie Smith, Barbra Streisand and Joanna Lumley, Muir's ex-house model. The first Jean Muir dress that Lumley owned was an LBD, now in the collection at National Museums Scotland.[28] The enduring vision of Miss Muir is of a

Fig. 3.6 (above)
Jersey dress and leather jacket by Jean Muir, shoes by Manolo Blahnik. Selected by Geraldine Ronson for Fashion Museum's Dress of the Year, 1979.
(© Fashion Museum Bath / Bridgeman Images)

Fig. 3.7 (page 62)
Jean Muir Ltd, British, 1966–1995.
National Museums Scotland K.2005.649.1392.1 and 2.
(Image © National Museums Scotland)

fashion designer to be labelled under 'classic'; however, beyond this image of refined sophistication she was a designer who was at the cutting edge of her craft. Miss Muir resolutely faced off the future, albeit with a cursory nod to the soigné sophistication of the 1930s – an era that was itself looking to streamline the world with the advent of the Art Deco movement. 'I love all the techniques of old, but the point of view is modern,' said Miss Muir. She was perhaps the ultimate Modernist, possessing an idealism that bordered on the puritanical. 'As in one's own life,' she once told me, 'one takes up the right kind of new feelings and eliminates the obsolete.' This continuous process of reappraisal and renewal shaped Miss Muir's elemental design philosophy and was best illustrated in her LBDs.

'The more you learn about clothes, the more you realise what has to be left off,' said Geoffrey Beene, most often credited as the 'Godfather of American Sportswear'.[29] Beene was another great exponent of the LBD, redefining it by patchworking together the most unlikely juxtaposition of fabrics – sheer *point d'esprit* tulle, leather, lace, and wool flannel. His designs were feats of meticulous manipulation. 'Simplification becomes a very complicated procedure,' he said, a message that chimed with Miss Muir.

Of course, Miss Muir's work was never as easy as it looked. The garments she created were sometimes the result of as many as forty separate pattern pieces, yet the finished effect was always of understatement. By cutting these architectural designs in a matte black jersey and soft leather, Miss Muir transformed them into fluid forms [Fig. 3.7]. She famously said: 'I do not drape jersey, I tailor it.' Miss Muir often framed geometric silhouettes with strips of leather and suede. Other looks were outlined in row upon row of contrast top-stitching or ribbons of metallic snakeskin. Her fascination with technique and fit (what she called the 'nitty-gritty')

gained her a distinguished fan club including Jean Paul Gaultier, Issey Miyake and Giorgio Armani. To date, Miss Muir's original clothes continue to be top sellers in vintage stores such as Rellik in London and Decades in LA, especially her LBDs. 'Jean Muir really provided the blueprint for minimalism in fashion,' British *Vogue*'s Kate Phelan once said, 'especially in her jersey dresses ... other designers would follow in her wake'.[30] Miss Muir's style-DNA can be found in the work of contemporary designers such as Calvin Klein, Hussein Chalayan, Phoebe Philo during her time at Céline, and Jil Sander.

Creating fashion that is informed by function has been Jil Sander's life's work, her aim to create uncomplicated clothes that reduced ornamentation to its essential minimum.[31] In the 1990s I wrote in *The Times* newspaper how, 'Season after season she continues to hone her collection, including all the right silhouettes, in all the right fabrics, in all the right colours'.[32] Black became a constant for Sander. In that particular collection, 'shapely black jackets that flowed into long, lean skirts were only bettered by black crêpe and chiffon evening dresses trimmed with even blacker feathers'.[33] 'I always had a strong handwriting, believing in a refined simplicity. You see wonderful women with beautiful spirit or intellect or personality and they don't want to be running around like little puppets,' said Sander.[34] 'Not everyone is a fashion freak .... I like to be artistic in the cutting and researching the fabrics but love to clean it down.'

Elsa Schiaparelli

It may come as something of a surprise to discover that this was also the *modus operandi* of Elsa Schiaparelli. 'Everybody thinks of Schiaparelli as the shoe hat and actually black dresses were her bread and butter,' says Rosemary Harden, Curator

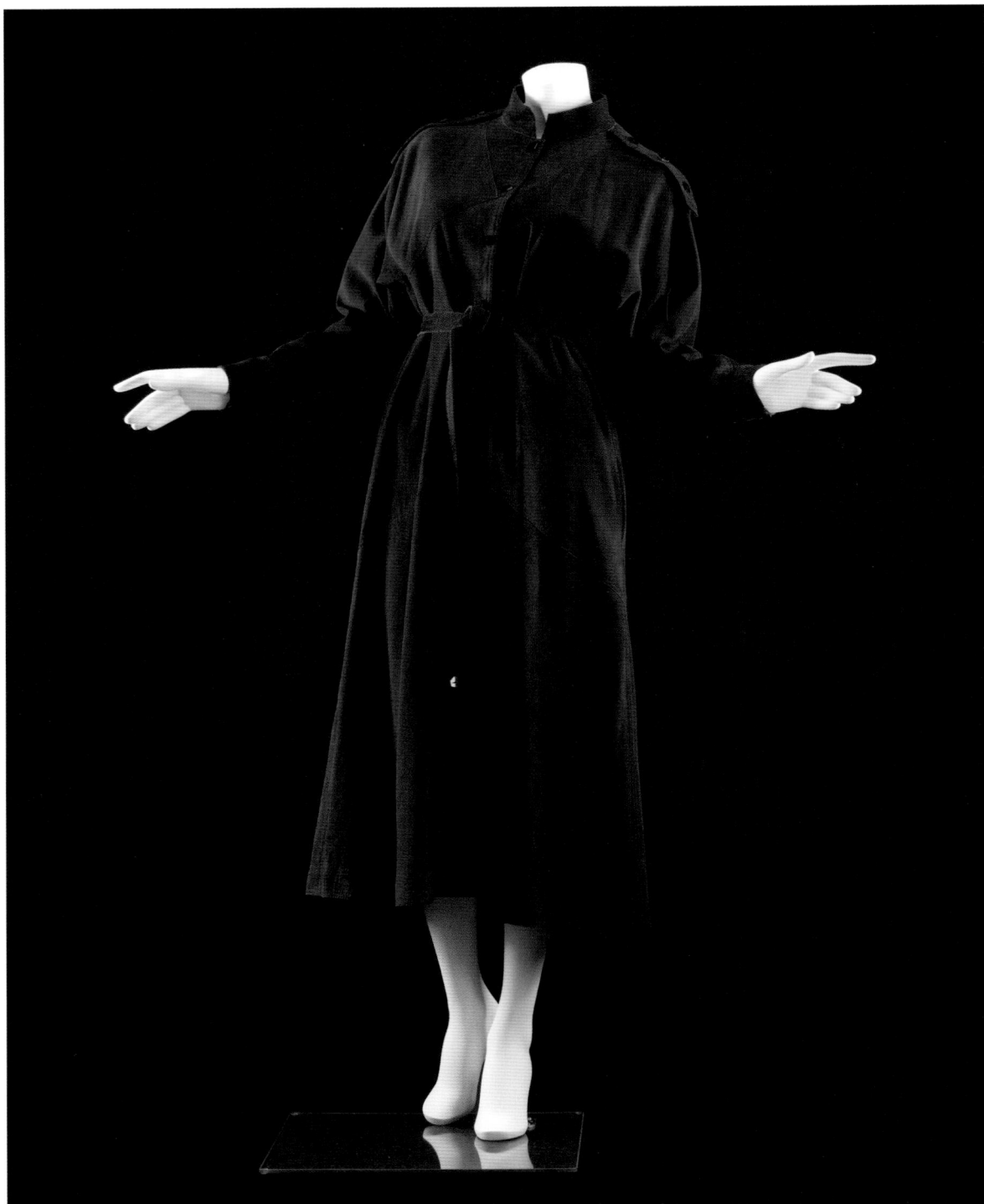

of Fashion Museum, Bath. 'Black dresses, I suspect, are every designer's bread and butter. In terms of Schiaparelli, one of her fabulous black dresses is the *Skeleton Dress* designed in 1938' [Fig. 2.7]. Although the designer questioned taste and often shocked society with her outlandish designs, she herself notes in her autobiography, *Shocking Life,* that her greatest fans were 'the ultra-smart and conservative women, wives of diplomats and bankers, millionaires and artists, who like severe suits and plain black dresses'.[35]

Schiaparelli designed her first evening dress, in black, around 1928, which she described as 'the most successful dress of my career. It was reproduced all over the world.'[36] In 1932 she went so far as to introduce black towels and beach pyjamas. While her bestselling fragrance was called *Shocking* after her signature 'shocking pink', and she gained publicity for her more eccentric designs, it was black that sold best and was also what she chose to wear: on a trip to New York, Schiaparelli is said to have worn all black, day in, night out.[37] This was a pragmatic choice that seems to run through the wardrobes of many female designers from Donna Karan, Sonia Rykiel and Katharine Hamnett, to *Zero*'s Maria Cornejo and sustainability champion Phoebe English, all of whom are noted as consummate creators of LBDs. 'I had designed a very plain black dress,' wrote Schiaparelli, '[that] could be worn both at the office and at the theatre, the sort of dress I wear all day myself.'[38] Meryle Secrest notes, in her biography of the designer, that '[Schiaparelli's] ability to design eminently sensible clothes is one of her lesser-known talents'.[39] Unlike many designers Schiaparelli did not fear popularity. In 1938 she designed a black moiré and satin dress (no. 648), worn with a matching black jacket. The dress proved so popular that it was seen on six socialites, including a baroness, a countess and a princess.

Pierre Balmain

It has to be said that while LBDs are firm wardrobe favourites, they are not headline makers. In 2018 fashion journalist Robin Givhan wrote 'A layman's guide to understanding a Fashion Week runway show' for *The Independent.* During the article Givhan notes: 'But whether the shows are straightforward or avant-garde, they leave many civilians with questions.' On her list of the most common: 'What's with all the weird stuff?' Her response: 'Wouldn't you get bored looking at little black dresses?'[40]

This dialogue between designer and critic is nothing new. In his autobiography, the fashion designer Pierre Balmain despaired at the attitude of the press, noting there had been little attention paid to the French couture houses until the Occupation of Paris. 'By the time of the Liberation, the habit had taken hold and fashion had become news,' he wrote.[41] 'As a consequence the Press was eager for the sensational ... and eccentricity took pride of place over reason.' Balmain also noted that 'some journalists ... are completely baffled by simplicity'.[42] Within the fashion media it is commonly accepted that newspaper picture editors do not want to feature black on the fashion page. This is an edict which comes from the top, as anyone who saw the appearance of American *Vogue*'s editor-in-chief Anna Wintour in the documentary film *The September Issue* can attest. In one scene Wintour previews a sombre-looking collection designed by then Yves Saint Laurent creative director Stefano Pilati: 'So you're not really feeling for colour, Stefano?' she asks after scanning the clothes rail.[43] From her tone the designer, and audience, realise the question is rhetorical, and throughout the film Wintour continually cuts pages from fashion stories that feature black dresses. Yet, ironically, black is the favourite colour worn by the fashion pack.

Balmain experienced such resistance at the start

Fig. 3.8
Pierre Balmain suit worn by Vivien Leigh (third from left)
at Crystal Stars of Film Academy Awards.

(Keystone Press / Alamy Stock Photo)

of his career when he worked alongside Christian Dior in the couture house of the designer Lucien Lelong. He was keen to propose a black dress to Lelong. Though at first his sketch for the dress was rejected by the couturier, Balmain was encouraged by Dior to push the idea further and describe how he saw the finished piece. Balmain explained that he envisioned an afternoon dress in black crêpe. He was horrified when Lelong responded, 'But Pierre, I told you when you first came to me that you could use any material you liked, except black crêpe'.[44] Still, Balmain persisted, insisting on making a toile of the dress.[45] Even then Lelong was not convinced, threatening to cut the finished dress from the show at the last minute. However, once modelled by Lelong's favourite house model Janine, the dress did make it into the show and turned out to be a massive success, selling 360 copies. Ironically, the dress was given the name *Little Profit*.

Balmain set up his own business in 1945. Known for his good taste and understanding of elegance, his designs were often polarised by silhouettes that were either cigarette-slim or featured ballooning ballroom skirts held afloat by voluminous stiffened nylon petticoats. 'Pure elegance I rate very highly,' said Balmain, 'but I am not insensible to eccentricity.'[46] The imperious Diana Vreeland declared Balmain's designs to be the quintessence of couture. During his career Balmain garnered a faithful celebrity clientele that included the Queen of Thailand and Duchess of Windsor, Brigitte Bardot, Sophia Loren, and Vivien Leigh whom he described as his most loyal client in England. Balmain dressed Leigh for her roles in *The Deep Blue Sea* (1955) and *The Roman Spring of Mrs Stone* (1961). An LBD and matching jacket ensemble worn by Leigh [Fig. 3.8] is preserved in the collection at Fashion Museum, Bath.[47] 'It's the look that you associate with Nan Kempner, Lee Radziwell and Jackie Kennedy, with their big hair,' says Rosemary Harden, 'and the astronauts' wives at the end of the 1960s.'

Yves Saint Laurent

Throughout the last century there have been myriad designers of exquisite little black dresses from Coco Chanel and Christian Dior (who famously stated, 'I could write a book about black'), to Ann Demeulemeester, Jean Paul Gaultier, Martin Margiela, Vivienne Westwood and Yohji Yamamoto, to name only a few. If there is one designer who deserves acknowledgement, none has been more influential than Yves Saint Laurent (YSL) who is deemed 'the father of modern fashion'. 'To me, Yves Saint Laurent is the essence of elegance, a sure value, a reference,' confirms the photographer Nick Knight.[48]

Saint Laurent is celebrated as a supreme colourist and audacious, ostentatious decorator – the opulent splendour and fantastic revelry of his haute couture shows are the stuff of legend – and yet it is his relentlessly noir *Le Smoking* tuxedo ensembles and achingly soigné LBDs [Fig. 3.9] that formed the backbone of his collections. When the 18-year-old

Fig. 3.9
Yves Saint Laurent,
Haute Couture Autumn/Winter 2001.
(Photographer: Iain R Webb)

ingénue designer won first prize at the International Wool Secretariat competition in 1954, his winning design was a black cocktail dress. The competition was judged by both Pierre Balmain and Hubert de Givenchy, along with fellow couturier Jacques Fath. Tellingly, the very first dress Saint Laurent designed for his own couture house (launched in 1961) was also a knee-skimming black evening dress. Created specifically for Mrs Arturo Lopez-Willshaw, and bearing the model number 00001, the dress was fashioned from black embossed silk crêpe georgette with a jet-embroidered bodice. It also featured a slashed neckline decorated with a sash, tied in a bow on one shoulder. 'His fashion doesn't tamper with your personality, it promotes it,' explained Paloma Picasso, one of Saint Laurent's closest confidants.[49] This might also be part of a sales-pitch for the popularity of his LBDs. Actress Catherine Deneuve, who Saint Laurent dressed since he was first commissioned to create her wardrobe for Luis Buñuel's *Belle de Jour* in 1966, added rather enigmatically that, 'His day clothes help a woman confront the world of strangers'.[50] Continuing her praise, she observed how Saint Laurent has 'this impulse to serve a modern woman, to accommodate her life'.[51]

When Tom Ford was creative director at YSL ready-to-wear (1999–2004), it was the erotically charged *Belle de Jour* he turned to for inspiration for many of his eveningwear looks; specifically, it was the theme of his Autumn/Winter 2002 collection [Fig. 3.10]. A series of barely-there black dresses cut in satin and Chantilly lace, held together with well-positioned bows, caused American *Vogue*'s Sarah Mower to muse: 'What, after all, could be more provocative than a woman wearing expensive clothes that look as if they were made to be undone by a lover?'[52] Prior to Ford's tenure, a youthful Alber Elbaz held the role of creative director at YSL (1998–2001). Elbaz's vision for YSL was more restrained than Ford's – a black satin roll-neck chemise or slashed and draped jersey shift. When he latterly assumed the role of creative director at Lanvin in 2001, he reprised this more refined style with his 21st-century ruminations on Jeanne Lanvin's trademark 1920s *robe de style*. At the house of Lanvin, he too made the LBD a signature of his repertoire.

Saint Laurent returned time and time again to the LBD, offering endless interpretations, each exactingly realised. It is pertinent to refer to Saint Laurent's own lyrical definition of how to cut the perfect dress: 'It's perfection of line. It's perfection of material. It's how to work with a beautiful fabric, to give life to a wonderful material. To tame it by keeping it alive.'[53] With so many to choose from in his vast archive it is an unenviable task to highlight just a handful without appearing to dismiss obvious exceptions. Every fashion fan has a favourite. In 1966, *WWD* listed a long black velvet evening dress with re-embroidered white cotton collar and black satin cuffs, and a black wool jersey dress belted with gold buckle among the best sellers.[54] Then there is the audaciously saucy black sheer silk chiffon gown with a skirt of ostrich feathers from Autumn/Winter 1968; the subversive black lace keyhole dress from his 1971 *Forties* collection; the dramatically back-draped black velvet cocktail dress of Autumn/Winter 1983; or the simple stretch jersey from the *Rive Gauche* line, 1988 [Fig. 3.11]. It's a list that never ends.

Throughout his career Yves Saint Laurent had but one aim: 'My job is to work for women. Not only mannequins, beautiful women or rich women but all women.'[55] At a retrospective exhibition of his work titled *Yves Saint Laurent: 28 Années de*

Fig. 3.10 (opposite)
Tom Ford for Yves Saint Laurent *Rive Gauche*, Autumn/Winter 2002. *Elle* magazine, December 2002.
(Photographer: Iain R Webb)

Création (Musée des Arts de la Mode, 30 May–26 October 1986), a vast collection of the designer's black dresses were displayed spanning his career. Shown en masse, it was difficult to pinpoint the chronology of the dresses, so timeless were they – each one perfection, each different from the other, but held together by their uniformity: black. And, more importantly, any one of those black dresses, both little and long, could have easily stepped down from its podium and sashayed into the night, partying at the ever-popular *Maxim's* restaurant or the hip and trendy *Bains Douche* bar. Today, those vintage little black dresses have never been more in demand. Lucinda Alford again:

So when I go out in the evening I always choose Yves Saint Laurent or a Jean Muir jersey. So simple. Personally, I have about four Yves Saint Laurent LBDs that I've worn for the last twenty years. Every time I wear them I feel fabulous. For me it's all about Yves. It's *always* all about Yves.

Acknowledgement

Sadly, during the making of this book Lucinda Alford passed away.

Notes

1   Lucinda Alford, personal interview with the author; likewise, all subsequent citations by Alford.
2   'Frock of Ages', in *Observer Life,* 5 December 1993.
3   Elizabeth Wilson, *Adorned in Dreams: Fashion and Modernity* (rev. edition 2009 [1985, Virago]), p. 189.
4   Veronica Horwell, 'Azzedine Alaïa obituary', *The Guardian* (2017).
5   Rosemary Harden, personal interview with the author; likewise, all subsequent citations by Harden. See Fashion Museum, Bath, BATMC I.09.2339.
6   Linda Watson, *20th Century Fashion: 100 years of style by decade and designer, in association with Vogue* (1999), p. 95.
7   Design Museum Enterprise: *Fifty Dresses that Changed the World: Design Museum Fifty* (2009).
8   John Galliano, personal interview with the author.
9   Stephen Jones, original interview with the author; likewise, all subsequent citations by Jones.
10 *Evening Standard,* 15 March 1988.
11 Bias cut: a technique of diagonally cutting across the fabric to achieve a sensual drape.
12 Kim Bowen, *BLITZ* magazine, January 1990.
13 Fashion Museum, Bath, BATMC 95.430.
14 Philip Treacy, personal interview with the author; likewise, all subsequent citations by Treacy.
15 Paul Gorman, *The Look: Adventures in Pop & Rock Fashion* (2001), p. 103.
16 Fiona Dealey, personal interview with the author; likewise, all subsequent citations by Dealey.
17 Domenico Dolce and Stefano Gabbana, personal interview with the author; likewise, all subsequent citations by Dolce and Gabbana.
18 Mary Quant, personal interview with the author.
19 Quoted in Jenny Lister, *Mary Quant* (2019), p. 102.
20 *Ibid.*, p. 208.
21 Mary Quant, personal interview with the author.
22 Mary Quant, *Colour by Quant* (1984), p. 159.
23 Jasper Conran, personal interview with the author; likewise, all subsequent citations by Conran.
24 Harry Leuckert, personal interview with the author; likewise, all subsequent citations by Leuckert.
25 Watson, *20th Century Fashion* (1999), p. 199.
26 Jean Muir, personal interview with the author; likewise, all subsequent citations by Muir.

27 See *Very Jean Muir*, an Antelope production for Channel 4 (1993/94).
28 National Museums Scotland, K.2012.102.
29 Linda Watson, 'Geoffrey Beene', *The Independent* (2004).
30 Sinty Stemp, *Jean Muir: Beyond Fashion* (2007), p. 132.
31 See Noël Palomo-Lovinski, *The World's Most Influential Fashion Designers* (2010).
32 *The Times*, 15 March 1993.
33 *Ibid.*
34 Jil Sander, personal interview with the author for article published in *The Times*, 10 May 1993; likewise, all subsequent citations by Sander.
35 Elsa Schiaparelli, *Shocking Life* (2018 [1954]), p. 52.
36 *Ibid.*, p. 50.
37 According to *Vogue* coverage, February 1940, quoted in Valerie Mendes, *Black in Fashion* (1999), p. 43.
38 Schiaparelli, *Shocking Life* (2018 [1954]), p. 90.
39 Meryle Secrest, *Elsa Schiaparelli* (2014), p. 93.
40 Robin Givhan, 'A layman's guide to understanding a fashion week runway show', *The Independent*, 11 February (2018): <https://www.independent.co.uk/life-style/fashion/laymans-guide-understanding-fashion-week-runway-show-thom-browne-spring-summer-2018-giant-unicorn-a8201086.html>
41 Pierre Balmain, *My Years and Seasons* (1964), p. 175.
42 *Ibid.*
43 R J Cutler (director), *The September Issue* (2009).
44 Balmain, *My Years and Seasons* (1964), p. 80.
45 Toile: an initial prototype of a garment, usually made in calico.
46 Balmain, *My Years and Seasons* (1964).
47 Fashion Museum, Bath, BATMC I.24.72 & A.
48 Hady Sy and Beatrice Dupire, *Yves Saint Laurent, 40 Years of Creation* (1998), p. 22.
49 Yves Saint Laurent and Diana Vreeland, *Yves Saint Laurent* (1984), p. 33.
50 *Ibid.*, p. 34.
51 *Ibid.*
52 Sarah Mower, 'Saint Laurent Fall 2002 Ready-to-Wear', *Vogue* online (March 2002): <https://www.vogue.com/fashion-shows/fall-2002-ready-to-wear/saint-laurent>
53 Saint Laurent and Vreeland, *Yves Saint Laurent* (1984), p. 96.
54 Jéromine Savignon and Gilles de Bure with Pierre Bergé, *Saint Laurent Rive Gauche: Fashion Revolution* (2012), p. 31.
55 Saint Laurent and Vreeland, *Yves Saint Laurent* (1984), p. 117.

Fig. 3.11 (opposite)

Yves Saint Laurent *Rive Gauche*, 1988, *Evening Standard*.

(Photographer: Mark Lewis)

4
BLACK WILL TAKE ANY OTHER HUE

Makoto Ishizeki

'Is black hopeless? Doesn't every
dark thundercloud have a silver lining?
In black lies the possibility of hope.'[1]

In the 1980s, a 'new wave' of fashion came from the Far East. On the crest of the wave were Yohji Yamamoto and Rei Kawakubo of Comme des Garçons, who entered the Paris fashion scene in 1981. Those who witnessed their early collections strongly remember the garments that were seemingly unfinished or worn, partly holed, irregularly asymmetrical, indefinitely genderless and radically black.

When describing this epoch-making event in both Western and Japanese fashion histories, fashion experts and scholars, mainly in Japan, frequently mention the 'shock of black'. Whether their way of using the colour was shocking or not, throughout the 1980s Yamamoto and Kawakubo regularly presented collections with looks mostly consisting of black, beige and, frequently, dark colours like navy, charcoal and olive, and monochrome colour palettes became characteristic of these two designers.

Just some months after the first Paris collections of Yamamoto and Kawakubo, *Artforum* magazine featured a sartorial work on its cover for the first time: an armour-like bodice fashioned from beautifully curved rattan, contrasted with a glossy, pleated long skirt, conceived by Issey Miyake [Fig. 4.1]. The outfit's dominant colour was black. Their Japanese contemporaries, among whom Junko Koshino and Mitsuhiro Matsuda were high on the list, also attracted international journalists and buyers with their novel way of cutting, playful design and use of black. At this time in Japan, young women who loved these growing brands and who dressed all in black were called the *karasu-zoku* (crow tribe).

Although the etymological origins of the cliché, 'shock of black', are difficult to trace, examples of its usage can be found around the early 1990s at the latest, and it has certainly affected subsequent generations. Through this recognition of the creativity of Japanese designers, we have developed new perceptions of the colour black.

'Exotic' black: Japanese designers in the 1980s

'Hiroshima chic', the legendary but unfavourable tag attached to the work of Yamamoto and Kawakubo, was derived from the reactions of international, primarily French, journalists who reported on their collections in the early 1980s. A famous commentary, published in *Le Figaro*, criticised their Spring/Summer 1983 shows:

> *Tout a commencé jeudi dernier. Avec en hors-d'œuvre des spécialités japonaises servies par une firme niponne. «Comme des garçons». Sa vision apocalyptique du vêtement: des trous, des loques, des guenilles comme pour les survivants d'une catastrophe nucléaire. Une mode de fin du monde que l'on retrouvera chez Kansaï [sic] Yamamoto qui met en pièces des vêtements déchiquetés comme après un attentat à la bombe. Froid dans le dos.*[2]

In this report, full of sarcasm *à la française* and employing the 'end-of-the-world' expression often used at that time, experienced French journalist Janie Samet demonstrated her disgust for characteristic elements of the two designers' pieces. Scattered holes and creases, frayed edges, loose and distorted shapes, which could be associated with those of ragged clothes, seemed like 'Japanese

Fig. 4.1 (page 72)
Ensemble by Issey Miyake, *Artforum*, February 1982.
(© Issey Miyake, 1982 Spring/Summer Collection. Photo: Eiichiro Sakata. Cover, *Artforum*, February 1982)

Fig. 4.2 (page 73)
Comme des Garçons, Paris, Ready-to-Wear Spring/Summer 1983.
Photographer Michel Arnaud.
(Courtesy of the FIDM Museum at the Fashion Institute of Design & Merchandising, Los Angeles, CA)

ARTFORUM

FEBRUARY 1982 **SPECIAL ISSUE** $6.00

LAURIE ANDERSON
▶ Record & Jacket

ANDY WARHOL
▶ Centerfold

MARIE COSINDAS
▶ Pinball Graphics

Advertising's Architecture

of Heaven...

Vulgar Modernism...

Bop Art...   and more

specialities' in her eyes [Fig. 4.2]. However, she did not mention anything about the colours they had used, and no images of the garments were published alongside her report to show what they looked like.

Not only Yamamoto and Kawakubo but other 'Japanese' designers active in the West are often distinguished by their nationality and considered as one group: their approaches toward dressmaking are compared with the theory of Western (or Parisian) couture, and the characteristics of their individual works are homogenised and 'often traced to origins in culture, such as a Japanese aesthetic, Zen, or regional costume'.[3] Fashion historian Hissako Anjo explored the representation of Kawakubo's early collections in Paris as they appeared in French newspapers and magazines of the time. Anjo argued that to understand the 'shock' of Yamamoto and Kawakubo to the Western fashion scene, we must consider the historical background: there had been a remarkable increase in Japanese designers participating in Paris Fashion Week,[4] as well as an escalation of Franco- or Euro-Japanese trade frictions since the late 1970s.[5] Japanese designers were described not just in terms of new or veteran competitors in the international fashion scene, but rather as mysterious catalysts who came from a different world to influence Western fashion. In the eyes of conservative viewers, their creations seemed like dubious invaders of the Western fashion market, likely to follow motorcars, televisions, semi-conductors and other 'made-in-Japan' products that had crowded Western countries and driven them to implement protectionist policies at that time.[6]

The excerpt below is a typical text from this period, in which – referring to the same shows by Yamamoto and Kawakubo witnessed by Samet for *Le Figaro* – the writer looked not at the two designers themselves but at their country of origin, its culture and economy, against a background of dualism between the West and Japan (or the East):

En révolte contre l'Occident, sa domination économique (l'impérialisme américain) et sa domination esthétique (la mode française). Deux Japonais qui revendiquent le droit à leur propre culture et qui l'affirment avec violence.

Violence contenue chez l'un, à la manière bouddhique; violence agressive chez l'autre, à la façon samouraï. Yohji Yamamoto et Reï Kawakubo, c'est le bonze et la kamikaze. Pour qui garde les yeux ouverts et tente d'observer sans parti pris, leur démarche est claire: faire éclater le monopole occidental de la mode. [...] Notre mode construite, logique, à la limite cartésienne, est désormais confrontée à une mode floue, non ajustée, fluide en quelque sorte. Jusqu'aux couleurs (noir, gris, bleus délavés) qui sont comme des non-couleurs.[7]

The article explicitly contains the Western point of view of Orientalism, as analysed by academic and political activist Edward Said, that positions Japan in opposition to the West to accentuate the otherness of the former and fabricate the persisting superiority of the latter.[8] The observations above were visually reinforced by the accompanying photographs – baggy looks by Yamamoto and Kawakubo, 'carefully' selected from their collections, and the colours of the chosen garments were, no less, white and black.

Despite its long history in Western culture, black has also borne 'exotic' meanings, often originating from the non-Western world. The use and symbolism of black in early Islamic culture influenced – not radically, but gradually – the vogue for this colour in the Spanish court and its subsequent spread throughout Europe in the 16th and 17th centuries.[9] A natural dye, logwood, extracted from a tree of the same name (*Haematoxylum campechianum*) and imported in large quantities from Central America since the 16th century, attracted European merchants and dyers to its beautiful deep black until the invention of synthetic dyes. Art Deco artists of the 20th century were aesthetically influenced by two different non-Western regions: art and culture from across Africa and, more specifically, the layered and polished black surface of Japanese lacquer work. In the 1980s, a new 'unknown' black was brought to the West by a mass of Japanese designers.

Although they vary widely, these designers all have a pared [*sic*] down approach which Mary Russell of American *Vogue* calls 'Japanese Minimal,' inspired by 'Zen simplicity' or 'mu' (nothingness) as a new conceptual art.

Great restraint is shown in color. Currently Japanese designers are limiting themselves to a severe palette of grey and various shades of black which adds to the sculptural feeling in the clothes. New, natural colors with a muddy tone combine with voluminous shapes, wrinkles and slits for powerfully sombre elegance.[10]

Plural black: Yohji Yamamoto

Junichiro Tanizaki's essay, *In Praise of Shadows* (1933), is often referenced to demonstrate the peculiarity of Japanese designers using dark colours and their creative roots in Japanese traditional aesthetics. Looking at the modernisation and Westernisation of Japanese society in the early 20th century, the novelist rediscovers a modest beauty in shades of shadow which might have been omnipresent in old Japanese life. In fact, the essay reflects Tanizaki's nostalgia for the distinct identity of the Japanese aesthetic, which he associates with objects and traditions that he assumes to be vanishing from everyday life. The Kyoto Costume Institute applied the title of the essay to the first section of its travelling exhibition project, *Future Beauty: 30 Years of Japanese Fashion* (Barbican Art Gallery, London, 15 October 2010–6 February 2011, and Haus der Kunst, Munich, 4 March–19 June 2011).[11] The section was mainly dedicated to the black clothing of Yamamoto and Kawakubo, where 'the light and the darkness woven by thread, the shades of colour created when material sags and overlaps, skilfully incorporates shadows as a form of sartorial expression' [Fig. 4.3].[12] The concept of the exhibition, to portray the creativity of Japanese designers in the history of Western fashion, implies in no small part a nationalistic point of view. Although that could be considered to reproduce and strengthen the discourse of Orientalism, what the exhibition accentuated with reference to the essay was not so much the tradition of aesthetics, but rather their subtle sensitivity to various nuances in colours.

Yamamoto has been particularly and unchangingly associated with the colour black since the 1980s. Utilising a variety of shades, his little black dress elicits multiple readings of the colour. For his first show in Paris, Yamamoto used lots of black, as opposed to the vibrant colours seen in Japan's city streets; here it represented the quietness and minimalism of *Noh* theatre contrasted with the dynamism of *Kabuki*.[13] One year later his – and Kawakubo's – black was regarded as the colour of poverty and mourning in connection to their shapeless, frayed and torn garments. He also considers black as the colour of silhouette – neutral and meaningless – to emphasise a surface or texture. The refinement of this idea is culminated in his bustle coat of 1986; impressively photographed by Nick Knight, a flat, black profile of a model wearing the dark coat with a red bustle sparkling at her back, precisely demonstrates the coexistence of darkness and light [Fig. 4.4].[14] Since then, his style has retained a haute

couture touch, referencing classic shapes of historic Western female dress as well as signature works of master designers such as Gabrielle Chanel, Madeleine Vionnet, Christian Dior and Cristóbal Balenciaga, who distinguished themselves by their use of black signifying elegance and Modernism. Inspired by street fashion and sportswear, models were dressed by Yamamoto in simple, loose clothes for his Autumn/Winter 2001 collection. The garments were comprised of stretchy or soft materials, effectively layered to create voluminous shapes in the air as the models moved. The black mainly used here was no longer 'dark'; instead it represented something pared back, but functional and sophisticated.

Curious and often ironical, Yamamoto prefers to play with the symbolism of black rather than the aesthetics of its various shades. As a colour of minimalism, black visualises Yamamoto's ethos of eliminating excess, though this is not to be completely confined to one set style or image. Essential differences remain, from which arise a new richness and new connotations. Above all, he loves black because of its fullness, the very nature of the colour

Fig. 4.3 (above)
Future Beauty: 30 Years of Japanese Fashion (Barbican Art Gallery, London, 15 October 2010–6 February 2011).
(© Barbican Art Gallery, photo by Lyndon Douglas Photography)

Fig. 4.4 (opposite)
Yohji Yamamoto, Ready-to-Wear 1986.
(Nick Knight / Trunk Archive)

encompassing all the colours of the visible spectrum, and the ambiguity of its interpretations. In Wim Wenders' experimental documentary film, *Notebook on Cities and Clothes*, Yamamoto described his preference for black:

> Sometimes, black is the conclusion of the colour[s], because of the mixing, mixing, mixing …. Then, everything comes to black. So, [I am] quite interested in that sense. For me, it is like […] put[ting] everything in the water. To put everything in black and I forget them.[15]

Colourful black: Rei Kawakubo

Kawakubo is also conversant with the variety of black. Her use of achromatic colours – dominantly in different shades of black, navy, dark grey, beige and white, occasionally with light colours like pink, orange and lime green as accent colours – was so intense and consistent throughout the 1980s that, even now, we cannot help but link her creations with black, the most captivating colour amongst them.

It was with her Autumn/Winter 1988 collection that Kawakubo turned colourist, with a cryptic remark 'red is black'. Adorned with her favourite ethnic motifs, the collection featured a vivid red variously in combination with white and black [Fig. 4.5]. Did Kawakubo paradoxically intend to contradistinguish red from black to declare the end of her 'black period'? Certainly not. For Kawakubo, black is as colourful as red: among varied tones and textures from reddish to blueish, light to deep, glossy to matte, differences are microscopic but visually perceptible, as if our eyes are focusing in darkness. Just as she had previously publicly discussed using several kinds of black for her very early

Fig. 4.5 (above)
Comme des Garçons, Ready-to-Wear Autumn/Winter 1988.
(© Chris Moore Catwalking)

Fig. 4.6 (page 80)
Comme des Garçons, Homme Plus Menswear Autumn/Winter 2019, Paris Fashion Week.
(By Victor VIRGILE / Getty Images)

collections in Paris,[16] during the 1980s Kawakubo demonstrated the potential of black to be 'multi-coloured' by using a range of materials and dyeing techniques, as well as different finishing methods like layering, pleating, creasing and fraying.

Kawakubo is also interested in the strength of colours. She used black because at the time it looked new and she felt that it could be strongly expressed.[17] Certainly, her consistent artistic practice of creating striking black colours was provocative and unforgettable. With the statement 'red is black', she defined red as a very strong colour equivalent to black. As the fashion curator and historian Valerie Steele observed, since 1988 'Kawakubo has exploited the varieties of red – but always with her own sense of style. When she uses a brilliant saturated red, for example, it is perceived as an unexpected element of avant-garde fashion.'[18]

During the 1990s, Kawakubo's repertoire extended from variations of black to orchestration of the whole spectrum of colour. The Spring/Summer 1996 collection, *Kaleidoscope*, symbolised her exquisite tact in using colour: asymmetric compositions of colour and multi-coloured vertical and horizontal stripes, worn with large, vivid, fluffy wigs, moved around on the stage in a skilful symphony of colour, generating visual impact from the consonance and dissonance of different hues.

Even white is no less strong – as proven in Rei Kawakubo's Autumn/Winter 2018 menswear collection. Beginning with colourful prints of Superman cartoons, bird's-eye city views, camouflage and stone pavements, these were gradually but entirely wiped out with garments in white and beige. The looks were completed with unique, large sculptural masks of dinosaur fossils created by a Japanese plastic artist [Fig. 4.6]. Kawakubo titled this collection *White Shock*, emphasising black and white as two opposing colours:

In this collection [...], white served for the expression of strength, and I thought it would fit with dinosaurs by [Masakatsu] Shimoda.
—— For the expression of strength?
The colour of white represents something unknown and unsettled in the future and, at the same time, something the most innocent, and it questions us about the two. I, myself, think white symbolises strength or toughness. Whether it is about 'camp' or 'punk', rebellion is easily associated with an image of black. Power created by black is overwhelming as a material for expression.
—— As for the strength and pliancy belonging to black, these were invented by you.
I believe that, for now, expression with white can be strong. I found it primarily important to express an image of rebellion with white, not to extend it in black, and so I tried to.[19]

White can arouse fear when we have an encounter with the unknown, as in the story of Moby-Dick. Herman Melville dedicated a whole chapter of his novel to 'The Whiteness of the Whale', which appalled the narrator Ishmael. Speculating about things and phenomena known as being impressively white, his questions attempted to reveal the true nature of this colour:

Is it that by its indefiniteness it shadows forth the heartless voids and immensities of the universe, and thus stabs us from behind with the thought of annihilation, when beholding the white depths of the milky way? Or is it, that as in essence whiteness is not so much a color as the visible absence of color; and at the same time the concrete of all colors; is it for these reasons that there is such a dumb

blankness, full of meaning, in a wide landscape of snows – a colorless, all-color of atheism from which we shrink?[20]

Similar considerations may be true when it comes to black: it is the very visible absence of colour and, at the same time, the result of mixing subtractive primary colours.[21] With eternally and unlimitedly expanding dark voids, the sum of things becomes transcendental and gives us a feeling of awe. Black is thus colourless and colourful, meaningless and meaningful. At this point, white translates to black, and vice versa. So too can red; Kawakubo's mystical statement 'red is black' likens black to a chromatic colour. In her eyes all the colours are equivalent to and interchangeable with one another, and can be expressed in equally extraordinary ways.

Cosmic black: Viktor & Rolf

Today, the ways in which Japanese designers thought about and used black for their garments during the 1980s are commonly accepted for fashion design, as well as for a fashion exhibition concept. The Kyoto Costume Institute held a fashion exhibition titled *Fashion in Colors: Viktor & Rolf & KCI* (The National Museum of Modern Art in Kyoto, 29 April–20 June 2004; and the Mori Art Museum, Tokyo, 24 August–5 December 2004), for which the Dutch designer duo played guest curators. Their design concept carried the colour of the garments on display to the gallery's walls, platforms and floors, and even to the mannequins. The first section of the show was titled 'Black'. The shape of every exhibit – from riding habits of the 19th century, through Chanel's modern little black dress and feminised suits of the 1950s, to today's punk-influenced or iconoclastic styles – was obscured by its integration into the exhibition

set. Visually powerful, the impact of black was reinforced by projecting the film of Viktor & Rolf's sensational Autumn/Winter 2001 show, in which everything was blackened – from the walls to the catwalk, the garments to the models (literally from head to toe). The collection was titled *The Black Hole*. The duo – who continued to present such colour-themed collections as white (Spring/Summer 2002), blue (Autumn/Winter 2002), and red (Spring/Summer 2004) – were inspired by their personal feeling:

At a certain point we felt very negative and depressed, and we felt the only way to deal with it was to use that feeling creatively and to turn the negative into the positive. Since it felt so black inside us, we felt we had to drip the whole show in black paint, including the models. Like a black hole in the universe that sucks up all energy.[22]

Black absorbs light. It has the power to subsume the spectrum of visible colours to transform a material into a silhouette or shadow, a flat but deep surface without substance, and which conveys a sense of 'absence'. The designers took the black hole as the most ideal notion in the universe that could represent the inescapable gravity of the colour.

An attracting force felt in the 'Black' section of the *Fashion in Colors* exhibition changed its vector in the following section, 'Multicolour'. There sparkled a variety of colours and colouring techniques that have flourished in fashion for centuries: French silk brocade and Indian chintz of the 18th century, innovative synthetic dyes of the 19th, and the democratised and unchained use of colour in the present day [Fig. 4.7]. The brilliant effect of various colourful objects gathered in one gallery was amplified for eyes which had become accustomed to a faint light in the darkness of the

Fig. 4.7

Fashion in Colors: Viktor & Rolf & KCI
(The National Museum of Modern Art, Kyoto,
29 April–20 June 2004; and the Mori Art Museum, Tokyo,
24 August–5 December 2004).

(© The Kyoto Costume Institute, photo by Naoya Hatakeyama)

previous room. Contrasting the achromatic and the chromatic to 'turn the negative into the positive', Viktor & Rolf maximised the optical and psychological influence of colour.

Since the beginning of their career, Viktor & Rolf have been interested in the potential of darkness, or the immaterial 'silhouette = shadow' as an avenue of expression, which has produced conceptually exciting collections. *The Black Hole* collection is one of the most visually striking shows in their history, and certainly in the history of the fashion show in general. The *Zen Garden* collection of Autumn/ Winter 2013 represented the duo's affection for Eastern culture and attempt to interpret the theory of mindfulness derived from Buddhism. Inspired by the world-famous rock garden of Ryoanji temple in Kyoto, they conceived a tableau vivant performance. Models were clad in black dresses and variously posed by the designers on a stage resembling the garden with a graphical imitation of its distinctive waves of raked gravel. Wearing dresses of different silhouettes in the same colour, models were gathered into groups to mimic uniquely shaped stones dispersed in the zen garden [Fig. 4.8].

The stillness and simplicity recognised in this

monochromatic rock garden both encouraged and facilitated reflection on the part of the viewer. Japanese Zen Buddhists consider their garden as a projection of an ideal world, legendary land, or metaphysical cosmos, and often sit in front of it to practice *zazen* (seated meditation). As for Viktor & Rolf's collection, the designers' mindful posing of the models was intended to 'express a feeling of serenity and nothingness'.[23] A striking contrast between light and shadow brought an air of intense quietness to the stage, giving an air of dignity to

Fig. 4.8
Viktor & Rolf, *Zen Garden*, Haute Couture Autumn/Winter 2013, Paris.
(Reuters / Alamy Stock Photo)

every movement of the models, while the black clothing accentuated their unusual silhouettes. In this sense, the designers succeeded in theatricalising the spirit of the zen garden.[24]

Conclusion: in search of the potential of black

Black is universal. How the eye distinguishes colours is subjective, culturally acquired and genetically determined, while black is equally perceived as the state in which visible light is absent or completely absorbed. Black is also a colour of the universe, expressed in the black hole, which absorbs everything.

Black is multi-coloured. It is created by a mixture of dyes and pigments of different colours. In Japan, indigo and madder were historically employed to dye a fabric black.[25] Diderot's *Encyclopédie* from the 18th century explains that to obtain a beautiful black for wool involved first dyeing it blue, as dark as possible, before applying different natural black dyes like gallnut, logwood and sumac.[26] In printing, a harmonised blend of the four CMYK colours produces a 'rich black', while a regular black comes from a single black ink cartridge. Theoretically and empirically, we see chromatic colours, more than nuances, in black.

Black is multi-faceted. Its symbolism is complex, ambiguous and variable: a black garment can represent mourning, abstinence, industriousness, gravity, magnificence, sophistication, minimalism and ordinariness. It can equally represent uniformity, solidarity, independence, existentialism, rebellion, maliciousness, impurity, unfamiliarity and mysteriousness – any one of which characteristics can be adopted in the intertexture of the wearer's intention and the viewer's perception. Japanese designers in the 1980s, and their followers, redefined the use of black in fashion, affirming an openness to manifold interpretations of the colour. Ultimately, black is darkness, a darkness behind which exists and appears the unknown universe, akin to Pandora's box. What do we see in the gloom – evil or hope?

Notes

1 Derek Jarman, 'Black Arts: O Mia Anima Nera', *Chroma: A Book of Colour – June '93* (1995), p. 138.
2 Janie Samet, '6 jour de mode, 36 collections 4500 modèles', in *Le Figaro* (1982), p. 2.
[*Everything started last Thursday. For starters, Japanese specialties served by a firm from Nippon, 'Comme des garçons'. Her vision for garments is apocalyptic: holes, rags, tatters like for the survivors of a nuclear catastrophe. End-of-the-world fashion that we will find at Yohji Yamamoto, who fragments frayed garments like after a bomb attack. Chills down the spine.*]
3 Dorinne Kondo, 'Orientalizing: Fashioning Japan', in *About Face: Performing Race in Fashion and Theater* (1997), p. 57.
4 The daily newspaper, *Libération*, reported that ten out of almost 70 collections for Spring/Summer 1983 were presented by Japanese brands: Hiroko Koshino, Yuki Torii, Comme des Garçons, Junko Koshino, Yohji Yamamoto, Kansai Yamamoto, Issey Miyake, Junko Shimada, Hanae Mori, and Kenzo. See Michel Cressole, 'Sept japonais ethniques', in *Libération* (1982), p. 2. More recently, nine out of 94 collections for Autumn/Winter 2021 were by Japanese designers: see *Paris Fashion Week*: <https://parisfashionweek.fhcm.paris/fr/calendrier/>
5 Hissako Anjo, 'A Study of the Discourse on the early collection of Comme des Garçons: The distance between the image and position in the contemporary discourse and the recent discourse', in *Journal of the Japan Society of Design*, vol. 47 (2005), pp. 8–10.
6 Anjo points out that some articles commenting on Japanese fashion designers referred to the trade issues of the period between France and Japan (*Ibid.*, p. 10). Sometimes they were described as 'péril jaune' [yellow peril].
7 Ginette Sainderichin, 'Le bonze et la kamikaze', in *Jardin des modes* (1982), p. 5.
[*Revolting against the West: its economic domination (American imperialism) and its aesthetic domination (French fashion). Two Japanese who claim the right to their own culture and affirm it with violence. One with a suppressed violence like a Buddhist, the other with an aggressive violence like a samurai. Yohji Yamamoto and Rei Kawakubo are the bonze and the kamikaze. For those who keep their eyes open and try to observe without bias, their approach is obvious: to shatter the Western monopoly of the fashion market. [...] Our fashion, which is constructed, logical, almost in a Cartesian way, is henceforth confronted with a loose, unadjusted, partly fluid fashion. Even their colours (black, grey, faded blues) which are like non-colours.*]
8 Anjo, 'A Study of the Discourse on the early collection of Comme des Garçons' (2005), p. 11.
9 John Harvey, *Kuro no bunkashi* (2014), pp. 93–108.

10 Rebecca Voight, 'East Meets West in Paris', in *Passion* (1983), pp. 24–25. Interestingly, a Japanese journalist's impression of the Spring/Summer 1983 season was that the entire Paris and Milan fashion weeks had been outstandingly dominated by black and white. She referred to Jean-Louis Scherrer, Philippe Venet, Guy Laroche and Emanuel Ungaro as examples: Junko Ouchi, '1983 Spring-Summer Paris Collection', in *Katei gaho* (1983), p. 129.

11 The exhibition continued to travel to the Museum of Contemporary Art, Tokyo (2012), the Seattle Art Museum (2013), the Peabody Essex Museum, Salem (2013–14), the National Museum of Modern Art, Kyoto (2014), and the Gallery of Modern Art, Brisbane (2014–15).

12 Akiko Fukai, 'Future Beauty 30 Years of Japanese Fashion', in Catherine Ince and Rie Nii (eds) *Future Beauty: 30 Years of Japanese Fashion* (2010), p. 15.

13 Mariejo de Loisne, 'À l'est, du nouveau', in *Gap* (1982), p. 119.

14 Yamamoto and Azzedine Alaïa once had a very short talk about red and black:
YY: Red isn't a colour, it's a light.
AA: There are red reds, violet reds. Red is another black. I never get bored of it.
See Laurence Benaïm, 'Azzedine Alaïa & Yohji Yamamoto in conversation with Laurence Benaïm', in *A Magazine #2* (2005), p. 47.

15 Wim Wenders (dir.), *Notebook on Cities and Clothes* (2006 [1989]).

16 De Loisne, 'À l'est, du nouveau' (1982), p. 118.

17 Izumi Miyachi and Hiroyuki Kikuchi, '20 seiki donna jidai dattaka, pari mōdo heno chōsen', in *Yomiuri Shinbun* (1999), p. 11.

18 Valerie Steele, *The Red Dress* (2001), p. 11.

19 Toshiki Arai, 'Long Interview with Rei Kawakubo: *Koboreru shiroi tomeina shizuku*', in *Switch* 36:6 (2018), p. 24.

20 Herman Melville, *Moby-Dick; or, The Whale* [1851]. See: <https://melville.electronic library.org/moby-dick-side-by-side>

21 The complementary colours cyan, yellow and magenta are commonly referred to as the primary subtractive colours because each can be formed by subtracting one of the primary additives (red, green and blue) from white light. If you overlap all three in equal mixture, all the light is subtracted giving black.

22 The Kyoto Costume Institute, 'Viktor & Rolf: Self-portrait', in Akiko Fukai (ed.), *Fashion in Colors: Viktor & Rolf & KCI* (2004), p. 279.

23 Tokiotours (2013), 'Viktor & Rolf designed a "living" Zen rock garden, inspired by Kyoto's Ryoanji temple'. See: <https://tokiotours.wordpress.com/2013/07/06/viktor-rolf-designed-a-living-zen-rock-garden-inspired-by-kyotos-ryoanji-temple/>

24 It has to be said that, inevitably, this kind of adaptation – which could pose simplistic interpretations to some extent – leaves room for criticism in terms of orientalism or cultural appropriation.

25 Ujo Maeda, *Mono to ningen no bunka-shi 38 iro some to shikisai* (1980), p. 276.

26 'Teinture', in Denis Diderot and Jean le Rond d'Alembert (eds), *L'Encyclopédie* [orig. 1751]: <https://artflsrv03.uchicago.edu/philologic4/encyclopedie1117/navigate/16/74/>

LBD (SM)

Fiona Jardine

Supposedly, the little black dress is handed something like a power of attorney over those social occasions that extend beyond our trusted circle of intimates. A proxy for good taste, it is meant to assure us that we will be judged favourably by those that do not know us or by those who employ us. Its authority derives from restraint in form, quality in materials and restriction of palette to a single colour: black – the perfect foil for a judiciously selected gold chain, a string of pearls or a diamond spider. Mercilessly, it exposes shortcuts in every deviation from the plumb line. It is variously modest, confident, alluring and polished, invoking the long history of formal black clothing in order to play with the projection of power. The classic little black dress takes shape as something Modern, finding forbears in the functional simplicity of Coco Chanel's liberating designs, as discussed in chapter 1.

By the time Tess McGill (Melanie Griffith) donned the off-duty garb of her boss in *Working Girl* (1988), the little black dress – or something like it – had established itself as an essential in the wardrobe of every city professional hoping to negotiate 'the boys' club' on her own terms.[1] As a secretary, Tess has too much hair, too much make-up, wears too many patterns, too many ornaments, has too many friends – she is not taken seriously. When transferred to work with a female executive, Katharine Parker, for the first time Tess feels she might have some sisterly support in achieving her ambitions. Duplicitous Katharine, wearing a beautifully draped grey suit, wants her to dress better:

> I consider us a team, Tess, and as such we have a uniform. Simple, elegant, impeccable. 'Dress shabbily, they notice the dress. Dress impeccably, they notice the woman' [Coco Chanel].[2]

Chanel's little black dress provides a notional blueprint for an educated businesswoman at the top of her game in an era when greed was good. The interpersonal dynamics between Tess and Katharine are riven with class tension and are most saliently expressed through dress. When a ski-ing accident affords Tess the opportunity to reclaim a commercial initiative Katharine has stolen from her, she also gains access to Katharine's vast Upper East Side closet: there, among the luxurious satin gowns, a perfect, terrifyingly expensive, little black dress. Sumptuous in rich black velvet, sparsely studded with diamanté, it is coquettishly off-the-shoulder and full-skirted [Fig. 5.1]. It contrasts dramatically with the mannish suits and pie-crust collars worn by the smattering of other female executives at a work party she crashes. Alluding more to Madonna – riding the swell of third-wave feminism – than to Chanel, Tess, the imposter, has 'a head for business and a bod for sin'.[3]

La Moratoire Noire

If we shift focus back a decade or so previously, to Montreuil, a suburb of Paris, some miles from the elegant ashlar of 31 Rue Cambon – spiritual home of Chanel's little black dress – we find ourselves with 4000 others at La Main Bleue. A newly established nightclub, La Main Bleue occupies the basement of a shopping centre repurposed by architect Phillippe Starck and club promoter Jean-Michel Moulhac, who has moved his funk nights here. It is industrially scaled and industrially fabricated – tarp, steel, concrete, futuristic green laser light. The club has become a destination for Congolese 'sapeurs', migrants to the city who live close by.[4] Now, it is attracting an aristocratic and bourgeois fashion crowd, seduced by the sapeurs' dapper dress. On the night of 24 October 1977, the dress code is black

[Fig. 5.2]. The occasion? A party in honour of Karl Lagerfeld, who has just presented a collection for Chloé at Paris Fashion Week. Karl's recent work has been influenced by his acquisition of a chateau in Brittany, and the clothes he is making reference the 18th century: 'short capes over satin breeches, redingotes, long dresses out of Watteau, all shown on pale powdered girls with long waving hair caught in black velvet bows'.[5] The party – dubbed 'La Moratoire Noire' – was orchestrated by the beguiling Jacques de Bascher, an intense presence in Karl's life for nearly twenty years. There are photographs of de Bascher with Andy at the Warhol exhibition

at Musée Galliera during 1974; in 1978 he is pictured wearing a corset to Kenzo's glitzy birthday party. Kenzo himself is dressed in a black mesh sheath embroidered with glittering fronds. On the night of La Moratoire Noire, de Bascher is sporting breeches, mask and rapier, as if ready for a bout of fencing. The dance floor is a sweaty crush of dressed and undressed people in black velvet and strapless taffeta, flimsy lace and transparent tulle, leather fetish, tight vests, tight shorts, gimp gear. Hardcore disco and BDSM performances overlap in an orgiastic live show.

In the extreme collision of materials, styles and behaviours, La Moratoire Noire seemingly established grounds for a new version of the little black dress that transcends genres, genders and classes. It is in this light, a decade later, that Tess McGill's velvet and diamanté frock becomes a toned-down symbol of hedonism, rebellion and unscripted sexuality. The look and feel of that dress scrolls back through the history of La Moratoire Noire to a time before Modernity: the little black dress becomes Postmodern by reviewing its past. In contrast to its older cousin, the Postmodern little black dress manifests in fabrics and textures explicitly associated with private lives and parties, occasions when the codes of behaviour governing the presentation of an everyday, sober, public self are suspended. Worn by Tess, this little black dress speaks to a change in the nature of what it meant to be a working woman. Whereas the classic or modern little black dress is a well-mannered acknowledgment of the mores of Modern society – promising an orderly negotiation of those liminal, social spaces that require a restrained, polite approach to being off-duty – the Postmodern little black dress pulls upon earlier forms of dress associated with music-driven lifestyles. Silhouettes and trims that emphasise, exaggerate and eroticise the body threaten to transgress and destabilise the very behavioural codes its classic sibling promises to observe. In doing so, the Post-

modern little black dress tells us something about changes in what the sociologists Luc Boltanski and Eve Chiapello name 'the spirit of capitalism'.[6]

Bricolage and the literary pose

During the post-war period, dressing in black came to operate widely as a recognisable sign of a youthful desire to stand against incumbent interests. Representing the values of autonomy and transgression, the effacing intellectualism of a Beatnik sweater and the raw machismo of a leather biker's jacket exist on that continuum. In the 1960s, the quasi-militaristic visual identity of the Black Panthers typically combined black leather blazers and berets with shirts or turtle necks, a look that influenced not only the habits of left-wing students and political activists in the USA and Europe, but also – in the writer Tom Wolfe's opinion – attracted the attention of cossetted Manhattanites in a time of 'Radical Chic'.[7] Wolfe's satirical account of a fundraising soirée held at Leonard Bernstein's Park Avenue duplex, counterposes socialite Felicia Bernstein's chic little black dress [Fig. 5.3] with the radical invitation extended to members of the Black Panthers. Her attire is presented as socially intelligent, a considerate, cultured statement that stealthily reinforces her status at the top of the heap – an egalitarian doyenne of the Upper East Side. It registers as a sympathetic, notionally objective, point of sartorial contrast and control.

For all its anonymising convenience, its clerical and bureaucratic formality, in many European cultures black has long held explicit symbolic associations with rebellion and anarchism as 'a shade of negation ... a colour of mourning ... a colour of determination, of resolve'.[8] Black flags connect the 1871 Paris Commune to the student demonstrations of May 1968 and the Radical Chic anti-capitalist

Fig. 5.2 (above)
Soirée Moratoire Noire, 24 October 1977.
(Photo Philippe Heurtault)

Fig. 5.1 (opposite)
Actress Melanie Griffith as Tess McGill
in the film *Working Girl* (1988, Mike Nichols).
(AF archive / Alamy Stock Photo)

ideology of the Situationists – a group of artists and academics at the forefront of theorising the alienating effects of a hyper-mediated life. Boltanski and Chiapello identify May of 1968 as a crucial turning point in the spirit of capitalism which, in the wake of countercultural movements, notably Situationism, began to incorporate elements of artistic critique: the adoption of black dress as a default sign of teenage rebellion throughout the 1970s and '80s perhaps reflects that influence.[9] Situationism was, in part, conceived as a check on the mollifying effects of mass media; and as it gained status among Marxist students, theorists and artists, it began to influence the development of British punk through the pivotal figure of Malcolm McLaren, partner of the British designer Vivienne Westwood.[10] McLaren's interest in Situationism extended well beyond the slogans he and Westwood printed on clothes, although it certainly influenced those in both form and content. Importantly, Situationism determined the way he thought about himself as a latter day *flâneur*, a figure of possibility and urban drifter who descends to the Situationists via Joris-Karl Huysmans, Charles Baudelaire, and other 19th-century Parisian writers. *Flânerie* (as a male habit) is predicated on a studied lack of concern with appearance, pitching general dishevelment against fashion, employment, wealth, inheritances, and predetermined social status. It was this negation of the conventional, Modern standards of self-presentation that filtered into punk aesthetics. Apocryphally, Daniel Kane argues that the spiky cropped hair of revered American musician Richard Hell – acknowledged as an inspiration for the Sex Pistols' Johnny Rotten – can be read as

a direct homage to a passage in Baudelaire's poem *Le Gouffre* (The Abyss): 'Witness my hairs, time and again / Raised on my scalp because the wind of Fear went by ….'[11]

In the summer of 1977, year of Queen Elizabeth II's Silver Jubilee and the Sex Pistols' infamous Jubilee boat trip, London itself was dishevelled, still pocked with bombsites, in the crux of wider economic decline. Families who could afford to leave the city had done so, redistributing along suburban lines. Historic central districts had been left to crumble. At the same time, such dereliction offered young people the possibility of return to a free-booting life of *flânerie*, squatting or renting cheaply with friends, cultivating anti-establishmentarian political and artistic communities. Jon Savage recalls taking photographs around Ladbroke Grove and Portobello Road in 1977:

> The whole district [was] one huge building site …. Decaying squats lie cheek by jowl with old factories surrounded by fly-tipped waste. In its emptiness, austerity and gloom, it [was] an interzone waiting for something to happen, for the beasts to be unleashed …. This was how London felt at the time: coming, coming, coming down – a speed hangover merging into an apocalypse. But there was also a sense of possibility that new ways of thinking and being might grow from this emptiness – like the scented buddleia on the bombsites. For the young, and the radical, space gave freedom. It felt like you could take back your power.[12]

Of course, the means by which power may be taken, or freedom pursued, are variously and unevenly available, and in this respect the notable differences between the construction of the *flâneur* and the *flâneuse* are instructive. Unlike her male counter-

Fig. 5.3 (opposite)
Leonard and Felicia Bernstein with Field Marshall Donald Cox, a leader of the Black Panther Party, at the Bernsteins' New York penthouse apartment, 14 January 1970.

(© Stephen Salmieri)

part and his air of distracted ruin, the *flâneuse* – a figure more recently recovered from history – pays meticulous attention to the detail of dressing.[13] She adopts male attire in order to pass unnoticed through city streets and public places:

> ... I had made for myself a *redingote-guérite* in heavy grey cloth, pants and vest to match. With a grey hat and large woollen cravat, I was a perfect first-year student. I can't express the pleasure my boots gave me ... my clothes feared nothing. I ran out in every kind of weather, I came home at every sort of hour, I sat in the pit at the theatre. No one paid attention to me, and no one guessed at my disguise .... No one knew me, no one looked at me, no one found fault with me ....[14]

In this passage from her autobiography, George Sand describes the care and control she takes over her clothes: they repay her by protecting her from unsolicited attention or criticism. Sand's approach to dressing is the antithesis of dishevelment and, in this, the wardrobe of the *flâneuse* can be seen to perform much like the classic little black dress.

Tagged to *flânerie,* punk was essentially a way of wearing that sought to disregard fixed fashion forms. Yet the act of wearing and of designing was (and is) somewhat interchangeable, especially in London where, during the post-war years, fashion design was increasingly and inextricably associated with art schools. Zandra Rhodes, who studied textile design at the Royal College of Art in the 1960s, presented her punk-inspired *Conceptual Chic* collection in 1977, the same year the Sex Pistols – wearing Westwood – released *God Save the Queen* and sailed down the Thames. With this collection Rhodes combined references to the avant-garde couturière Elsa Schiaparelli with a nod to King's Road street style, detailing slashes with gold-plated chains and

safety pins [Fig. 5.4]. Schiaparelli and the Situationists connect through Surrealism and détournement: in Rhodes' hands, 'Shocking Pink' was indexed to Schiaparelli's signature colour, but in the hands of Poly Styrene, 20 years old in 1977 and leader of the punk band X-Ray Spex, it presented itself as DayGlo. Poly wore second-hand and homemade outfits as she worked a stall in Beaufort Market, selling 'plastic trash, mainly kitsch jewellery and bags, old army cast-offs'.[15] Under Poly's aegis, demure blouses and softly comforting cardigans became punk. Her pose, which was never dishevelled, carried through in an attitude and approach to personal styling which made no distinction between life and art: 'Clothes are never really you, that's why people wear them. [Be]cause you can just create an image with clothes. They are just part of a façade which is good fun to play with sometimes.'[16] The practice of bricolage, so essential to understanding how subcultural dress functions, is one of subverting everyday objects and materials in order to communicate with affiliates. Poly's way of wearing spoke from the margins, indicating new and feminist ways of inhabiting and reforming the world, of refusing to go along with it.

Sex and AtomAge

In September 1976, a year before the night of La Moratoire Noire, the Sex Pistols, self-styled as 'London's Most Notorious Band', visited Paris to play at Le Chateau du Lac, a club operated by the family of Jean-Michel Moulhac (who went on to open La Main Bleu). Johnny Rotten wore a black Westwood bondage suit and the gig was advertised

Fig. 5.4 (opposite)
Zandra Rhodes, *Conceptual Chic* collection, 1977.
(Polly Eltes Punk 1977–78, in Basement 242;
Photo © Joe Gaffney)

using screen-printed imagery of the naked, smoking boy that featured on T-shirts and muslins sold by Westwood and McLaren at this time. SEX, their shop on the King's Road, was an environment designed to simulate the kind of 'adult' back room or seedy basement you might find a couple of miles away in Soho [Fig. 5.5]. They had already occupied the site for some years in a series of incarnations – Paradise Garage, Let It Rock and Too Fast To Live Too Young To Die – selling vintage porn alongside rockabilly clobber, customised T-shirts and brothel creepers. They learned how to make clothing by reworking or repairing existing garments, using domestic machines and techniques, hand-knitting simple jumpers. Punk expected people to 'DIY' – to start a band, to publish fanzines, to repurpose and customise clothes:

> ... people began to dress in rips and holes, safety pins and staples through flesh as well as cloth, to wrap their legs in plastic bin liners and trash bags, to drape their shoulders in remnants of curtains and couch coverings left on the street. Following the lead of McLaren's designs for the Sex Pistols and the Clash, people painted slogans up and down their sleeves and pants legs, across jackets, ties and shoes: the names of favourite bands and songs, passwords like 'ANARCHY' or 'RIOT' .... [17]

Ripped, glued and graffitied, fabric and paper were reused and reworked in ways that demonstrated their fundamental commonality. Coupled with this originary attitude, at SEX, Westwood and McLaren moved decisively towards using clothes to court controversy, selling their own designs alongside genuine fetishwear. It is in this context that subcultural fashion – clothing designed or worn to represent an oppositional position – began to make explicit connections to sex as a profession and recreation. Punk extrapolated the aspects of 19th-century *flânerie* that esteemed prostitutes, actresses and artist's models – rather than the *flâneuse* – as the female principle. [18] It embraced ostentation, artifice, vulgarity, and sexually transgressive dress as liberating.

One of the suppliers to SEX, John Sutcliffe, had been manufacturing leather 'weatherproofs for lady pillion riders' since 1957. [19] His business, AtomAge, moved into the burgeoning rubber trade in the late 1960s. By the time Westwood and McLaren stocked AtomAge, Sutcliffe had a degree of cultural currency, having supplied artist Allen Jones with bondage-style harnesses to dress *Hatstand*, *Chair* and *Table* (1969), a series of sculptures that pose female mannequins as furniture [Fig. 5.6]. The lushly explicit AtomAge catalogues and magazines carried articles and stories of interest for rubber enthusiasts and were an essential service connecting individuals isolated by their kink. Writing *The Outer Fringe of Sex* in 1970, Maurice North observed that in the 20th century 'rubber fetish' was not only the most prevalent of all the forms of sexual fetishism he had studied in the UK, USA and Northern Europe, but the only one specially catered for commercially. [20] Quoting a specialist outfitter – more than likely AtomAge itself – he relays that the labour intensive production of individually fitted bondage gear ...

> may sound painstaking, but we are painstaking people and [it is] the only possible way to be able to offer individual service to

Fig. 5.5 (opposite)

Pictured from right: Vivienne Westwood, Jordan, Chrissie Hynde, writer Allan Jones, Danielle, and Sex Pistol Steve Jones, 1976.

(David Dagley / Shutterstock.com)

Fig. 5.6
Allen Jones, *Chair*, 1969.
(*Chair*, 1969, Allen Jones / Photo: Tate)

'standardised' clothes themselves are the result of skilful handcraft. Some of Chanel's peers – Paul Poiret, for example – jealously distrusted the simplification of design.

The emergence of rubber as a material is co-extensive with Modernity, as rooted in the 19th century as the Baudelairean *flâneur*. Latex, the plant sap from which it is derived, is a plantation crop, grown extensively on colonised land in Malaysia and the Congo. Rubber was a keystone material in the expansion of the automobile industry – no Model T Ford could run without rubber tyres. Bonded to woven substrates, it lent its waterproofing properties to an array of clothing designed for military campaigns, travel and outdoor sporting pursuits. Like 19th-century crinoline dresses coloured mauve, produced using the first chemical dye process, rubberised clothing was initially a source of curiosity and status before its reputation sullied.[23] Rubber was used in underwear – corsets, jock-straps, girdles – to support the body and aid deportment. Its malleability meant that it was ideal for moulding and casting, so it was used to make prosthetics, dildos and anti-onanism devices, which, ironically, facilitated sex play.[24] The stuff of prophylactics, the sheer intimacy of rubber's relationship with the human body means that it evokes responses in complex nostalgic, erotic and corporeal terms: in fashion, it raises fetish as a presumption. To shock Middle England, Westwood and McLaren traded on an ambient appreciation of rubber's kink qualities – it is less SEX that sells than citation.

individual people. In a mass-produced world, we treat our customers as people and not as sales units or something equally gruesome.[21]

Consistent with the Situationist position, Westwood too appreciated the repudiation of mass-production and impersonal consumerism as gruesome: 'I [don't] go to Hong Kong or somewhere and get something made up cheaply, I rely on English craftsmen to make things for me and I think that people do appreciate what they are actually paying for.'[22] Fundamentally, the bespoke nature of the fetish trade shares an approach to production with couture: both require expertise to work with atypical materials, novel patterns and specific bodies; both attend to the individual demands of their clientele. When Chanel's little black dress is described as the fashion equivalent of the Model T Ford (see p. 13), it is seen to embody a notion of standardisation that runs counter to fussy materials at a formal, ideological level, even when such

Merchandise

Punk's defining year and – some might say – its last hurrah, was 1977. SEX became Seditionaries, signalling a change in orientation and in commercial intent. Stephane Raynor, an associate of Westwood and McLaren, opened a new shop, BOY, also on the King's Road. He previously had an interest in selling on vintage rockabilly shirts and denim jackets, as well as involvement with Acme Attractions, a store catering for London's subcultural music and club scene. At Acme, Philip Sallon – later of Blitz Club fame – made clothes assisted by Billy Idol, perhaps the archetypal BOY and mainstream rebel, a bleach blonde pastiche of the King of Rock 'n' Roll. BOY sold Seditionaries T-shirts in what Raynor claims is one of the 'first streetwear collaborations ever', although he set about inhabiting trends rather than reinventing fashion or acting as an impresario for insurgency.[25] Recognising value in the SEX aesthetic, Raynor painted the interior of BOY black and laid it with black rubber flooring. He nailed Dr. Martens boots to the walls and hung medicine cabinets on chains from the ceiling. The shop was raided by police on the day it opened, generating useful publicity. Alarming to parents and ideal tabloid fodder, as punk became a mainstream pop phenomenon, BOY had an eye for the young adults and teenagers running up and down King's Road:

> We turned BOY into an experience, a place where kids went to get away from home, a space that spoke to them, where they could express themselves, a hedonistic mind fuck, a space and time to meet others, compete with them, dress like them, the kids that could hardly wait for the weekend so they could be back there, be who they really wanted to be. This was BOY and once you stepped through the door you were transported into another world, you became part of the In Crowd. We created a kind of sacred atmosphere, likened to a church, a religion. A movement so strong you could feel the presence of some other power. The power of thousands of visitors, customers, pilgrims, devotees and loyal fans.[26]

For a time in the early 1980s, Raynor was involved in PX and PX2, New Romantic sister shops to BOY, selling a promiscuous array of frilly shirts, pleated peg trousers, vintage brooches, hats and so on. He saw his engagement in retail as an opportunity to capitalise on the amalgamation of all the British music-led subcultures surrounding him, from Teddy Boy to punk, goth and raver.[27] Perhaps it is not surprising then that BOY is best known today as a logo-driven brand. Throughout the 1980s, BOY gained endorsements from numerous musicians, celebrities, clubbers and fans: Madonna and Pet Shop Boys wore BOY baseball caps, cycling shorts and vests. In effect, BOY operated more like branded sportswear than catwalk, boutique or market stall fashion – plastic bags and garment tags branded with the BOY logo became covetable items in themselves. In the decade that followed the establishment of the shop, Raynor was able to monetise the BOY logo and establish it globally as a generic signifier of London street and club style [Fig. 5.7]. The logo sometimes included a schematic eagle, drawn with its wings outstretched, and latterly this imagery has been likened to Nazi symbology.[28] Raynor is evasive about the origins of the eagle, stating only that it was found in 'history books', but the image has been banned in the EU on the grounds of substantial similarity.[29]

It is possible to spot echoes of the BOY typography in designer Virgil Abloh's use of text. His brand, Off-White, gained cult-status by printing Helvetica Bold statements on garments and on

accessories. These are not slogans, but statements of fact: stiletto-heeled over-the-knee boots carry the statement 'FOR WALKING' along the length of their calf. Abloh explained his approach with reference to the ready-mades of Marcel Duchamp, notional grandfather of conceptual art. Duchamp's ready-mades were certain everyday objects – a urinal, bottle rack, snow shovel – elevated to art by the artist's decision to exhibit them. Citation, mischievous in the work of Westwood and McLaren, is, in this instance, disarmingly blunt. In art historical terms, if punk finds affiliation with the Situationists and Surrealism, Abloh finds it with Dada. Abloh's satirical 'LITTLE BLACK DRESS' is just that – no frills – a slogan printed in white Helvetica Bold type on basic, black viscose jersey. It puns on punk and fast fashion, as a no-brand branding strategy. For Nancy Troy, an expert in European Modernism, Chanel's little black dress heralds the era of mass-produced fashion as something standard, simple and easy to copy: Abloh's little black dress marks the absolute exhaustion of that trajectory, a deep irony on the idea of uniform.[30] If Westwood's black bondage suit represents a transition from Modern to Postmodern, Abloh's LBD is symbolic of Global Capitalism's (desperate) endgame.

Terrorist Chic

Raynor's use of shock tactics – fetishwear in SEX, and BDSM at an event like La Moratoire Noire – exemplified what Michael Selzer, writing in 1979, termed 'Terrorist Chic'. With this title, Selzer self-consciously instituted a link to Wolfe's essay on 'Radical Chic'; but whereas Wolfe implied a fascination with the glamour and integrity of the politically engaged, Selzer described Terrorist Chic as an ennui which defines the post-industrial, Postmodern condition where that results from the 'oppressive monotony of middle-class life':[31]

> ... Terrorist Chic expresses fascinated approval of violence, brutality, sadomasochism, evil and degeneracy in general; it apotheosizes meaninglessness and indecency .... [Terrorist Chic has] succeeded in transforming into a publicly acceptable posture what hitherto had existed only in furtive and antisocial privacy. Degenerate fantasies of sex and violence are not new; making them a fashionable pose *is* something of a departure in culture.[32]

Selzer was more appalled by high-gloss decadence than dive bar punk. Unlike Radical Chic Manhattanites who maintain a veneer of concern for social causes, for Terrorist Chic Manhattanites abundance is anaesthetising; and in an effort to find something – anything – interesting, they attach glamour to the performance of extreme behaviour. This, Selzer says, is reflected in the 'macabre and menacing' fashion imagery splayed across the pages of *Vogue*, or dressing the windows of the upmarket New York department stores and boutiques [Fig. 5.8]:

> ... Bendel's window shows three women in evening clothes – one a tie-dyed number that looks as if it were splattered with blood – standing, as if cowering, in the corner of a room. At their feet another woman is sprawled on the floor. She seems very dead, and whatever was in the bottle in her hand has turned her body green .... [At Bonwit Teller]

Fig. 5.7 (opposite)
BOY LONDON goods on display in the shop window of SICK in Redchurch Street, London.
(Loop Images Ltd / Alamy Stock Photo)

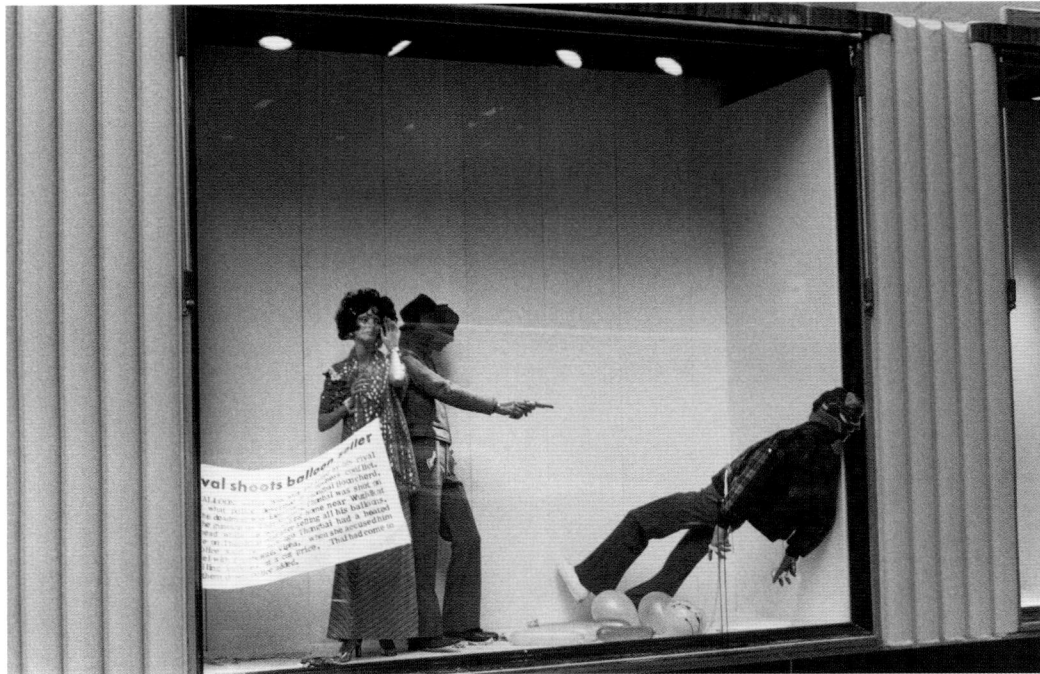

a window is criss-crossed with black masking tape to make it look like a cell .... Up a few blocks, at Halston's, we find five glossy metallic mannequins attired in incongruously wispy and delicate evening gowns. The room is bare of furniture, but a portable TV set and record player sit on the floor. Someone has smashed them and a large number of champagne bottles ....[33]

Selzer's descriptions recall the fashion shoots and photographs that are central to the plot of the slick horror, *Eyes of Laura Mars* (1978). Set in the world of high fashion, the film features Faye Dunaway in the titular role as a highly successful fashion photo-

grapher who begins to experience disturbing premonitions of death. In the film's opening scenes, Laura is seen preparing to attend the opening of a large, museum exhibition of her work – 'Has this gone too far?' the posse of frantic journalists enquire.[34] The photographs that perform as the controversial, violent and sexy work of Laura Mars are in some cases the actual work of Helmut Newton, one of the photographers that Selzer identifies as a master of Terrorist Chic. Women in Newton's photographs are manicured, lithe and leisured, bored by the palatial surroundings they move through, overtly sexualised and frequently posed full frontal. Technically, Newton's preference is for the classicism of boldly lit black-and-white photography that lends his subjects hauteur and means that, compositionally, jackets, suits and slips register as black shapes in sharp contrast to white, aristocratic skin. His photographs might be seen to present an idea of the little black dress as the narrow androgynous tailoring of Yves Saint Laurent's *Le Smoking*, an evening suit worn bare-breasted:

Fig. 5.8

Installation view of the 'Balloon Seller', window #10 in the exhibition *Lynn Hershman: 25 Windows, a Portrait/Project for Bonwit Teller.*

(© 2021. Digital image, The Museum of Modern Art, New York / Scala, Florence) understated, yet as sexually transgressive as the designs of Westwood and McLaren.

Eyes of Laura Mars was set in New York just as disco was becoming commercialised. Predicated on going out to dance, disco dressed up where punk dressed down and *Eyes of Laura Mars* is contemporaneous with the ambitions of the crowds begging entry to the legendary nightclub, Studio 54. The original Studio 54 opened in April 1977, expiring with a final party in February 1980. Selzer's descriptions of it recall the night of La Moratoire Noire:

> Money and squalor ... punk and elegance ... celebs and just plain beautiful folk ... 54 is the Grand Central of on-time trends, the spot where everyone comes to do his [*sic*] own thing no matter whether it is straight or gay or in-between or autosexual or menage-ing à trois or anything else you can think of. Excitement. Shock. Thrill. That's what 54 is all about. The General Assembly of weirdness and glamour, but without a Security Council to call things to a halt. A living, dancing, doping fantasy market where the one word that is not allowed is 'no'. A laboratory for probing the outer limits of who we are.[35]

A little black dress worn here might be imagined as a Halston sheath in licentious, unforgiving satin, a minute away from falling to the floor. It is a loose descendant of the famous Givenchy gown Audrey Hepburn wore as Holly Golightly in *Breakfast at Tiffany's* (1961).[36] Arguably, a variant of the Studio 54 aesthetic entered everyday life in the form of disco pants inspired by the shiny, cauterising trousers sported by 'Bad Sandy' (Olivia Newton-John) in *Grease* (1978) as she emerged foot first, clad in black, to ride the Shake Shack at the Rydell High fair.[37] A decade later, Bad Sandy's 'Tell me about it, stud' translates to Tess McGill's 'head for business

and a bod for sin', as the disco pants become a velvet cocktail gown, and the seduction of the school hunk becomes an ascent of the corporate ladder.

Goth

Selzer comments in *Terrorist Chic* that at Studio 54:

> The door has been torn off the subterranean Gothic closet of fetish clothing the Soho weekly news discloses. Chains, black leather, feathers, velvet and lace – not to mention Nazi uniforms – have tumbled out in wanton profusion only to be reassembled on the floor of 54: 'the habits of nuns, the robes of priests and monks, the clothes of construction workers, firemen and military along with S&M gear and women in garter belts and corsets who look as if they have stepped out of a Richard Lindner painting ....'[38]

In the early 1980s, the term 'goth' began to creep into common parlance to describe those camp aspects of punk that were indebted to the ambiguously gendered, decorative self-presentation of David Bowie, Marc Bolan and Suzi Quatro. On an episode of Thames Television's *Today* programme in 1977, made famous by the Sex Pistols' profanity-littered encounter with presenter Bill Grundy, Siouxsie Sioux – dressed and made up as a Pierrot – augured her future as the Queen of Goth. By the end of the decade, she had embraced a wardrobe that established black as a baseline for the decorative interplay of fishnet, rubber, lace, velvets and brocades, defining a look that persists to the present day. Grounded in punk, goth extrapolated the decadent, hedonistic elements that characterised disco, coupled them with ideas derived from countercultural interests in transgressive behaviours, and wound its way through images of heath-blasted Romanticism to the turn of the century.

Goth is now a perennial influence in couture, which is attracted to the drama and extravagance of archaic fabrics and silhouettes inspired by corsetry and frock coats, trailing skirts and clumpy boots. With black as a unifying principle, diverse and heterogeneous materials are handled texturally in a rebuff to the desire for singularity, simplicity and 'good' taste that Poiret saw as the consequences of Chanel's horrific assault on fashion. Anthropologists Annette Weiner and Jane Schneider remark on the disenchantment of cloth under capitalism, whereby (19th-century) mass industrial production divorced textiles from long-established homespun, rural and ritualistic origins.[39] Power-loomed cloth, consistent and flat, is seen to be less human than that woven by hand. Even in its most reduced circumstances, goth-inspired fashion mourns that loss of enchantment, the loss of arcane and idiosyncratic production, the loss of unnecessary frills. Reviewing an exhibition dedicated to Balenciaga at the Metropolitan Museum of Art in 1973, Kennedy Fraser delights in the designer's connoisseurship of fashion fabrics:

> He drew freely on the experience of the great French silk weavers, and we are reminded, in the exhibition's catalogue, of the old, romantic names of tulle, zibeline, bombazine, cloqué, matelassé, taffeta, broché, organza, marquisette, and point d'esprit, and of a time, before blends and synthetics, when a heroine could tell her maid 'to lay out the bayleaf faille'.[40]

Here Balenciaga is a goth *avant la lettre*, prefiguring the work of someone like Gareth Pugh. In Pugh's hands, Balenciaga's extravagant black Chantilly babydoll dresses of the late 1950s – which Valerie Mendes suggests were inspired by the 1956 film

Baby Doll – become tented fantasies for a post-punk generation [Fig. 1.8].[41] His Autumn/Winter 2013 collection makes a literal nod to punk's bin bag aesthetics while celebrating the high drama of Victorian silhouettes: expressive autonomy and self-possession rendered as exquisitely crafted Gothicism.

Batcave and The Gargoyle

By 1982, the goth scene in London centred on Batcave, a weekly night hosted in a nightclub at 69 Dean Street, Soho. It was a fitting address, one that gave the Blitz Kids their first run out:

> ... the crowd was mainly suburban art-school students who had become disillusioned with punk but liked a challenge and channelled a punk spirit by gleefully customising their outfits. It was always more punk to wear something no one else was wearing than to buy garments off the peg.[42]

From 1925, throughout the age of austerity until its gradual post-war decline, 69 Dean Street had housed The Gargoyle Club which distinguished itself as an elite avant-garde 'anti-club' for society and the literati ...

> an antic theatre of social, sexual and intellectual challenge – of thrust and counterthrust, of bravura display and emotional piracy ... the only common ground where all branches of the arts and media might meet; and through its tolerance of age, class and of sex in all its variants, the Club established an emphatic social breakthrough.[43]

Historically, Soho has been a region of London

marked by the intertwined, overlooked economies of dance, dress and sex, a state of mind as much as a physical place. Its cosmopolitanism, its European qualities, marked Soho as a foreign place, a step or two beyond the pale.[44] Having entertained Tallulah Bankhead and Matisse in its hey-day, by the 1970s The Gargoyle was a low-rent strip-club. Michael Luke notes, sadly, that The Gargoyle's ultimate conversion into a film studio in the 1980s was preceded by 'a number of once a week ventures … ending in 1982 in a Sixties Soul Disco hosted by David Ogilvy, a former pageboy to the queen'.[45] Another of these ventures happened to be Batcave.

At Batcave it was as if the decadences and dress code of La Moratoire Noire were transmogrified by the youth that gravitated to central London from suburbs and provincial towns. Jonny Slut, keyboardist in Batcave's house band, Specimen, exemplified the Batcave look and attitude: encased, like Siouxsie Sioux, in gender-bending rubber, feathers and fishnets [Fig. 5.9], Jonny wore heavy kohl and panstick under his spectacular 'Deathhawk' hairstyle. As Jonathan Melton, Jonny had read about Batcave at his home in Chatteris, Cambridgeshire, 'carrot capital of England', and promptly determined to make it his destination.[46] He moved to London and found work as a screen printer with Sue Clowes (who dressed Boy George), and later as printer and sometime model for BOY. Batcave was a highly visual, highly performative scene that loved to see itself in the music and style press – *The Face, Flexipop, Smash Hits, NME, Melody Maker*. Jonny lived in a Somers Town squat, complete with DIY parodies of the aforementioned Allen Jones *Hatstand* sculptures that featured in *BLITZ* magazine dressed in AtomAge gear. Madonna apparently dropped by when she first appeared on *Top of the Pops* in 1984, sporting a dance-inspired look that teamed black leggings with a distressed vest and black leather wristbands. Her layers of lace and string in *Desperately Seeking Susan* (1985), a film peppered with cameos from cult punk personalities, mix 'Bad Sandy' with the Batcave look, inspiring a generation of American teenagers to dress paradoxically as mainstream outsiders.[47]

Concurrent to the establishment of Batcave, Raynor published the *Big Black Catalogue*, reflecting BOY's latest goth obsessions. In the catalogue, Jonny is pictured in a graveyard wearing a black latex rubber vest and leggings designed by Theresa Coburn, who had recently arrived in London from Newcastle. While the design of AtomAge garments was led by the requirement to serve the fetish, and SEX's representation of fetishwear was rooted in acts of deliberate transgression, Coburn incorporated references to fetish already refracted for fashion through punk and pop culture. Requoting in this way, from an eclectic range of sources, is a defining characteristic of goth, which – in anticipation of Abloh's expressionless branding – gaily abandons any residual claims to authenticity that punk might have made. Collaborating with Jonny, Coburn played with the draping and elastic qualities of rubber, teaming it with marabou trim and recalling the lost, feminised, 'softer fetishes' that Valerie Steele sees characterising gothic fashion.[48] Rubber appealed to Coburn and Slut because, unlike leather, they regarded it as an ambiguous material. Jonny said:

> I [did not] want to be pigeonholed into the label 'gay', which to me implied the leather scene around Earl's Court and Bronski Beat. I think a lot of the more interesting 'gay' artists of the time – Boy George, Marc Almond, Pete Burns – rebelled against that too.[49]

The dialectics that exist between leather and rubber might be seen to reiterate in notions of the Modern and the Postmodern, the authentic and the ironic.

Fig. 5.9
Jonny Slut wearing latex ensemble by Theresa Coburn.
(© Ted Polhemus)

Leather wears authenticity in its creases and scuffs, morphing to the shape of the body that wears it. As a simulation and substitution, rubber is immanently forgetting the body underneath. It does not hold wrinkles in the same way as leather, it does not really age, although it perishes quickly and tears easily. Like glass, 'the miracle of a rigid fluid', rubber expresses vulnerability and mediates the relationship between industry, technology and the body in a very visceral manner.[50] If punk's skinhead tendencies, stiff denim and leather 'valorised a rigid male body', the tensility of pliant rubber which – having no bias – stretches equally in every direction, styled the body as a supple androgyny, making it behave differently and giving rise to the more fluid movements associated with goth dance.[51]

Pop styles

Reviewing the fashion year in 1984, Ted Polhemus and Lynn Procter commented that Batcave's 'pop sleaze bandwagon' popularised the idea of fetish and rubberwear for the 'unsuspecting populace', crediting the 'Soft Cell/Specimen' trend with bringing it to more mainstream attention:

Rubber is [...] seen in our society as a fetishistic material but until this year [1984] it certainly [was not] the sort of thing pin-ups might wear and any comment about rubber macs and such like would be derisive. Quite why leather should have a better press is hard to say – except that, despite its origins on docile cattle, leather's associations with aggressiveness via bikers' leathers underlines the fact that dominance and aggression are better thought of than submission and [...] passivity which is more readily linked with rubber.[52]

The same year, they published *Pop Styles*, an alphabetic taxonomy of the hairstyles, footwear, materials, trends and clothes they saw characterising the dress of pop stars and their fans over the previous 20 or 30 years. Jonny, wearing a silver latex spider's web designed by Coburn, illustrates a section titled 'Ripped and Torn – one wonders if things can go any further?' According to Polhemus and Procter, unlike 'mainstream fashion', whose meaning and form is seemingly dictated by a select group of remote industry experts, pop styles (idealistically) originate in 'little gangs and subcultures' before clothing manufacturers, dressmakers and backstreet cobblers '[push] facsimiles into production'.[53] The classified sections of music magazines and newspapers, which indicate a 'common language of signs and symbols' that 'communicate tastes and philosophies, desires and dreams', testify to the significant part played by mail-order businesses in supplying fans with clothes and accessories they wanted to wear in imitation of the bands or stars they followed.[54] In 1979, it was possible to obtain Seditionaries muslins – 'As worn by the Sex Pistols (£9.25 inc. P&P)' – from BOY through ads placed in *Sounds* or *NME*.[55] As a form of marginalia, classifieds testify to a fertile (sub)cultural hinterland.

Polhemus and Procter approached the subject of fashion as anthropologists and were essentially embedded within the subcultures they wrote about. They believed that 'pop styles', emblematic of subcultural dress, function as 'anti-fashion', ironically more like the ceremonial dress of Queen Elizabeth II or Chanel's 'Model T Ford' than the seasonal directives issued by the fashion industries.[56] 'Anti-fashion' is conceived as a cultural context that exists beyond, or in some way opposed to, the essentially capitalist motivations of mainstream fashion. In terms of punk, this was expressed in a tension between fixed forms and ways of wearing, and is what made Poly Styrene's approach to dress so genuinely radical. Polhemus and Procter understood the dialectics between anti-fashion and fashion as those between continuity and rupture, with rupture the grist in the capitalist mill. Punk presented an accelerated rupture, one that – idealistically – claimed for itself a new continuity, a new authenticity. Polhemus and Procter's pop styles – dressing to express affiliation with a genre, band or singer – represent affiliation based on a shared subcultural interest and, for fans, this felt like permanence.

Fashionably unfashionable

'Fringe times are crucial,' declares Tess McGill as she sizes up the cocktail gowns in Katharine's closet.[57] In the 1980s, those white-collar executive roles Tess was chasing were, like cloth, also disenchanted. Off-duty networking at parties where people are tangentially connected through work became crucial to success in an organisational environment that reconstitutes itself through ever-changing accumulations of mutual interests. Between the late 1960s and early '90s, what Boltanski and Chiapello perceive as the new spirit of capitalism emerged as organisations incorporated the formerly countercultural values of autonomy, creativity and opportunity.[58] This was in opposition to the predictability that characterised the industrial capitalism of, for example, Henry Ford. In what they dubbed 'the projective city', the reliability and understatement of the 'Fordist' little black dress can be a hindrance if it is seen to be too formal, fixed and 'boring'. In the new spirit of capitalism, individuals are required to demonstrate acumen and originality rather than obedience and loyalty, and the little black dress responds in exaggerated silhouettes, a flurry of frills, the sheen of latex, a wild heterogeneity of attitude and form. In the words of Tess McGill, it '... makes a statement. Says to people, confident, a risk-taker, not afraid to be noticed'.[59]

In the early years of the 21st century, the 'anti-fashion' common ground between the little black dress and subcultural style is one that could be seen to put the brakes on media-driven fashion cycles. Any absolute bifurcation between fashion and anti-fashion is, of course, absurd, something that Polhemus and Procter acknowledge, and the little black dress is perhaps a statement of the 'fashionably unfashionable' *par excellence*. From the outset, aspiring to the status of a universal form for 'everywoman', it was emblematic of modernity: it was supposed to be timeless. Claiming purview over the principle of good taste, it resisted the seasonal, trend-led changes of colour and silhouette that gave other clothes their place in a wardrobe. A restricted palette or a stable form refuses the exhausting pace set for fashion and, in this, the classic little black dress shares a characteristic with the subcultural dress that, ironically, might otherwise be seen to oppose it: the little black dress is a form of resistance in and of itself.

Notes

1   Mike Nichols (dir.), *Working Girl* (1988).
2   *Ibid.*
3   *Ibid.*
4   Alice Augustin, 'Dark Nights at Paris's La Main Bleue', *Red Bull* (2017): <https://daily.redbullmusicacademy.com/2017/09/la-main-bleue-feature>
5   Joan Juliet Buck, 'Karl Lagerfeld: the private life of a public fantasy', in *Vogue* (1 August 1979), p. 222.
6   Luc Boltanski and Eve Chiapello, *The New Spirit of Capitalism* (2007).
7   Tom Wolfe, 'Radical Chic: That Party at Lenny's', *New York Magazine* (1970), pp. 26–56.
8   Howard Erlich (ed.), *Reinventing Anarchy, Again* (1996), pp. 31–32.
9   Boltanski and Chiapello, *The New Spirit of Capitalism* (2007).
10 Guy Debord, *The Society of the Spectacle* (2014).
11 Daniel Kane, 'Richard Hell, *Genesis: Grasp*, and the Blank Generation: From Poetry to Punk in New York's Lower East Side', *Contemporary Literature* 52:2, p. 343.
12 Astrid Proll (ed.), *Goodbye to London: Radical Art and Politics in the 70's* (2010), p. 17.
13 Lauren Elkin, *Flâneuse: Women Walk the City in Paris, New York, Tokyo, Venice and London* (2016).
14 *Ibid.*, p. 109.
15 Celeste Bell and Zoë Howe, *Dayglo: The Poly Styrene Story* (2019), p. 45.
16 Poly Styrene in Ted Clisby (dir.), *Who is Poly Styrene?* (1979).
17 Greil Marcus, *Lipstick Traces: A Secret History of the Twentieth Century* (2011), p. 65.
18 J-K Huysmans, 'Dance Night at the Brasserie', *Parisian Sketches* (2004 [1880]), pp. 47–65.
19 Jonny Trunk, *Dressing for Pleasure ... The Best of Atom-Age 1972–1980* (2010).
20 Maurice North, *The Outer Fringe of Sex* (1970), p. 62.
21 *Ibid.*, p. 87.
22 Vivienne Westwood, interview with Janet Street Porter, 18 December 2012: <https://www.youtube.com/watch?v=rp8M-fley0s>
23 See Simon Garfield, *Mauve: How one man invented a colour that changed the world* (2011).
24 Manuel Charpy, 'Craze & Shame: Rubber Clothing during the Nineteenth Century in Paris, London, and New York City', *Fashion Theory* 16:4 (2012), see pp. 433–60.
25 Stephane Raynor, *All About the Boy* (2018).
26 *Ibid.*, p. 32.
27 *Ibid.*, p. 54.
28 Daniel Marriott, 'Extremist Symbolism in Fashion – A Cultural Statement or Unacceptable? You Decide ...', *Huffington Post* (2012): <https://www.huffingtonpost.

co.uk/daniel-marriott/extremist-symbolism-in-fashion_
b_1930025.html>

29 Paolo Passadori, 'The Streetwear Brand BOY declared
    invalid ...', *Lexology* (2020): <https://www.lexology.com/
    library/detail.aspx?g= 55e4343c-bb1f-46dd-b746-7c3a481
    dd614>

30 Nancy J Troy, *Couture Culture: A Study in Modern Art and
    Fashion* (2003), p. 316.

31 Michael Selzer, *Terrorist Chic: An Exploration of Violence
    in the Seventies* (1979), p. xiv.

32 *Ibid.*

33 *Ibid.*, pp. 28–29.

34 Irvin Kershner (dir.), *Eyes of Laura Mars* (1978).

35 Selzer, *Terrorist Chic* (1979), p. 73.

36 Blake Edwards (dir.), *Breakfast at Tiffany's* (1961).

37 Randal Kleiser (dir.), *Grease* (1978).

38 Selzer, *Terrorist Chic* (1979), p. 74.

39 Annette B Weiner and Jane Schneider (eds), *Cloth and
    Human Experience* (1989), p. 13.

40 Kennedy Fraser, *The Fashionable Mind: Reflections on
    Fashion 1970–1983* (1985), p. 88.

41 Valerie Mendes, *Black in Fashion* (1999), pp. 72–73.

42 Dave Haslam, *Life After Dark: A History of British Night-
    clubs and Music Venues* (2015), pp. 267–68.

43 Michael Luke, *David Tennant and the Gargoyle Years*
    (1991), p. xi.

44 Judith R Walkowitz, *Nights Out: Life in Cosmopolitan
    Londo*n (2012), p. 3.

45 Luke, *David Tennant and the Gargoyle Years* (1991), p. 199.

46 Mick Mercer, *Gothic Rock: All you ever wanted to know ...*
    (1993), p. 99.

47 Susan Seidelman (dir.), *Desperately Seeking Susan* (1985).

48 Jessica Burnstein, 'Material Distinctions: A Conversation
    with Valerie Steele', in Lauren M E Goodlad and Michael
    Bibby (eds), *Goth: Undead Subculture* (2007), pp. 257–76.

49 Theresa Coburn and Jonathan Melton, 'London calling:
    subculture in the early 1980s', *Back to the Future: 1979–
    1989* (2019): <https://digital.nls.uk/1980s/society/
    london-culture/?fbclid=IwAR3JcPmnVLDrttmGKnutq
    GEtw7xDK-wTGE4FiTniBxthimJ76vO7E20SAP0>

50 Jean Baudrillard, *The System of Objects* (2005), p. 41.

51 Burnstein, 'Material Distinctions ...', in Goodlad and
    Bibby (eds), *Goth: Undead Subculture* (2007), pp. 257–76.

52 See Emily White (ed.), *The Fashion Year, Vol. 2* (1984).

53 Ted Polhemus and Lynn Procter, *Pop Styles* (1984), p. xx.

54 *Ibid.*

55 Anon., *Sounds*, 10 November 1979.

56 Ted Polhemus and Lynn Procter, *Fashion and Anti-
    Fashion: An Anthology of Clothing and Adornment* (1978).

57 Nichols (dir.), *Working Girl* (1988).

58 Boltanski and Chapiello, *The New Spirit of Capitalism*
    (2007).

59 Nichols (dir.), *Working Girl* (1988).

FASHION, TECHNOLOGY AND THE LBD

Pamela A Parmal

Designers including Madeleine Vionnet, Cristóbal Balenciaga, Christian Dior and Yves Saint Laurent – all masters of their craft – turned to the little black dress when expressing the essence of an idea, whether a specific cut, silhouette or technique. Today's designers, including those who explore the world of high-technology (referred to as high-tech hereafter), are no different. Whether exploring new methods of manufacture, performance-enhancing materials, or the use of semi-conductors and micro LEDs, the little black dress is a staple in the design vocabulary that allows the technology to shine.

The colour black has had particular resonance within the creative and tech worlds and has been adopted as a quasi-uniform by many. Architects, gallerists and contemporary art curators wear black clothing as an aesthetic badge of honour. Steve Jobs in his black Issey Miyake mock turtleneck sweaters became a poster boy for the tech industry. For Jobs the custom-made black turtleneck served as a uniform, typically worn with his blue Levi's® 501 jeans and grey New Balance trainers. He found a jumper he liked, stocked his wardrobe, and solved the problem of deciding what to wear. Although he did not explicitly comment on the aesthetics of his choice, the black turtleneck gave him a casual elegance, aligned him with creative professionals, and set him apart from business people in tailored suits.

Jobs frequently turned to black in the early designs for Apple and for what can be considered the ultimate technological achievement of our age, the iPhone – what we might term the LBD (Little Black Device) of the tech world. Of course, black was not the only option for those investing in the new iPhone technology: graphite, white and, by 2013, a range of coloured phones were issued with the iPhone 5c. With the introduction of the iPhone 7 in 2016, available in black or matte black, and with its now softly curved edges and successfully integrated camera and home button, the company introduced a sleek, refined and powerful tool whose simple, iconic design suggested the mysteries to be found in the black monolith of *2001: A Space Odyssey* (1968). While the black iPhone remains a staple, with each new model the colour options continue to change, driving the desire among consumers to own the latest release and newest fashionable accessory. Apple has thus been successful in tapping into fashion as a powerful marketing tool.[1]

Astute recognition of the power of fashion by Apple and other tech companies contrasts sharply with the current ethos among designers working on high-tech apparel. Some developers work to enhance the performance of garments with little concern for contemporary fashion, producing odour-eating socks, breathable athletic wear, and clothing that monitors our blood pressure, or the pollution in the atmosphere around us. Others are developing new technologies for manufacturing and customisation, which allow for one-of-a-kind garments tailored to an individual's size and taste. In an ironic twist, the clothing industry is striving for performance and individuality, while high-tech products with mass appeal like smart phones have become the new fashion arena.

This essay focuses specifically on apparel designers who eschew the fashion merry-go-round and are pushing the limits of technology to develop clothing that is custom-fit, custom-designed, or is a vehicle for self-expression. While many of these cutting-edge technologies and the resultant clothing are still experimental and better suited to the catwalk or the laboratory than a shop rail, the work of contemporary designers is moving us towards a more sustainable future in which the wearer is placed at the centre rather than the latest catwalk obsession.

3D printing

3D printing is one arena in which designers and technologists have experimented in the hope of creating more sustainable and customisable clothing. Described as 'fashion's high-tech priestess' by *Dazed* magazine, Dutch designer Iris van Herpen often collaborates with scientists to create her forward-looking fashion.[2] Her high-concept, haute couture collections fuse an interest in fashion, art, architecture and engineering with cutting-edge technologies and fields of science as diverse as particle physics, robotics and microbiology. Pushing the boundaries of fabric innovation, she began combining scientific techniques with traditional craft when she started 3D printing in 2009, becoming among the first to send 3D-printed clothing down the runway in 2010. In 2013 she featured two 3D-printed dresses in her *Voltage* collection. The sculptural *Anthazoa* cape and skirt, now in the collection at the Museum of Fine Arts Boston,[3] was made on a new 3D printer that allowed for the use of multiple materials in the same job – in this case, polyurethane rubber and acrylic.[4] Van Herpen collaborated on the look with Stratasys Ltd, a leading developer of 3D printers, and Neri Oxman, an architect and designer who leads the Mediated Matter Group at the Massachusetts Institute of Technology (MIT) in Boston. The second 3D-printed look was developed in collaboration with the Belgian company Materialise, a pioneer in developing additive manufacturing software which controls the printing process, and the architect Julia Koerner whose 3D clothing more recently appeared in the film *Black Panther* (2018). Both van Herpen garments pushed the boundaries of 3D printing at the time, taking a process more suited to parts manufacture and adapting it to create softer, more flexible structures that could be worn on the human body.

The design that was created in collaboration with Koerner and Materialise was made using a new 3D printing technology – selective laser sintering (SLS) [Fig. 6.1]. According to Koerner, its 'architectural structure aims to superimpose multiple layers of thin woven lines, which animate the body in an organic way'.[5] The thin layers, made possible by SLS, created a more flexible and transparent structure, thus making a more wearable garment designed to 'flow across the body like a woven web'.[6] In the SLS method of 3D printing, a laser fuses together particles of plastic, metal, ceramic or glass to create a solid structure. The powdered material is placed in a printer bed, and the laser, directed by a 3D digital model of the finished product, selectively fuses the powder while scanning across the bed. When a pass is completed the bed is lowered, a new layer of powder is placed on top, and the process repeated. Because the unfused powder remains in place, the gaps between the sintered material are supported so that complex geometries can be created – like the multiple layers found in van Herpen's design. Van Herpen and other young fashion designers, such as the New York collaborative ThreeASFOUR and Rem D Koolhaus for United Nude shoes, have continued to experiment with 3D printing, but because of the limitations of the technology their designs have rarely found their way off the catwalk and into a wardrobe.

Among the young designers who have most thoughtfully and successfully incorporated 3D printing into their work, establishing a blueprint for the future, are Jessica Rosenkrantz, a Harvard-trained biologist and architect, and Jesse Louis-Rosenberg, a MIT-trained mathematician and designer. The two founded the company Nervous System in 2007, where they focus their considerable talents on developing generative design processes based on those found in the natural environment – such as the growth of a plant or algae – and using contemporary technologies to digitally

fabricate their products. In 2013, Rosenkrantz and Louis-Rosenberg introduced *Kinematics*, an innovative line in which large flexible objects, like a dress, can be created on a 3D printer [Fig. 6.2]. The three basic concepts behind their *Kinematics* line were the development of a hinged mechanism which could be 3D printed in one piece and not require any construction, now possible with selective laser sintering; a computer simulation process that could compress the finished product into a smaller more efficient shape for printing; and finally,

Fig. 6.1 (left)
Iris van Herpen, Look 7 Haute Couture Spring/Summer 2013.
(Iris van Herpen dress from *Voltage* collection, 3D printed in collaboration with Materialise)

Fig. 6.2 (right)
Kinematics dress by Nervous System.
(Photo by Steve Marsel Studio)

a web-based app which would allow the consumer to customise the product. With these three components in place, they introduced an integrated clothing design and manufacturing process, in which garments are completely customisable and manufactured on demand.

A *Kinematics* garment begins with the web-based app *Kinematics Cloth*.[7] The customer enters their measurements into the *Shape Explorer* app, which generates a digital mannequin in their size onto which the desired garment is digitally 'fitted'. The consumer then follows a series of steps to choose their preferred style of garment, making decisions regarding the shape, style, number and colour of the hinged components that will complete the final design. This digital garment is then fed into the computer simulation, which folds it into a structure that can be 3D printed. By allowing for complete customisation in relation to taste and fit, whilst also eliminating the waste created in traditional clothing manufacture by printing on-demand, Nervous System has created a model for the future. This on-demand process eliminates not only the fabric wasted in pattern-cutting, but also the problem of unsold stock – most of which ends up in landfill. Yet, while Nervous System's *Kinematics* line is a road map for the future, the synthetic materials currently available for 3D printing result in clothing unsuited to long-term wear and comfort.

While the problems with the inflexible nature of the materials used in 3D printing have yet to be solved, some designers continue to experiment with the technique, more recently developing new ways in which to ornament cloth. ThreeASFOUR, a trio of transnational artists who use fashion as their primary medium, first experimented with the technology in 2013 and recently featured clothing embellished with 3D-printed designs in their Spring/Summer 2020 collection. For this collection they took inspiration from nature, in what seemed to be a move away from their earlier emphasis on technology. However, two dresses were constructed from a fabric that mimicked the play of light and colour on the wings of the Greta-Oto butterfly – the effect was recreated by 3D printing thousands of photopolymer cells onto the surface of the cloth [Fig. 6.3]. Each cell was composed of a clear lens with strips of colour beneath, so that as the fabric moves the colours shift accordingly as the garment catches the light.

It remains in question whether this switch to using 3D printing to embellish cloth rather than as a tool for manufacturing is an admission of defeat. As more sophisticated materials are developed for use in 3D printing, the technology might one day hold the answer to more sustainable and customisable clothing.

Digital technology

Historians of technology often claim that Joseph Marie Jacquard's 1804 loom-patterning mechanism, controlled by punched cards, was the first binary technology to operate a machine and heralded the beginning of the computer age. Further technology related to the weaving and patterning of textiles followed; but, more recently, the Jacquard mechanism's descendant – digital technology – has had a profound impact on the manufacture of textiles and apparel, causing designers to think differently about the process of clothing design and construction. This has been especially true for Japanese fashion and textile designers, who are among the most innovative of the last quarter of the 20th century.

Fig. 6.3 (opposite)
ThreeASFOUR, Look 15 *Human Plant* collection Spring/Summer 2020, New York Fashion Week.
(Thomas Concordia / Getty Images)

Textile innovators Junichi Arai, Makiko Minagawa and Reiko Sudo began to experiment with digital technology in the 1980s, considering how it could be used to create innovative textile designs and materials. Arai's digitally designed and jacquard-woven textiles so impressed fashion designer Issey Miyake that he refused to cut them and told Arai he should sell the cloth as it was.[8]

Miyake's reverence for cloth is basic to understanding his design philosophy. In fact, 'a piece of cloth' has now become one of the company's main tenets. It informed the creation of several of Issey Miyake lines such as *Issey Miyake Pleats Please* and *A-POC (A Piece of Cloth)*. *Issey Miyake Pleats Please*, which launched as a brand of its own with the Spring/Summer 1994 collection, was a collaboration with Makiko Minagawa, who developed a process of digitally engineering clothing which would be constructed before pleating. An oversized, sewn garment was then sandwiched between Japanese paper (washi) and mechanically pleated. The line represented Miyake's first attempt at creating a universal garment that could be worn by anyone and put functionality first: light and wrinkle-proof, the garments are easy to care for, and fold into a compact size for easy storage and packing.

Miyake also collaborated on innovative clothing lines with textile engineer Dai Fujiwara, who joined Miyake's company in 1994 after graduating from the Tama Art University in Tokyo. Shortly after Fujiwara started working for Miyake, he began experimenting with digitally programming an old knitting machine discovered in an abandoned barn outside of Tokyo. Miyake became intrigued by the work, which eventually led to the development of *A-POC* (launched February 2000). Fujiwara programmed the knitting machine to create a larger tube of cloth into which was integrated a jigsaw puzzle of garments and accessories: one tube could include a pair of trousers, a top, a handbag and even mittens [Fig. 6.4]. The knitting machine 'stitched' together the seams of the embedded clothing, integrating the two layers of the tube. After purchasing the cloth tube, the customer could cut out the garments and customise them by making the sleeves long or short, creating a V-neck or round neck, or by changing the length of the hem; because the seams were integrated into the cloth, no sewing was necessary. With the notion of producing self-tailored clothing through mass production, Miyake's intention was to unleash 'the freedom of imagination'.[9] By closely laying out the pattern pieces onto the knitted tube, it had the additional benefit of reducing the waste created by traditional cut-and-sew garments. However, while *A-POC* clothing was collected by museums, such as The Museum of Modern Art and The Metropolitan Museum of Art in New York,[10] it was not a commercial success and the line was discontinued. Undeterred, Miyake's fascination with reconceptualising fashion and the manufacturing and design process continued and still underpins the brand ethos. In his later years, Miyake stepped away from designing annual collections to focus his attention on the Issey Miyake Design Studio and Reality Lab, which was founded in 2007 to experiment with new technologies and to create innovative and sustainable clothing.

Yuima Nakazato, who has been called a neo-futurist in fashion design, is another Japanese designer exploring new methods of clothing manufacture and customisation.[11] Nakazato envisions a time when, 'Eventually, each and every garment will be unique and different'.[12] His vision for customised clothing as the future of fashion began in

Fig. 6.4 (opposite)
A-POC ensemble, by Issey Miyake, on view as part of the exhibition *Items: Is Fashion Modern?*, The Museum of Modern Art, New York (1 October 2017–28 January 2018).
(Zuma Press Inc. / Alamy Stock Photo)

2016, when he showed during Paris haute couture week for the first time as an official guest designer selected by couture's governing body, the *Fédération de la Haute Couture et de la Mode.* Nakazato is only the second Japanese designer in history to be chosen to show as part of the official couture calendar, and in 2016 became the first since Hanae Mori retired 12 years prior. The *UNKNOWN* Autumn/Winter 2016 collection featured garments inspired by a trip to Iceland and what Nakazato saw as the country's other-worldly landscapes.[13] Merging traditional Japanese craftsmanship with state-of-the-art technology, Nakazato set out to recreate this 'out of planet experience' of Iceland's natural wonders.[14] Each garment was constructed from thousands of cells made of intricately cut, reflective film printed with photographs of Icelandic ice-scapes. The film was then folded into three-dimensional forms, as in origami, to form the cells that were linked together to create the final piece [Fig. 6.5].

Nakazato has expanded upon this idea of creating unique garments from individual cells with his proprietary 'Unit System', a modular approach inspired by observations of natural crystal and molecular structures, which creates modifiable garments.[15] In his follow-up Spring/Summer 2017 collection, *IGNIS AER AQUA TERRA,* thousands of these Units followed one of four elements – fire, air, water or earth. While the *UNKNOWN* and *IGNIS AER AQUA TERRA* collections used iridescent film to stunning effect, Nakazato still strove for more wearable clothing that could make its way into the marketplace. His Autumn/Winter 2017 collection, *FREEDOM,* offered a breakthrough in his concept. It showcased clothing inspired by the 1950s, an era characterised by two completely opposite styles: the haute couture of Christian Dior that revived elegance and luxury after the Second World War, and democratic blue jeans, a mass-produced, globally popular garment. Each look was made up of thousands of small Units of only two shapes, one square and the other with a curved side, cut from wearable fabrics such as cotton, wool, nylon and leather. The desired silhouettes were mapped out of the two basic shapes using digital modelling and the final garments constructed by hand-pegging the Units together at the corners, dispensing with the need for needle and thread [Fig. 6.6].[16]

While Nakazato's Units allowed for complete customisation, the technique necessitated long hours to assemble the garments and did not eliminate waste in the way Nakazato had hoped. He continued to push his ideas around Unit Constructed Textiles, but with more of a focus on sustainability: the following Spring/Summer 2018 collection featured upcycled clothing made from discarded industrial textiles, such as that used in airbags and parachutes. The clothing was still constructed from Units, but now the wearer could add or remove those Units at will to change the sleeve from long or short, or to raise or lower a hem, moving towards Nakazato's goal of creating tailor-made garments which harmonise with the individuality of each wearer. Two years later, his Spring/Summer 2020 collection illustrated this ongoing commitment to more sustainable clothing technology, for which he collaborated with scientists to incorporate biologically developed materials into his work, disrupting the guarded tradition of haute couture. One

Fig. 6.5 (opposite)
Yuima Nakazato, Haute Couture Autumn/Winter 2016.

Fig. 6.6 (page 118)
Yuima Nakazato, Haute Couture Autumn/Winter 2017.

(Both images – Courtesy: YUIMA NAKAZATO / Photo Credits: SHOJI FUJII)

such material was Brewed Protein – developed by the Japanese bio-tech firm Spiber: it is made from genetically programmed proteins created during a microbial fermentation process bio-engineered by Spiber. In total, three new biodegradable materials that do not contain any petro-chemicals were developed for Nakazato: a fabric similar to cotton, a fibre resembling hair, and a yarn.[17] Building on their Unit System technology, Nakazato's team went on to experiment with the pioneering technique of 'Biosmocking', a digital textile-modelling method capable of achieving three-dimensional textures on Brewed Protein textiles. In addition, for Spring/Summer 2020 Nakazato debuted a new garment construction technique called TYPE-1, using clasps made of 99 per cent sustainable, plant-derived materials.

Digital mapping, printing, even bio-engineering, are thus providing a means for designers to explore material innovation and alternative methods of clothing construction that hold promise for a more sustainable future.

Integrated technology

Another means of customising contemporary fashion is by the introduction of electronics, semi-conductors and LED lights – not only into the finished looks, but into the raw fibres and textiles from which they are made – to create programmable garments that allow for individual expression. Like the modern T-shirt or baseball cap branded with slogans that visually communicate messaging, these new garments have the power to digitally 'speak' to other devices or communicate a range of images or ideas at the command of the wearer – the very latest in making a personal statement.

Among the leaders in integrating smart technology into clothing designs are Francesca Rosella and Ryan Genz of London-based label CuteCircuit. The company has created haptic garments that hug the body and aid the hearing-impaired, as well as clothes that can send and receive phone calls and Bluetooth signals, and light up the night. Genz and Rosella first met in 2001 at the Interaction Design Institute in Northern Italy. They shared an interest in using technology to amplify the body's senses, producing their first collaboration, the *HugShirt*, in 2002. The world's first haptic telecommunication wearable, the *HugShirt* continues to evolve with new designs each season. Each version is embedded with sensors that capture the strength, duration and location of the touch, skin warmth and heart-beat rate of the sender of the hug – an intervention in fashion which became chillingly relevant in the context of the Covid-19 pandemic that introduced physical-distancing measures and discouraged human touch. As the sensors receive a digital signal via CuteCircuit's *Q* app, it causes the actuators to provide a physical sensation in specific areas of the body, reproducing the feeling of a hug sent by another user.[18] More recently CuteCircuit used the same haptic technology to develop the *SoundShirt*: 16 micro-actuators, microscopic devices that amplify the data and transmit a measured amount of energy, are integrated into the fabric of the shirt. The actuators receive a digitised audio signal captured during an orchestral performance by microphones set below the stage and translate these signals into haptic sensations that change in intensity, travelling across the arms and around the torso. The shirt creates an immersive experience for the wearer, allowing hearing-impaired people to feel the music.[19]

CuteCircuit specialises in the creation of advanced smart textiles in which micro-electronics such as LEDs, sensors and actuators are seamlessly integrated into the cloth. They pride themselves on the lack of wires. Their ingenuity knows no bounds: CuteCircuit's more futuristic designs have included the *M-Dress* (2007), which combined a fashion classic with the next big thing in tech by embedding digital technology into an elegant silk jersey little black dress that was also a functioning mobile phone. The *M-Dress* accepts a standard SIM card, inserted into a small slot in the garment's label; the phone can be operated through body gestures, allowing the wearer to receive and make calls without them having to carry a mobile in their pocket or purse.[20] Their keynote, that 'simplicity is elegance', mirrors the design ethos of Coco Chanel, who popularised the LBD with her simple black day dress of 1926, as outlined in chapter 1 of this book.

CuteCircuit's use of programmable micro-LEDs has led to some of their most dramatic designs, which can play a choice of videos via the *Q* app and Bluetooth technology, or receive text messages and Twitter posts. Between 2009 and 2015 they created a series of particularly high-profile garments which fused technology, wearability and interactivity in one. Their first internet sensation was a dress embedded with micro-LEDs, worn by the singer Katy Perry to The Metropolitan Museum of Art's Costume Institute Gala in 2009. This was followed by the *Twitter Dress*, worn by Nicole Scherzinger in 2012 to a launch party for the British telecommunications company EE and the introduction of the UK's first 4G mobile network. The dress was Bluetooth-enabled, allowing it to receive tweets; 2000 micro-LEDs in the bodice and skirt played the tweets in real time. It is perhaps no coincidence that the *Twitter Dress* – like the *M-Dress* – is an elegant black dress in its own right: a floor-length evening dress made from delicate black French chiffon *changeant*, embellished with over 2000 triangular Hematite Swarovski elements.[21]

As Georgina Ripley discusses in chapter 1, black is the perfect ground on which to experiment with sensory detailing, whether traditional embroidery, glittering jewels or wearable technology. It is a

design trope CuteCircuit has returned to with its *Graphene Dress* (2017). A collaboration between fashion and science – developed in conjunction with scientists at the National Graphene Institute in Manchester and intu Trafford Centre – it marked the world's most technically advanced LBD, the first to incorporate the Nobel Prize-winning material. Hailed as a wonder material, Graphene is tough but stretchable like rubber, lightweight, conductive and transparent. CuteCircuit's innovative dress design reflected the properties of Graphene – specifically taking inspiration from an electron microscope view of the material, which displays hexagonal crystal-like formations, mirrored in the 3D-printed translucent appliqués applied to the finished dress. Graphene's properties were exploited for functionality too: the interactive smart dress captured the wearer's breathing patterns, illuminating parts of the dress through transparent conductive film and changing the colour of the dress's LED decoration. A shallow breath turned the LEDs from orange to green, a deep breath from purple to turquoise.[22]

More recently, CuteCircuit created another version of the Twitter dress for Spanish supermodel and actress Nieves Alvarez, who wore it on the red carpet. A Bluetooth-enabled haute couture dress composed of thousands of programmable micro-LEDs and sequinned panels, it too takes the classic LBD as the basis of its design [Fig. 6.7]. Asymmetrically cut panels of black silk organza and black sequins are combined with inserts of laser-cut, colour-changing polyurethane film and luminous Magic Fabric (CuteCircuit's own micro-LED fabric). Like previous examples of CuteCircuit's wearable technology, it is controlled by the *Q* app to display moving patterns and animations, customising the garment according to mood or taste [Fig. 6.8].

Until recently this technology was purely experimental, better suited to museum displays and concert performances, but Genz and Rosella have continued to refine their technology so that subsequent models of their micro-LED garments can be more easily controlled by the wearer via their *Q* app. CuteCircuit now retails programmable clothing and accessories for men and women, including T-shirts, evening dresses and handbags.

Digital textiles and wearables hold the most promise for the future and, unbeknown to most of us, this technology has been under development by laboratories around the world and adapted for use by the military, as well as medical, athletic-wear and other companies. AFFOA, or Advanced Functional Fabrics of America, is among the leaders in this field. Lead by Yoel Fink, this innovation laboratory has developed a technique for integrating semiconductors into fibres. According to AFFOA, 'recent breakthroughs in fibre materials and manufacturing processes will soon allow us to design and to wear fabrics that see, hear, sense, communicate, store and convert energy, regulate temperature, monitor health and change colour – heralding the dawn of a "fabric revolution"'.[23] The basis for AFFOA's work is transforming traditional fibres into highly sophisticated network devices and systems. In their high-tech laboratory, also fitted out with the latest weaving and knitting technology, AFFOA has developed a system of integrating semi-conductors into monofilaments. These new fibres can be programmed in multiple ways and themselves integrated into wearable, functional garments and accessories. One of AFFOA's earliest marketable products is the *LOOksPack* backpack, each woven in a different plaid incorporating their pioneering high-tech fibres. Each backpack is uniquely encoded, thus becoming programmable communication devices that speak to one another via the *LOOks* app: if someone with the app scans another user's pack, they can view an augmented reality avatar of the pack's owner; the information is delivered to the app, and vice versa. The *LOOksPack* only hints at the future possibilities of this technology.

Technology is redefining dress for the 21st century. Everything from the materials and the manufacturing processes to the function of clothing is being questioned by leading mathematicians, technologists, engineers and clothing designers. While much of the work is experimental, it reveals a future in which clothing will take on new functions such as monitoring blood pressure or heart rate, as well as eliminating odour or regulating temperature. These practical applications hold promise for the increased functionality of clothing, but new technologies can also be harnessed aesthetically, customising garments to suit the wearer's size, taste and personality. What will this mean for fashion's most classic of garments, the little black dress? We have seen how companies like CuteCircuit turn to the LBD as the blank canvas best suited to showcasing innovation. In 2019, Montreal-based fashion designer and professor at the University of Quebec, Ying Gao, unveiled robotic clothing that reacts to the chromatic spectrum. The project *Flowing Water, Standing Time* created garments capable of recognising colours in their immediate surroundings, and which are 'at once liquid and chameleon-like, adapting to the slow rhythm of their ever-changing environment'.[24] Tellingly, while one ensemble was

Fig. 6.7 (page 122)
Nieves Dress by CuteCircuit, London, England, 2018.

Fig. 6.8 (page 123)
Sketch for *Nieves Dress* by CuteCircuit, London, England, 2018.

Fig. 6.9 (page 125)
Ying Gao, *Flowing Water, Standing Time*, 2019.
(© Malina Corpadean)

sequinned
fabric

LEDs
on Bust
(stop at
waist)

CUTECIRCUIT
for
(Nieves
Alvarez)

Translucent fabric

© CUTECIRCUIT 2016

created in a patchwork of ethereal pastel tones, another was off-black [Fig. 6.9]: more evidence that black can help sharpen a designer's eye. Kate and Laura Mulleavy of the label Rodarte once said that 'the creation of the black dress is the purest form of expression for a designer. The absence of colour allows one to focus on the fundamental elements of design: texture, tone, and silhouette.'[25] As the fundamental elements of design evolve as fashion explores a more sustainable future, hopefully this push toward customisation, individuality and performativity will not lead to the demise of the little black dress, but instead encourage new iterations of this ever-evolving wardrobe staple.

Notes

1   Mary Meisenzahl wrote, 'The iPhone is available in 6 colours, including purple for the first time ever – here's how to decide', *Business Insider* (2019): <https://www.businessinsider.com/apple-iphone-11-colors-purple-green-yellow-white-black-red-2019-9> See also Fiona McCormack, 'Apple's iPhone Marketing Strategy Exposed', *Business 2 Community* (2013): <https://www.business2community.com/marketing/apples-iphone-marketing-strategy-exposed-0661613>

2   Mhairi Graham, 'Iris Van Herpen: Fashion's hi-tech priestess', *Dazed* (2015): <https://www.dazeddigital.com/fashion/article/24899/1/iris-van-herpen-fashion-s-hi-tech-priestess>

3   Museum of Fine Arts Boston, 2013.1487.1-2

4   <https://www.irisvanherpen.com/haute-couture/voltage> *Voltage* collection, Look 10.

5   Emilie Chalcraft, 'Voltage by Iris van Herpen with Neri Oxman and Julia Koerner', *dezeen* (2013): <https://www.dezeen.com/2013/01/22/voltage-3d-printed-clothes-by-iris-van-herpen-with-neri-oxman-and-julia-koerner>

6   Van Herpen, *Voltage*: <https://www.irisvanherpen.com/haute-couture/voltage>

7   See <https://n-e-r-v-o-u-s.com/kinematicsCloth/>

8   Mio Yamada, 'The Future of Fabrics Woven with the Past', *The Japan Times* (2013): <https://www.japantimes.co.jp/culture/2013/02/21/arts/the-future-of-fabrics-woven-with-the-past/#.XkwVRtL7QdU24>

9   Dana Thomas, 'The Epoch of A-POC', in *Newsweek* (2002).

10 The Metropolitan Museum of Art 2015.417 and 2015.418 are examples of uncut lengths from larger rolls: 2014.544a-m shows a complete cut ensemble, including top, bra, skirt, briefs, socks, mittens, armbands, cap and handbag; 2014.454, 2011.560.1a, b and 2011.560.2 are examples of ready-made, customised garments cut from the roll. In addition, see The Museum of Modern Art, 841.2005.1-4.

11 Neo-futurism was originally a late 20th to early 21st century architectural style that has spread throughout art and design. It is seen as a departure from the referential style of Postmodernism, and represents an idealistic approach to the future, aiming to rethink the aesthetics and functionality of rapidly growing urban areas.

12 For Yuima Nakazato, 'Brand Philosophy' (n.d.), see: <http://www.yuimanakazato.com/about.html>

13 Yuima Nakazato, 'Couture Autumn/Winter 2016–17 [UNKNOWN]': <http://www.yuimanakazato.com/collection/couture_aw2016-17.html>

14 *Ibid*.

15 Yuima Nakazato, 'Couture Spring/Summer 2020 [COSMOS]': <http://www.yuimanakazato.com/cosmos/>

16 See 'Yuima Nakazato haute couture Fall/Winter 2017/18', on *Fashion Feed* for a film of the process: <https://www.youtube.com/watch?v=rn DxDqeJfsQ>

17 Ann Binlot, 'Yuima Nakazato introduces fermented microbes and digital fabrication to the guarded tradition of haute couture,' *Document* (2019): <https://www.documentjournal.com/2019/07/what-is-biocouture-meet-the-japanese-designer-yuima-nakazato>

18 See <https://cutecircuit.com/the-hug-shirt/>

19 See <https://cutecircuit.com/soundshirt/>

20 See <https://cutecircuit.com/mdress/>

21 See <https://cutecircuit.com/twitter_dress_nicole/>

22 See <https://cutecircuit.com/news/graphene>

23 See <https://go.affoa.org>

24 'Ying Gao unveils Robotic Clothing that reacts to the Chromatic Spectrum', *Visual Atelier 8* (2019): <https://www.visualatelier8.com/fashion/2019/10/3/ying-gao-robotic-clothing>

25 André Leon Talley, *Little Black Dress* (2012), p. 19.

THE 'POST-POSTMODERN' LITTLE BLACK DRESS

Georgina Ripley

In Justine Picardie's 2005 article for *The Guardian* on black in fashion, she remarked that 'in the circling language of fashion, black is a recurrent feature, more constant in its forceful repetitions than anything else in the lexicon'.[1] This volume has outlined the fashion for black as it is embodied in the cultural phenomenon of the little black dress, demonstrating how its chameleonic character has ensured it remains a firm fixture on the catwalk. The scope of the chapters evidences that the little black dress is symbolic of how fashion relates everyday lives to the broad sweeps of history; but together they also show that in the history of fashionable black, 'The Little Black Dress attributed to Coco Chanel plays only a very small part'.[2]

Black is variously either in fashion or, in recent years, on trend as a kind of anti-fashion indicative of a growing weariness for mercurial trends. Fashion, as Osman Ahmed declared, 'had already become deeply unfashionable long before coronavirus rendered it officially *démodé*'.[3] Reporting on the Autumn/Winter 2020 collections amidst the Covid-19 pandemic, the November 2020 issue of British *Vogue* noted black had 'gained a poignant new edge', described as 'dramatic and tender', and designated a 'pragmatic and poetic choice'.[4] In attempting to consider what part the LBD might play in our sartorial futures, this final chapter explores the cyclical trend for black in the context of the present-day industry – one increasingly grappling with the imperative to consider its impact on people, society and the planet, against the backdrop of a global health crisis and significant social upheaval. In a sense, it acts as a sequel to chapter 1, which provides a broad overview of the LBD in its Western context but, as such, tells a limited story. This chapter aims to reconcile the historical study of fashion in the West, situated primarily within a postcolonial, 'Euromodern' perspective, with the reality of a global fashion system of production, distribution and consumption.[5] At the same time, it embraces contemporary environmentalist perspectives to map what a sustainable future might look like for the LBD. Ruminating on the possibilities for a fashion industry post-Covid-19, Osman Ahmed asked, 'When does the future begin? As soon as the past ends.'[6] However, this chapter argues that in fact the temporal entanglements of fashion ensure a place for both tradition and modernity in revitalising the industry – and that the LBD will endure in fashion precisely because it bridges these polarities.

Fashion in time and place

Picardie's 2005 memoirs open with a chapter on her mother's wedding dress – a French cocktail ensemble from an expensive boutique in Hampstead, bought for her wedding in 1960, eight months before her daughter was born. It is remarkable for its colour, black. The dress was a narrow, corseted sheath, with a skirt of black mohair sitting just shy of knee-length and a black satin bodice. Picardie questioned her mother's rationale for such a purchase, asking, 'How useful is a French cocktail dress to a pregnant girl living in a rented one-bedroom flat in Hampstead?'[7] Her suggestion, that her mother's dress was 'her way of declaring ... she was a chic European now; that she had left behind the safe conformity of her colonial upbringing', cements the idea of the LBD as the epitome of style, injects it with a frisson of danger and marks it out as, notably, *European*.[8]

Fashion critic Suzy Menkes called the LBD 'emblematic of Gallic chic'; while in 1984 Diana Vreeland remarked that 'Girls today look the same all over the world, but they start in the streets of Paris. A girl in America, in Japan, in Germany would rather look like girls in the streets of Paris than anyone else.'[9] The mid-19th century invention of haute couture assured Paris' synonymy with style, consolidating the West's claim to a monopoly over fashion. It is a claim that Jennifer Craik terms the 'European-dictator (ethnocentric or cultural superiority) model of fashion' – and one which has overwritten Asia as a leader in the textile trade in the previous centuries.[10] The apparent globalisation of fashion, often couched in terms of economic inevitability, is argued to perpetuate an imperialist ideology that ignores the transnational flow of ideas, and promotes a clothing system founded on Eurocentric ideals of beauty, gender ideologies and secular principles of modesty. That the 'mainstream' fashion industry is still presided over by the 'big four' fashion cities of Paris, London, Milan and New York underestimates the importance of thriving fashion weeks launched elsewhere which are shaped by localisation as much as by the global political economy – such as in Johannesburg in 1997, Shanghai in 2003, Seoul in 2010 and Lagos in 2011. In 2021, *Business of Fashion* reported that the industry and economic fallout of the pandemic is 'recentering the global fashion sector from the United States and Europe to Asia',[11] leading to what Simona Segre Reinach acknowledges as a 'complex new cultural construct enriched by the Asian interpretation, which is rapidly influencing the image and identity of European fashion'.[12] It is a significant evolution in the history of dualism between Asia and the West, which Makoto Ishizeki outlines in chapter 4 on the increasing presence of Japanese designers at Paris Fashion Week in the 1980s. With the balance of power tilting away from the West, it is stirring up broader transnational scepticism towards an ideological construct of a Western modernity 'that is not consistent with present-day reality'.[13]

European colonisers throughout the 16th–19th centuries encountered the unfamiliar dress forms of countries including China, India, Japan and various African nations. Characterised as 'costume',

they were typified as unchanging and traditional, distinguishing the 'ethnographic present' from the '"perpetual future" associated with Western fashion's constant rush to the next season'.[14] The essentialising idea of fashion as rapid and continual change establishes a false notion that fashion is relentlessly innovative, engendering much discussion by cultural theorists about the superficial binary between linear time, understood to denote progress and modernity, and cyclical time, interpreted as stalled, or degenerative, and associated with tradition.[15] The little black dress encapsulates this ambivalence as it simultaneously absorbs and resists fashion's proclivity for newness and is thus both the embodiment and the antithesis of this notion of Western 'modernity'.

Transnational perspectives

The idea of Post-Postmodernism is rooted in the simple premise that we no longer live in the era of Postmodernism. Yet formal attempts to define this paradigm shift remain elusive, shared across competing cultural and philosophical movements from Pseudo-Modernism to Metamodernism and Transmodernism. Particularly applicable to the study of global fashion is one of the key tenets of Transmodernity, which acknowledges the interconnectivity of everything in a global society, demonstrating a respect for diversity and a dismantling of hierarchies between cultures. A synthesis of both Modernity and Postmodernity, it proposes a useful framework within which to consider fashion, itself the sum of cultural, technological, socio-political and historical interactions. In her book *New African Fashion*, Helen Jennings acknowledges how African aesthetics have been shaped by forces including imperialism, the transatlantic slave trade, and patterns of migration and globalisation. As such, they evidence how all garments, fabrics and accessories of dress are, as Victoria L Rovine observed, 'the result of global interactions and historical change; in short, they are part of fashion systems'.[16] These systems necessarily widen the lens through which we should seek to interpret the colour black.

Black power

> Should Blackness have as much meaning as it does and how negative and positive is it? And what are the other connections to this term and to this colour …?[17]

The work of conceptual artist Fred Wilson has questioned the notion of Blackness in the 21st century in the face of enduring Western definitions of black as 'wicked' and white as 'pure' – as is memorably captured in the dictionary scene in Spike Lee's film *Malcolm X*, in which Baines teaches 'Detroit Red' the symbolism of language.[18] In 1960s America, revolutionary movements emphasising racial pride, defence against racial oppression, self-determination and economic empowerment took the term 'Black' for their political slogans. The Black Power Movement, rooted in the 1950s, made it into the cultural lexicon in 1966 with the founding of the Black Panther Party by Bobby Seale and Huey Newton in California to challenge police brutality. Professor of dress, diaspora and transnationalism, Carol Tulloch, has described how this use of the term Black in the 1960s was seen as 'a rallying call for self-definition' to reclaim history and identity among the Black community and was central to the agenda of the Black Power Movement.[19] The Black Panthers' 'urban militant' uniform was an expression of their solidarity, and an accessible way into joining the front [Fig. 7.1]: black leather jackets, black trousers and their signature black berets 'formalised

the uniform of all black' and has ensured the legacy of the colour black in Black Lives Matter protest clothing today.[20]

It is because the Black body is both 'problematically visible' and 'paradoxically invisible' that the Hollywood film of the Marvel comic *Black Panther* (2018) represented such a significant cultural shift for the Black Lives Matter movement [Fig. 7.2].[21] As a celebration of Black life and global Black diaspora, it was the first film to have an African American director and predominantly Black cast. Created by Marvel visionaries Stan Lee and Jack Kirby in the 1960s, King T'Challa was their first Black superhero, reflective of an 'African American mythology that was being forged in the 1960s of independent and liberated Black people'.[22] His origin story reflects the history of colonialism in Africa, albeit with one significant twist: the East African Kingdom of Wakanda remains unconquered. By constructing it as free from colonialist narratives, the costume too is free from struggles over race, gender, tradition and imitation. Oscar-winning costume designer Ruth E Carter melded cultural aesthetics from all over the Continent, with distinct colour palettes and motifs conspicuously reflecting African customs and exemplifying the film's celebration of Afrofuturism.[23] In Lorraine Henry King's view, Carter's departure from superhero costuming tropes was most significant:

> Like other superheroes, Panther conformed to the genre expectation of wearing a costume so tight it could be described as a second skin; but there was also a new respect established for the black primordial skin on which the costume sat.[24]

Referring to the power of skin as both vehicle and metaphor, Lorraine Henry King's research has meant 'interrogating the readings of fear, racism and fetishization around Black skin', and creating

new interpretations apart from 'old tropes of naked-ness, shame, subjugation and slavery'.[25] Thus Black in this context is emphatically synonymous with empowerment and solidarity, and represents a dis-mantling of stereotypes by 'placing positive repre-sentations of the Black body as heroic within main-stream conversation'.[26]

Life-giving black

In her book on the black dress, Valerie Steele wrote:

> Throughout human history, black has been associated with night and, by extension, death and nothingness. Nor is this simply the result of racism, since traditional African symbol-ism makes precisely the same association. Night *is* black, just as blood is red.[27]

While Black is indisputably night, the varied dress in the African context historically draws from deep local roots and demonstrates intimate connections to clothing across the peoples of different regions, which extends to more nuanced interpretations of colour symbolism. In ancient Egypt, for example, as in other parts of Africa and Asia, black was simul-taneously symbolic of life and death. Writing of the colour black as the 'colour of the bowels of the earth and the underground world', Michel Pastoureau wrote that in pharaonic Egypt 'this chthonic black

is neither diabolical nor harmful'.[28] In contrast to the singularly negative connotations of hell, death and the devil, bestowed upon the colour in the early Christian period, in many other ancient cultures black can be regarded in both a good and a bad light. Pastoureau wrote that 'it is linked to the fertile aspect of the earth; for the dead, whose passage to the beyond it ensures, it is a beneficial black, the sign or promise of rebirth'.[29] Ancient Egypt was it-self referred to as 'the Black Land', distinguishing the fertile banks of the Nile from the surrounding desert, or 'Red Land'. It was red that was associ-ated with the forces of evil, while divinities related to death were almost always painted black, such as the jackal-god Anubis, and deified Kings and Queens were generally represented with black skin, 'a colour that was not the least bit depreciatory'.[30]

Among the Bamana of Mali in West Africa, the symbolism of black in the decoration of bogolan or bogolanfini (mud cloths) is intertwined with com-plex narratives of femininity and fertility, and proves an insightful case study to probe the complex global histories of black [Fig. 7.3]. In Bamana culture there are three basic colour categories – red (*bilen*), white (*jè*) and black (*fiyn*). Red is associated with blood and transformative power. White is related to death (and thus also with Islam, since Muslims wear white in mourning), but *jè* can also mean clear or clean and, in a sexual context, pure or faithful.[31] However, the binary understanding of black and white does not exist as it does in Western interpretation – *fiyn* is usually only used to describe colours across a spectrum of hues from blue to deep black, rather than expressly applicable to certain behaviours or characteristics.[32] The Bamana instead view black as a rich, productive colour, associated with a fertile, wet earth. To make the cloths, the women dye locally made cotton cloth with leaves, before painting it with a fermented mud solution. The leaves are deeply imbued with symbolism: they are used for

Fig. 7.1 (opposite, above)
Black Panthers line up at a Free Huey rally in DeFremery Park in West Oakland, 1968.
(© 2022, Stephen Shames / Courtesy Steven Kasher Gallery)

Fig. 7.2 (opposite, below)
Actor Chadwick Boseman as T'Challa in the film *Black Panther* (2018, Ryan Coogler).
(Moviestore Collections Ltd / Alamy Stock Photo)

Fig. 7.3
Woman's skirt of cotton mud cloth: West Africa, Mali,
Beledougou region, Bamana people, made by Djowari Suko,
1987. National Museums Scotland A.1988.39.

(Image © National Museums Scotland)

cooking, for making medicines, and historically as part of burial rituals. Less tangibly, and more forbiddingly, they were also associated with *fura ci* – translated loosely as the act of excision and referring to an ensemble of rituals which included a woman's transfer to her husband – sometimes interpreted as 'breaking of the leaf'.[33] Connecting women's sex and fertility to the earth in this way is not accidental. Sarah Brett-Smith explains that 'in the past, the dark colour of mud cloth probably functioned as a metaphor for the richness, ease, and fertility desired by the women who wore it'.[34] This is rooted in the symbolic practice of young girls wearing a short skirt with open sides (*m'pògò*) dyed solid black with mud, as soon as they began to menstruate (as well as immediately after childbirth). In this way, femaleness was connected with a dark and dangerous power – Brett-Smith hypothesizes that 'the black underskirt was associated with the power of untouched female genitalia and the idea of an inchoate matrix of darkness as a symbol of female generative capacity'.[35]

Global anxieties of liberated womanhood

This positioning of femininity as something to be feared or controlled within a society founded on hierarchy and masculine power is cross-culturally shared, as discussed in chapter 1 in relation to 1920s Europe. Ilya Parkins relates this anxiety back to the positioning of women and femininity that called their subjugation into question and considers it analogous to the political agenda to dispel ideals of emancipation from colonial oppression.[36] The idea of the 'new woman' was deployed within women's liberation campaigns around the world, from Japan and USA, to the UK and France. In some instances – such as in China and India – the symbolic modern woman was part of a broader modernising discourse, where the 'transformations, real or perceived ... became a focus for debates about the state of the nation and its progress'.[37] Thus the international modern woman, just like the 1920s European dressed in her democratic LBD, became the target of accusations of promiscuity intended to impede any notions of a truly liberated womanhood.

The Chinese counterpart to the Western flapper, the *modeng* girl, sported *qipao* and high-heels, permed or bobbed her hair, and wore lipstick and face powder. The early *qipao* – arguably the LBD's equivalent – emerged during the politically and socially turbulent end of the Qing dynasty (1644–1911) in the late 19th and early 20th centuries, and is fundamentally 'linked to the redefinition of the female body during the crucial period of the development of Chinese modernity'.[38] An ankle to knee-length dress, with an asymmetric closure across the chest and a high mandarin collar [Fig. 7.4], the modern *qipao* variously integrated stylistic features from Han and Manchu traditional dress as well as Western fashion, with its slimmer silhouette and higher hemlines. The historian Antonia Finnane interprets the dress as a modification of the single *changpao* (long robe), worn by the male literati, and thus representative of a bid to claim equal status with men.[39] Consequently, it has been declared a 'masculine, anti-traditionalist female dress', credentials equally applicable to Chanel's LBD.[40] The *modeng* bore the additional burden of association with the ascendancy of Western ideas of modernisation, carrying negative connotations

Fig. 7.4
Soong Qingling wearing the *qipao* in 1925.

of 'superficial Westernisation, hedonism, even avarice'.[41] Government pushback to the changing fashions in early 20th-century China 'created a line between the intellectual idea of a modern woman and the promiscuous seductress' – the politics of women's bodies causing fluctuations in the style and meaning of the *qipao*, similar to how the Western LBD metamorphosed from Chanel's liberated ideal of womanhood to Dior's commodified femininity.[42] Removed from its previously revolutionary and modernising spirit, by the 1930s the *qipao* symbolised the 'homely femininity of a good wife and mother who turned to traditional social values' as the New Life Movement, established in 1934, sought a return to traditional Confucian teaching and Christian values of feminine virtue.[43] Yet simultaneously, the allure of the *qipao* was marketed and celebrated in the advertising sector, as well as in Shanghai and Hollywood films.

After the Fall

Western interpretation of black has been underscored by the early Christian Church's inference of black as synonymous with sin, as explored by Lynne Hume (chapter 2), and the notion of sin is itself reliant upon narratives of gender and the body, as in biblical interpretations of Genesis 1–3. In the story of Adam and Eve, the state of paradise is a state of nakedness, free from artifice, avarice and deceit until 'traditional Judeo-Christian thought stemming from the Old Testament description of the Fall imposed a morality upon the exposure of the shameful naked body'.[44] Although there are divergent readings of the Fall across the three Abrahamic faiths, the cultural importance of modesty in relation to women's clothing is far-reaching, and the interplay between revealing and concealing underscores the division between the public and private spheres. However, for the designer Carli Pearson, founder of Cimone, who has played with Christian religious references in her fashion collections [Fig. 2.4], there is a sexual tension equally imparted by the notion of concealing and 'the provocative notion of the untouchable' that complicates the sex/modesty dichotomy in women's dress.[45]

The modest body

Black is often integral to notions of modesty, as in relation to the Catholic priest's cassock and the nun's habit, as discussed by Hume. Her essay also references Jean Paul Gaultier's *Chic Rabbis* collection, in which female models walked a menorah-lined catwalk in clothing evocative of the characteristically black canonical attire of Hasidic men. In Judaism, the choice of black underpins the principle of *tzniut* (modesty); Eric Silverman described how the black clothing 'symbolises the mystical goal of renouncing the self in order to reunite with the divine', as well as emphasising 'conformity and collectivism over individualism'.[46] In relation to Jewish women, *tzniut* makes distinct outer beauty from inner – or the public from the private self – protecting women from eroticised standards of secular beauty and men from sexual temptation. Among the Orthodox, *tzniut* also protects the sanctity of motherhood; as the bearers of life, women are considered 'holier than men' and so 'need layers of protection'.[47] Interpretation differs as to whether modesty in Jewish dress empowers women to have control over their sexuality, or whether it 'amounts to little more than male power dressed as female honour'.[48] Thus, much like the modest dress of Islamic cultures, it can be variously understood as either a gift or a burden, but it is equally critiqued as patriarchal ideology.

The Muslim veiling tradition encompasses multiple types of covering according to the regional and cultural preferences of Islamic societies across Africa, and West, Southwest and Central Asia. Garments are varied and include the (commonly black) chador; the burqa and niqab, which cover or partially cover the face; and the abaya, a long voluminous robe, traditionally black or dark in colour, and often worn with a light matching veil (shayla). Worn for cultural or religious imperative, the veil is designed to be self-effacing and to diminish physical suggestion; black therefore suggests modesty, or as an expression of religious affiliation it reflects the 'numinous' individual – a mystical spiritual or religious quality. However, veiling is a longstanding clothing tradition with a more complex history, believed to have originated in Assyrian (now Iraqi), Persian (now Iranian) and Byzantine cultures, long before the birth of the Islamic religion in 7th century CE. At one time, veiling was a signifier of social status – working women and prostitutes were denied veiling, while Susan B Kaiser wrote that upper-class women wore the veil to shield the '"impure" gaze of commoners'.[49] As the practice came to be an important Islamic and nationalistic symbol of identity, Islamophobia and secular views of humanitarianism and feminism have clouded understandings of veiling in the West, causing the all-encompassing, once primarily black attire to be solely viewed as a mark of oppression.[50] In fact, the core issue remains one of bodily autonomy, with the fight to be allowed to publicly wear the hijab in multi-faith societies as vital as the fight for the right to choose in countries where it is compulsory.

In the United Arab Emirates in particular, a growing multicultural hub for international design, the abaya has emerged as an object of high fashion available in an array of cuts, colours, and embellished fabrics. It has given rise to the female-driven trend for 'abaya-as-fashion' – fashionable adaptations of the plain abaya into garments expressive of individual taste. Seen by conservatives to privilege fashion over piety, and thus worn not necessarily to veil but to display, it unsettles Islamic modesty ideals promoting uniformity and anonymity for women.[51] Elizabeth Shimek wrote that the abaya-as-fashion is a 'paradox within this paradigm', with even the uniform black abaya serving as a template on which to elaborate, a blank canvas for designers to paint upon, with endless possible variations.[52] It is precisely this function that continues to draw designers to the LBD; and as much as Chanel's dress of 1926 transgressed social constructs of gender while outwardly remaining within the boundaries of accepted gendered forms of dress, the abaya-

Fig. 7.5
(Abaya by Effa Fashion)

as-fashion acquiesces to cultural edicts for modesty, even while it challenges those structures. In the context of modernisation, conservatives have reproached the new abaya for undermining the traditional social order, participating in global fashion trends and seeking to align with a new transnational and cosmopolitan culture. Yet, the international designs of Effa Abaya Couture [Fig. 7.5], one of Dubai's most prestigious abaya-as-fashion designers, have become so popular they are known colloquially as the 'Little Black Dress of the

Middle East', which, Shimek wrote, draws 'a striking comparison between the once-plain abaya and a symbol of female beauty and sexuality in the West'.[53]

Meanwhile, Western cultural anxiety around the tradition of veiling is steeped in hypocrisy, particularly as mask-wearing was commonplace during the pandemic, contradicting anti-veiling attitudes. Kaiser addresses the issue of double standards between Western high fashion and religion, asking, 'What are the relationships among ethnicity, religion, nation and gender? And how do gender and other subject positions intervene and become entangled in contexts of colonialism and other power relations?'[54] In 2016, Dolce & Gabbana released its first line of abayas and hijabs – however, it was criticised for reinforcing the idea that Western designers control or legitimise global fashion.

On the Met Gala's red carpet in September 2021, Kim Kardashian wore a full-body, all-black Balenciaga ensemble, comprised of a trained T-shirt over a body-suit with a matching mask which obscured her features, while concealing – yet in its starkness, ultimately being more revealing of – her physique. Her look was praised by *Vogue* for rewriting red carpet rules and for lending the reality star anonymity – something conversely at the root of anti-Muslim discrimination in the West, where the act of concealing is counterposed to the relative value of revealing.[55] While some commentators likened the ensemble to the full-body coverage afforded by the burqa, sheathing Kardashian's body head-to-toe in contour-hugging black arguably alluded more to the gimp suits of the fetish scene than the modesty of veiling. Either way, its favourable reception by the fashion press underscores the inconsistent attitudes towards sexuality and modesty within different cultural contexts, an ambivalence inherent in the colour black.

The fetishized body

Writing in 2007, Valerie Steele remarked, 'Today, every designer who pushes the boundaries of fashion must address the power of black', where 'Beauty and horror kiss'.[56] It seems that in fashion, black cannot escape its more lascivious connotations. Previous chapters in this book have highlighted instances of the paradoxical intersections of fashion and femininity, whereby styles can be interpreted as simultaneously degrading and empowering, or alternately as respectable or dangerous.[57] This dichotomy in dress is further encapsulated in headlines following the Autumn/Winter 2020 fashion shows: 'Lace or Latex? London Fashion Week's 2 Biggest Trends Couldn't Be More Polarising.'[58] Tim Blanks reported that Creative Director of Yves Saint Laurent, Anthony Vaccarello, had 'pushed all Yves's emblematic tokens of bourgeois fetishism to his own limit' with his emphatic use of latex in a collection where black was the strongest accent, resonating across sheer lace bodies, leather culottes and one notable black, décolleté, latex slip dress [Fig. 7.6]. Blanks identified an 'undeniable sexual charge – the dominatrix in her element', as the show notes referred to 'a tension between discipline and pleasure'.[59] The shiny, erotic latex was juxtaposed with respectable tailoring and styled with luxurious cashmere and lace, both softening its hard edges and invoking a sensorial stimulation in the tactility of clashing textures. In the context of Harvey Weinstein facing sentencing following convictions for rape and sexual assault, Blanks observed that it 'felt like an appropriate moment to consider how #MeToo fitted into this dominatrix fashion niche'.[60]

As observed by Iain R Webb in chapter 3, Yves Saint Laurent was a tastemaker for modern fashion, influential in transforming the LBD – or its *Le Smoking* equivalent – for his female clients. He brought together austerity and elegance and utilised

Fig. 7.6
Yves Saint Laurent, Ready-to-Wear Autumn/Winter 2020.
(Sipa US / Alamy Stock Photo)

the phallic power of the tailored silhouette to re-dress gendered boundaries of fashion – an approach in some sense prefaced by Chanel's female dandyism. For Spring/Summer 2022, Vaccarello's 'second-skin' all-black two-pieces and jumpsuits recalled Fiona Jardine's description (chapter 5) of the 'Bad Sandy' trope of womanhood immortalised in *Grease* (1978), set against the backdrop of a Postmodern turn in fashion imagery and the countercultural havens of disco and Studio 54, and Club Kid culture.

Yet this discourse of an empowering sexualisation of the female body is complexified by broader historical and global forces such as colonialism. The Western fashion industry has routinely cast Black women and women of colour 'in the role of exotic, mysterious muse' – they are, as Rebecca Arnold writes, 'Almost always seen through the filter of white Western fantasies of the eroticised "other", their cultures have been merged into a generalised sense of sexual potential and the frisson of danger in the unfamiliar'.[61] As skin is one of the most important erogenous zones, the predominantly black, second-skin materials of fetish fashion – appropriated by 'Bad Sandy' – have a certain power because they both imitate and encase human skin, marking the boundaries of the body, and exploiting the association of black with perversion and rebellion. When the eroticised subject is Black skin, the notion of an objectified femininity inevitably intersects with narratives of colonial power structures, the eroticised 'other' and Western fetishization of the Black body.

The gendered body

This volume's narrative of the LBD has inevitably focused on themes of heteronormative femininity, taking Parkins' view of fashion as a 'rich and compelling *mediator* of larger questions concerning the relationship of women and femininity to modernity'.[62] This relationship is integral to contextualising the mythic status of Chanel's LBD, but it risks reducing fashion to another binary – that of the masculine and the feminine – when in fact, fashion 'is important in revealing the perverse masquerade of gender itself'.[63] As the feminist, Gay Liberation and Black Civil Rights movements 'drove stakes into the heart of traditional moral opinion on representation' in the second half of the 20th century, Arnold concluded that 'the simple dichotomy of masculine/feminine had gradually been eroded ... undermined by the shifting power structures of industrialised society and the crumbling of empires'.[64] A more 'dissonant eroticism' in fashion representation had developed, with blurred gender identities and fluid sexualities enabled by queer subcultures and their assimilation into fashion. Gender theorists, from Simone de Beauvoir to Judith Butler, have posited now well-established arguments that recognise gender to be a social construct. It follows that just as women have historically subverted so-called gendered signifiers of dress by adapting and adopting masculine fashions – as with Chanel's LBD and the *qipao* – men might also procure feminine styles for themselves. Once seen as 'the perfect weapon for liberated womanhood', the little black dress of today must encompass a broader understanding of gender expression.[65]

Hazel Clark and Leena-Maija Rossi have traced popular feminine masculinities (outside of drag) back to the 1980s.[66] When Jean Paul Gaultier put men in skirts on his catwalk in 1984, the style was criticised for flirting with a notion of transvestism, though it in fact drew upon the male national dress of the Scottish kilt. Just like the sensibility of camp, now sanitised by its assimilation into high fashion, men in skirts has lost the power to shock; however, neither has lost the power to re-energise the status quo. For Mal Burkinshaw, Head of Design at Edinburgh College of Art, dispelling myths of gendered clothing is at the root of his work: 'I prefer to design with transparent black materials and lace, allowing me to challenge preconceptions about the sexualisation of black and the biased gendering constructs of lace as a more "feminine" material.'[67] Fashion designer Marc Jacobs' appearance on the 2012 Met Gala red carpet in a sheer, black lace shirt-dress, worn with white boxer shorts, black socks and diamanté-buckled dress shoes, caused a stir, proving that lace – particularly black lace – still holds a uniquely feminine, and eroticised, status. The question arises of what might be considered the (heteronormative) male equivalent to the little black dress, and a well-cut suit seems the logical comparison, drawing a line between Chanel's falsely unassuming LBD and the Brummellian dandy's fastidious sobriety in dress at the turn of the 19th century. Both have endured in fashion, but perhaps never so artfully expressed as when they were combined in a sharply tailored tuxedo jacket, overtop a full-skirted, strapless velvet gown and white dress shirt with frilled cuffs and traditional bow tie, worn by Billy Porter on the red carpet for the 91st Academy Awards [Fig. 7.7]. Created by the American designer Christian Siriano, the evening gown challenged but remained within the rigid Hollywood 'black tie formal' dress code. For Porter, his collaboration with Siriano was especially significant because, 'I'm not a drag queen, I'm a man in a dress'. He added, 'What is masculinity? What does that mean? Women show up every day in pants, but the minute a man wears a dress, the seas part.'[68]

Clothing, tied as it is to the body, is the greatest tool in renegotiating gendered identities for it marks the boundary between the physical, or biological body, and the social body – that which is subject to social, cultural and moral pressures, and which so often constrains perception of the physical body.[69] The black dress has repeatedly appeared in this lexicon and continues to be deployed – most recently in Raf Simons' Spring/Summer 2022 collection, which included several black dresses modelled by a racially diverse but

Fig. 7.7 (opposite)
Billy Porter wears a tuxedo gown by Christian Siriano to the 91st Academy Awards Oscars Governors Ball in Hollywood, 24 February 2019.
(REUTERS / Alamy Stock Photo)

otherwise homogenous cast of androgynous models. Perhaps it is because the obscurity of black as a non-colour, so often chosen for a cloak of invisibility, enables limitless opportunities for self-expression; as Burkinshaw said, 'As a style statement you can't hide your personality behind black and I think it pushes people to look more at who you are'. It is just as *Vogue*'s Global Editor-at-Large, Hamish Bowles, observed: it is 'small wonder that Gabrielle "Coco" Chanel, that commandingly powerful character, revelled in its possibilities as a sartorial foil to her coruscating persona'.[70]

The future of the LBD

Predicting the trajectory for post-pandemic fashion for *The Economist* in 2020, Luke Leitch titled his article 'The End of Modernity'.[71] With fashion shows comprehensively cancelled for the first time since the Second World War, and factories shuttered, it marked at the very least a pause in the self-perpetuating vicious circle of newness that holds the modern industry to ransom. On top of the relentless pace of innovation, journalist Alec Leach added that 'fashion's many, many sins were laid bare for all to see. Whitewashed runways, cultural appropriation, sizeism, vast power imbalances, reckless consumption, wasteful business models – fashion week had it all.'[72] Nevertheless, the slew of fashion headlines that declared the pandemic to have revealed the ugly truth of the industry and announcing it time for a 'reboot', were quickly replaced with a collective scratching of heads as initially strident industry calls for change quietly petered out. The pandemic represents a significant yard-stick against which to measure the industry's capacity for structural change. The economic and environmental fallout has precipitated a cultural unravelling, shifting the emphasis onto social challenges, such as social justice and human rights issues. Labour rights violations in the fashion industry exposed the fragility in supply chains and inequality for garment workers, centring concerns about replication and perpetuation of colonial practices in the industry's extraction of labour and resources and its discarding of waste. Bandana Tewari, writing for the *Business of Fashion*, declared that 'garment workers have, in essence, become as commoditised as the raw materials that the British extracted from colonial India'.[73] In Western culture where we have been socially conditioned to desire newness, it is possible to draw a line between consumerism, colonialism and climate change. Fashion must change, but just how can the LBD be a vehicle for that change?

Twenty-first century modern

With the spotlight now on anthropogenic climate change, international Black Lives Matter protests, Covid-19 and the inevitable economic fallout, contemporary fashion has once again veered towards the sexual provocation of glamour, which has long been associated with periods of instability and neurosis. This time however, Eugene Rabkin argues that '"Look, don't touch" is the ethos that pervades fashion's exhibitionist post-pandemic look', one that views sexuality as agency and sexy attire as an expression of body positivity.[74] Notably, Albanian womenswear designer Nensi Dojaka, whose deconstructed LBDs are intricately cut to reveal the body just so, won the prestigious LVMH prize in 2021 [Fig. 7.8]. Her rise has been meteoric since graduating in 2019; *Vogue* reported that her black, asymmetric, mini-dress was on global fashion shopping platform Lyst's index of the ten hottest women's products for the first quarter of 2021.[75]

Black has appeared on both virtual and in-

Fig. 7.8

Model Paloma Elsesser walking at London Fashion Week for Nensi Dojaka Ready-to-Wear Autumn/Winter 2022.

(Shutterstock / Shutterstock.com)

(Autumn/Winter 2021); and in the alluring danger of Maria Grazia Chiuri's dark fairytale collection for Dior (Autumn/Winter 2021).[76] Fashion mid-pandemic was swinging between extremes, a trend for hyper-classicism that functioned almost as anti-fashion brushing shoulders with a longing for freedom – whether that be for the outdoors, for libertarianism, for carnal sensuality, or for going 'out-out'. Christopher Kane has stepped into the void left by Azzedine Alaïa and Thierry Mugler, with his 'fetish-y, sensual fashion play', manifest for Autumn/Winter 2022 in wipe-clean, black PVC, cut-away dresses.[77] Significantly, the most iconic LBD of the present might come to be such purely for the cultural moment it represented – for Fashion Museum's 'Dress of the Year' 2021, Ib Kamara and Gareth Wrighton selected a black-and-white silk georgette Armani dress with lotus flower embroidery. Worn by Meghan, Duchess of Sussex for her world exclusive interview with Oprah Winfrey, viewed by more than 60 million people worldwide, it was chosen for surely the same reason Princess Diana's 'Revenge' dress or Liz Hurley's Versace number are etched into our minds:

> In today's hyper-stylised pop culture, the Dress of the Year now has the potential to also be 'meme of the year' and we both latched upon Meghan and Harry's now iconic interview with Oprah as the definitive anti-establishment moment that will forever endure in the British collective consciousness.[78]

In these specific conditions of Modernity, the collections garnering accolades are those that communicate the humanity and tactility of couture, redolent of fashion's shift towards sustainability, or a sense of activism, which Amy de la Haye identified as the single most defining feature of contemporary fashion.[79] This was captured for the *Vogue* annals

person catwalks in various guises: as a surreally proportioned coat punctuated with spikes by Viktor & Rolf (Autumn/Winter 2020); in Simone Rocha's 'curiously exuberant, in a kinky way' biker leathers with the pull-out cover of the September 2020 issue of British *Vogue*, which celebrated the faces of British activism for its theme of hope, led by model Adwoa Aboah and the footballer Marcus Rashford dressed in all-black ensembles, with Aboah donning the countercultural Black Panthers' beret.

In 2020, Cameroonian designer Imane Ayissi made his Paris couture debut, the first designer from sub-Saharan Africa to be invited to participate, where his critical attention to ethical artisanship and 'Made in Africa' fashion proposed a more sustainable, transnational pathway for the future. Latterly, Pierpaolo Piccioli's 'Anatomy of Couture' collection for Valentino (Spring/Summer 2022) revolutionised the couture atelier, designing his creations on ten differently proportioned house models as opposed to the one, typically slender, silhouette, in stark contrast to the singular canons of beauty in any given era. Chanel's LBD of 1926 was created for a modern woman aiming to liberate herself from patriarchal control, but yet she conformed to prevailing heteronormative feminine beauty standards, with her supple, youthful and slender figure. In contrast, Piccioli identifies modern beauty in diversity. In an interview with *Vogue* he said: 'For me, the modernity of couture doesn't mean the modernity of beauty, because beauty is beauty. But it means that the approach is different. You embrace humanity.'[80] And how did this show open? With 57-year-old supermodel Kristen McMenamy modelling a black mini-dress with a plunging, moulded sweetheart neckline and flirtatious, frilled hem.

A slowing down

The Slow Fashion Movement is encouraging consumers to break up with fast fashion: studies show that wearing a garment for twice as long would lower greenhouse gas emissions from all clothing by 44 per cent.[81] In this context, a wardrobe classic such as the LBD – a reliable, multifaceted and timeless garment – becomes a powerful source of sustainability. In 2009, Sheena Matkeiken founded the Uniform Project, a pledge to wear and restyle the same little black dress for 365 days, using only vintage, handmade or donated accessories to explore sustainability through the versatility of a wardrobe staple. Her chosen style was a button-down, reversible, A-line dress, which could also be worn front to back, or as an open tunic. The principle of using the LBD as a base garment is testament to its capacity for limitless possibility. As Robin Givhan noted: 'For years, designers spun whimsical garments that tantalised the imagination but mostly didn't sell; it was their more pragmatic styles that made the cash registers sing.'[82] This is one reason Rosemary Harden, Curator of the Fashion Museum in Bath, believes designers return time and again to the LBD – simply, 'black dresses, little or otherwise, sell!'[83]

Conversations around sustainability in fashion have naturally entered the virtual world, as fashion makes inroads into the metaverse, finding commonality in ideas of agency, fantasy and self-expression. Since progress is tied to industrialisation, which is afforded by new technologies of production and consumption, it thus follows that new technologies have an important role to play in fashion's future, as explored by Pamela Parmal in chapter 6. However, developments in science and technology also offer sustainable solutions away from the digital, as a means of preserving the haptic sensibility of making clothes. British designer Phoebe English's Spring/Summer 2022 collection, *Here: An Alternative Route*, marked the studio's new approach to incorporating regenerative design into its fashion practice, replenishing rather than extracting resources [Fig. 7.9]. In a sense, it encapsulates fashion's temporal paradox – a going back to the

Fig. 7.9

Model Kaigin wears the *Inky Gather Dress* by Phoebe English, *Here: An Alternative Route* collection Spring/Summer 2022.

(Photographer: Asia Werbel)

earth, to the literal roots of fashion, to regenerate clothing in a cyclical and entirely different way to those exploiting the productive and progressive capacities of new digital technologies. Sustainable and natural dyes seemingly threaten the future of the LBD, with pure black being an especially difficult colour to achieve. For English, who has always centred her design process around the colour black, the path to developing her signature *Inky*, derived from locally foraged oak galls and logwood

sourced from sustainably managed forests, took four months and endless dye samples. She sees that innovating the LBD in the 21st century will be just one aspect of how our relationship to clothes will change to end the cycle of excessive consumption:

> Designers are solution-based problem solvers. Fashion helps to form and inform what is deemed fashionable and what is deemed unfashionable, it is enormously influential, and I hope can see its power for potential shift towards a priority over preservation, over an endless 'new'. Preservation must become the new black.[84]

Award-winning eco designers Vin + Omi are similarly masters of utilising waste. For their Autumn/Winter 2020 collection *RESIST*, they worked with King Charles III's Highgrove estate – dead hydrangea heads were combined with latex and linen to produce jackets; willow and ash cuttings were woven into baskets; and horsehair was woven into garments. Waste nettles were naturally dyed and incorporated into the collection, forming the letters to spell out 'RESIST' on their catwalk finale: an ominous, hooded black gown, specially created for National Museums Scotland's exhibition on the little black dress [Fig. 7.10]. It is evident that change oriented to slow fashion does not compromise associations between change and progress, but rather, as Rita Felski has argued, 'Cyclical time and linear time are not opposed but intertwined; the innovations of modernity are made real in the routines of everyday life'.[85] Predicting the future of the LBD once again returns us to the interrelationship between Modernity, fashion and temporality, in which 'movement toward the future becomes the utopian end or purpose of the present'.[86]

Back to black

Writing in 2020, journalist Anna Murphy asked, 'Are trends dead? Or rather, are we in a post-trends age?'[87] The 'perma-trends' identified year in, year out caused her to question how fashion was to square the circle of delivering constancy with just enough novelty. Enter the little black dress. If the essays in this book prove anything, it is the LBD's infinite capacity to bridge this divide between constancy and novelty, with its myriad iterations and endless possibilities. Designers will always turn to black; indeed, few garments 'have continued to inspire designers with such disparate points of view' as the LBD.[88] As a textile designer, English spoke of how black allows her to focus on the elements of texture, shape and form alone. Likewise, Pearson reaches for black for her architectural silhouettes, where 'the presence of black allows me to see the sharp lines and outer frame clearly and crisply, the illusion of an imposing tower'. Both English and Burkinshaw have shared their fascination with how black responds to light, absorbing the details of design; as such, Burkinshaw encourages his students to look at the surface effects of black, by contrasting the tones and effects of satins and silks, sheer and matte, or textural embellishments. To all three designers, black is reassuring. For English, it is courtesy of its versatility and enduring presence: 'It can be there, and it can be not there, it can be a canvas, or it can be the feature. It doesn't age, you can be present, or you can be invisible, it lasts forever, and you will always wear it.' For Pearson, it is manifest in its familiarity:

> ... in my collections it serves as a full stop, or a corner, a pathway to keep the narrative moving forwards .... Black also has a universality that makes it very wearable. In this sense, unusual shapes that we create become more palatable and easier to understand and define.

Burkinshaw finds that he prefers to work with a colour 'that connects me to the design process and I don't associate black with any particular mood or feeling'. Overwhelmingly, they agree on Pearson's observation that black 'is a palette cleanser of sorts. It strips away any unnecessary noise, removing the clutter.'

In putting the question of what defines the quintessential LBD to the editor, curator and collector Hamish Bowles, he pinpointed that 'Fiendishly complicated simplicity seems to be the hallmark of the most successful little black dresses in my collection'. It is a style reinstated in fashion at seminal moments – Tim Blanks compared Helmut Lang's reign in the 1990s to Coco Chanel 'for the way he brought realness into fashion ... his vision and art direction brought everyone back to the real and meaningful essence of fashion'.[89] The present day – with a global demand for fashion to be more aware of its footfalls in the culture – feels like one of these times. Writing of the 21st century, Amy de la Haye and Valerie D Mendes identify a dearth of the radical fashions that peppered the later years of the last century, remarking it has 'not spawned any major "outsider" styles. Emerging trends across the entire fashion spectrum are immediately spotted and consumed by an astute and rapacious fashion industry, propelling it forwards with ever increasing speed.'[90] This is certainly true of the LBD, which has absorbed countless mainstream and subcultural trends in its century in fashion's limelight. Yet perhaps, as Jardine concludes, its perpetual existence in fashion is a form of resistance in and of itself.

While the relentless pace of contemporary fashion is under the microscope, it is nevertheless true that 'the constant shifting nature of fashion, its rapid turnover of styles, allows the fluid definitions of gender, sexuality, ethnicity, status and class that populate a culture in transition, to be captured and revealed'.[91] Addressing fashion's bid for newness is thus heavily nuanced. The true issue lies in how historically we have fallen into the binary trap – the concepts of ethnographic 'costume' versus Western 'fashion' presupposes that we can in fact establish a hierarchy between local fashions. The binary of linear and cyclical temporalities that set one up as the central tenet of modernity versus the keystone of tradition (and therefore backwardness) is reductive. As Reinach concluded, the contradictions inherent in this binary model, though always evident, 'are exploding in our time, highlighting a model of greater complexity'.[92] Perhaps this is why it is necessary to seek new paradigms for our Post-Postmodern era. Implicit in the LBD's enduring appeal is the idea it can be all things to all people, just as American *Vogue* anticipated in 1926 when it heralded it as 'the frock that all the world will wear'. In such fragmented times it is difficult to predict anything of fashion, but one thing is clear: if fashion can continue to remix fragments of the past into something that will resonate into the future – as designers have done for more than a century with the little black dress – it will continue to prevail. For all that fashion prizes novelty, as Robin Givhan wrote, 'Fashion, an industry that is forever racing forward, sees its future in its past'.[93]

Acknowledgements

I am indebted to Dr Qin Cao, Dr Margaret Maitland, Dr Sally Tuckett, Dr Sarah Worden and Friederike Voigt for their contributions to this chapter, and to Georgina Johnson for her insights into the Uniform Project. My sincerest thanks go to Hamish Bowles, Mal Burkinshaw, Phoebe English, Rosemary Harden, Miles Lambert and Carli Pearson.

Fig. 7.10
RESIST dress by Vin + Omi for National Museums Scotland, Autumn/Winter 2020.
(© VIN + OMI)

Notes

1   Justine Picardie, 'The darkness', *The Observer* magazine (2005): <https://www.theguardian.com/lifeandstyle/2005/aug/28 fashion.shopping1>

2   Valerie Steele, *The Black Dress* (2007).

3   Osman Ahmed, 'What will the fashion industry look like post-Covid 19', *i-D* (2020): <https://i-d.vice.com/en_uk/article/z3eaz4/what-will-the-fashion-industry-look-like-post-covid-19>

4   Harriet Quick, 'Why Black Is Back On The Style Agenda As AW20's Most Faultless & Seductive Shade', *Vogue* (2020): <https://www.vogue.co.uk/fashion/article/ode-to-black>

5   Lawrence Grossberg's 2010 definition of 'Euromodern', which particularly foregrounds Western Europe, North America, Australia and New Zealand, is discussed in Susan B Kaiser, *Fashion and Cultural Studies* (2019 [2011]), p. 32.

6   Ahmed, 'What will the fashion industry look like post-Covid 19' (2020).

7   Justine Picardie, *My Mother's Wedding Dress: The Life and Afterlife of Clothes* (2006 [2005]), p. 2.

8   *Ibid.* Picardie's mother married aged 21, newly arrived in London from South Africa.

9   Suzy Menkes, 'The Colourful History of the Little Black Dress', *The New York Times* (2013): <https://www.nytimes.com/2013/08/06/fashion/06iht-fbblack06.html>; and Yves Saint Laurent/Diana Vreeland, *Yves Saint Laurent* (1984).

10 Jennifer Craik, *The Face of Fashion: Cultural Studies in Fashion* (1994), p. xi.

11 Vikram Alexei Kansara, 'From West to East: Recentering the Fashion World', *Business of Fashion* (2021): <https://www.businessoffashion.com/briefings/retail/from-west-to-east-recentering-the-fashion-world/>

12 Simona Segre Reinach, 'Ethnicity', in Alexandra Palmer (ed.), *A Cultural History of Dress and Fashion in the Modern Age* (2021 [2018]), p. 156.

13 *Ibid.*, p. 158.

14 Victoria L Rovine, 'Viewing Africa through Fashion', in *Fashion Theory: The Journal of Dress, Body & Culture* 13:2 (2009), p. 134.

15 Ilya Parkins, *Poiret, Dior and Schiaparelli: Fashion, Femininity and Modernity* (2012), p. 25. See also Caroline Evans and Alessandra Vaccari (eds), *Time in Fashion: Industrial, Antilinear and Uchronic Temporalities* (2020), pp. 9–13.

16 Helen Jennings, *New African Fashion* (2011), p. 8; Victoria Rovine quoted in Reinach, 'Ethnicity' (2021 [2018]), p. 158.

17 Carol Tulloch, 'Style–Fashion–Dress: from Black to Post-Black', in *Fashion Theory* 14:3 (2010), pp. 280–81.

18 Spike Lee (dir.), *Malcolm X* (1992).

19 Tulloch, 'Style–Fashion–Dress' (2010), p. 280.

20 Darnell Lisby, quoted in Sara Radin (2019), 'How Colour in Fashion Has Been Used Throughout History to Display Political Solidarity', *Teen Vogue*: https://www.teenvogue.com/story/color-color-fashion-history-political-solidarity>

21 Tulloch, 'Style–Fashion–Dress' (2010), p. 281.

22 Jordan Evans, 'Black Panther, Black Power, and the Black Nationalist Tradition', *African American Intellectual History Society* (2018): <https://www.aaihs.org/the-black-panther-black-power-and-the-black-nationalist-tradition/>

23 Melena Ryzik, 'The Afrofuturistic Designs of "Black Panther"', in *The New York Times* (2018): <https://www.nytimes.com/2018/02/23/movies/black-panther-afrofuturism-costumes-ruth-carter.html>

24 Lorraine Henry King, 'Black skin as costume in *Black Panther*', *Film, Fashion and Consumption* 10:1 (2021), p. 267.

25 *Ibid.*, p. 273.

26 *Ibid.*, p. 267.

27 Steele, *The Black Dress* (2007).

28 Michel Pastoureau, *Black: The History of a Color* (2008), p. 30.

29 *Ibid.*

30 *Ibid.*

31 Sarah C Brett-Smith, *The Silence of the Women: Bamana Mud Cloths* (2014), pp. 60, 80–81. Spellings of *bilen, jè* and *fiyn* as written by Brett-Smith. For further information on alternate spellings of bogolan and bogolanfini, see Victoria L Rovine, *Bogolan: Shaping Culture through Cloth in Contemporary Mali* (2001).

32 *Ibid.*, p. 81.

33 *Ibid.*, pp. 50–52.

34 *Ibid.*, p. 60.

35 *Ibid.*, p. 118.

36 Parkins, *Poiret, Dior and Schiaparelli* (2012), p. 31.

37 Louise Edwards, 'Policing the Modern Woman in Republican China', *Modern China* 26:2 (2000), p. 116.

38 Helena Heroldová, 'Allure of the Body: Chinese Qipao', *Annals of the Náprstek Museum* 35:1 (2014), p. 30.

39 Antonia Finnane, *Changing Clothes in China: Fashion, History, Nation* (2008), p. 144.

40 Heroldová, 'Allure of the Body' (2014), p. 30.

41 Edwards, 'Policing the Modern Woman in Republican China' (2000), p. 133.

42 Adrienne Cox, 'The Qipao: Defining Modern Women in the First Half of the 20th Century', University of Kansas: History honours thesis (2019), p. 36

43 Heroldová, 'Allure of the Body' (2014), pp. 23–27.

44 Rebecca Arnold, *Fashion, Desire and Anxiety: Image and Morality in the 20th Century* (2001), p. 67.

45 Carli Pearson, e-mail to author 17 May (2021); likewise, all subsequent citations by Pearson.

46 Eric Silverman, *A Cultural History of Jewish Dress* (2013), p. 114.

47 *Ibid.*, p. 111.

48 *Ibid.*, pp. 87, 111.

49 Kaiser, *Fashion and Cultural Studies* (2019 [2011]), p. 94.

50 In 1966, Norman Daniel wrote 'there is no subject connected with Islam which Europeans have thought more important than the condition of Muslim women': quoted in Zachary Lockman, *Contending Visions of the Middle East: The History and Politics of Orientalism* (2004), p. 69.

51 Noor al-Qasimi, 'Immodest Modesty: Accommodating Dissent and the "Abaya-as-Fashion" in the Arab Gulf States', *Journal of Middle East Women's Studies* 6:1 (2010), p. 63.

52 Elizabeth D Shimek, 'The Abaya: Fashion, Religion, and Identity in a Globalized World', *Lawrence University Honors Projects* 12 (2012), p. 12.

53 *Ibid.*, p. 23.

54 Kaiser, *Fashion and Cultural Studies* (2019 [2011]), pp. 93–94.

55 Janelle Okwodu, 'Kim Kardashian's Met Gala Look Rewrote the Red Carpet's Rules', *Vogue* (2021): <https://www.vogue.com/article/kim-kardashian-balenciaga-met-gala-2021-look>

56 Steele, *The Black Dress* (2007).

57 See chapters 1 and 5 in this book.

58 Kara Kia, 'Lace or Latex? London Fashion Week's 2 Biggest Trends Couldn't Be More Polarising', *Popsugar* (2020): <https://www.popsugar.co.uk/fashion/london-fashion-week-autumn-winter-2020-trends-47246582>

59 Tim Blanks, 'Shiny Erotic Definitions at Saint Laurent', *Business of Fashion* (2020a): <https://www.businessoffashion.com/reviews/fashion-week/shiny-erotic-definitions-at-saint-laurent/>

60 *Ibid.*

61 Arnold, *Fashion, Desire and Anxiety* (2001), p. 95.

62 Parkins, *Poiret, Dior and Schiaparelli* (2012), p. 16.

63 Caroline Evans, quoted in Lorraine Gamman and Merja Makinen, *Female Fetishism: A new look* (1994), p. 10.

64 Arnold, *Fashion, Desire and Anxiety* (2001), pp. 101–105.

65 Chloe Fox, *Vogue Essentials: Little Black Dress* (2018), p. 12.

66 Hazel Clark and Leena-Maija Rossi, 'Clothes (Un)make the (Wo)man – Ungendering Fashion (2015)?', in Andrew Reilly and Ben Barry (eds), *Crossing gender boundaries: Fashion to Create, Disrupt and Transcend* (2020), p. 207.

67 Mal Burkinshaw, e-mail to author 31 January (2020); likewise, all subsequent citations by Burkinshaw.

68 Christian Allaire, 'Billy Porter on Why He Wore a Gown, Not a Tuxedo, to the Oscars', *Vogue* (2019): <https://www.vogue.com/article/billy-porter-oscars-red-carpet-gown-christian-siriano>

69 See Joanne Entwistle, 'Fashion and the Fleshy Body: Dress as Embodied Practice', *Fashion Theory* 4:3 (2000), p. 327; Kaiser, *Fashion and Cultural Studies* (2019 [2011]), p. 149.

70 Hamish Bowles, e-mail to author 31 January (2020); likewise, all subsequent citations by Bowles.

71 Luke Leitch, 'The end of modernity: what will fashion look like after the pandemic?', *The Economist* (2020): <https://www.economist.com/1843/2020/07/24/the-end-of-modernity>

72 Alec Leach, 'Fashion week as we know it is dead. Or is it?', *i-D* (2020): <https://i-d.vice.com/en_uk/article/bv83qa/fashion-week-as-we-know-it-is-dead-or-is-it>

73 Bandana Tewari, 'Op-Ed. How Fashion perpetuates Modern-Day Colonialism', *Business of Fashion* (2020): <https://www.businessoffashion.com/opinions/global-markets/op-ed-how-fashion-perpetuates-modern-day-colonialism/>

74 Eugene Rabkin, 'Op-Ed. Sex Doesn't Sell. Voyeurism Does', *Business of Fashion* (2021): <https://www.businessoffashion.com/opinions/marketing-pr/op-ed-sex-doesnt-sell-voyeurism-does/>

75 Kati Chitrakorn, 'Award-winner Nensi Dojaka on her future in the fashion business', *Vogue* (2021): <https://www.voguebusiness.com/fashion/award-winner-nensi-dojaka-on-her-future-in-the-fashion-business>

76 Tim Blanks, 'London's Creativity Lights Up Dark Times', *Business of Fashion* (2021): <https://www.businessoffashion.com/opinions/fashion-week/londons-creativity-lights-up-dark-times/>

77 Sarah Mower, 'Christopher Kane Fall 2022 Ready-to-Wear', *Vogue* (2022) <https://www.vogue.com/fashion-shows/fall-2022-ready-to-wear/christopher-kane>

78 Meredith Clark, 'Meghan Markle's Oprah interview outfit named Fashion Museum's dress of the year', *The Independent* (2022): <https://www.independent.co.uk/life-style/oprah-meghan-markle-interview-outfit-b2022604.html>

79 Amy de la Haye and Valerie D Mendes, *Fashion Since 1900* (world of art) (2021), p. 310.

80 Anders Christian Madsen, '"I Want to Embrace Different Proportions": Pierpaolo Piccioli's Body Diverse Valentino SS22 Haute Couture Show', *Vogue* (2022a): <https://www.vogue.co.uk/fashion/article/valentino-haute-couture-ss22>

81 Amrita Mitra, 'Unravelling the Story of the World's Cast-Off Capital', *Slow Fashion Movement* (2021): <https://www.slowfashion.global/blog/34/unravelling-the-story-of-the-worlds-cast-off-capital>

82 Robin Givhan, 'Fashion was broken even before the pandemic. A reboot could be just what it needs', *The Washington Post* (2020): <https://www.washingtonpost.com/lifestyle/style/fashion-retail-business-bankrupt-stores/2020/06/12/463572b0-9c56-11ea-ac72-3841fcc9b35f_story.html>

83 Rosemary Harden, e-mail to author 11 February (2020).

84 Phoebe English, e-mail to author 13 October (2020); likewise, all subsequent citations by English.

85 See Parkins, *Poiret, Dior and Schiaparelli* (2012), p. 33.

86 *Ibid.*, p. 28.

87 Anna Murphy, 'Is this the end of fashion trends?', *The Times* (2020): <https://www.thetimes.co.uk/article/is-this-the-end-of-fashion-trends-c6c2j677q>

88 Talley, *Little Black Dress* (2012), p. 19.

89 Tim Blanks, 'Anthony Vaccarello Reveals Collaboration with Helmut Lang', *Business of Fashion* (2020b): <https://www.businessoffashion.com/articles/luxury/anthony-vaccarello-saint-laurent-helmut-lang-collaboration/>

90 De la Haye and Mendes, *Fashion Since 1900* (2021), p. 308.

91 Arnold, *Fashion, Desire and Anxiety* (2001), p. 124.

92 Reinach, 'Ethnicity' (2021 [2018]), p. 158.

93 Givhan, 'Fashion was broken even before the pandemic' (2020).

BIBLIOGRAPHY

Publications

Anczyk, Adam (2017): 'The Art of Borrowing: Interpreting contemporary Pagans' ritual fashion', in Adam Anczyk and Joanna Malita-Król (eds) (2017): *Walking the Old Ways in a New World: Contemporary Paganism as Lived Religion* (Katowice, Poland: Sacrum Publishing), pp. 183–207.

Arnold, Rebecca (2001): *Fashion, Desire and Anxiety: Image and Morality in the 20th Century* (London: IB Tauris).

Balmain, Pierre (1964): *My Years and Seasons* (London: Cassell).

Banz, Claudia, Cornelia Lund and Beatrace Angut Oola (eds) (2019): *Connecting Afro Futures: Fashion x hair x Design* (Bielefeld: Kerber Verlag).

Baudrillard, Jean (2005): *The System of Objects* (London: Verso).

Beetham, Margaret (1996): *A Magazine of Her Own? Domesticity and Desire in the Woman's Magazine, 1800–1914* (London: Routledge).

Bell, Celeste and Zoë Howe (2019): *Dayglo: The Poly Styrene Story* (London: Omnibus Press).

Boltanski, Luc and Eve Chiapello (2007): *The New Spirit of Capitalism* (London: Verso Books).

Brett-Smith, Sarah C (2014): *The Silence of the Women: Bamana Mud Cloths* (Milan: 5 Continents Editions).

Breward, Christopher (2003): *Fashion* (Oxford History of Art) (Oxford: Oxford University Press).

Breward, Christopher (2016): *The Suit: Form, Function & Style* (London: Reaktion Books).

Breward, Christopher and David Gilbert (eds) (2006): *Fashion's World Cities* (Cultures of Consumption) (Oxford: Berg).

Burnstein, Jessica (2007): 'Material Distinctions: A Conversation with Valerie Steele', in Lauren M E Goodlad and Michael Bibby (eds), *Goth: Undead Subculture* (Durham, NC: Duke University Press Books), pp. 257–76.

Carter, Ernestine (1977): *The Changing World of Fashion, 1900 to the Present* (London: Weidenfeld and Nicolson).

Clark, Hazel and Leena-Maija Rossi (2020): 'Clothes (Un)make the (Wo)man – Ungendering Fashion (2015)?', in Andrew Reilly and Ben Barry (eds), *Crossing gender boundaries: Fashion to Create, Disrupt and Transcend* (Bristol/Chicago: Intellect), pp. 201–18.

Cosgrave, Bronwyn (2012): *Vogue on Coco Chanel* (*Vogue* on Designers) (London: Quadrille Publishing).

Craik, Jennifer (1994): *The Face of Fashion: Cultural Studies in Fashion* (London: Routledge).

De la Haye, Amy and Shelley Tobin (1994): *Chanel: The Couturiere at Work* (London: V&A Publishing).

De la Haye, Amy and Valerie D Mendes (2021): *Fashion Since 1900* (world of art), 3rd edn (London: Thames & Hudson).

Debord, Guy (2014) (trans. Ken Knabb): *The Society of the Spectacle* (Berkeley: Bureau of Public Secrets).

Design Museum Enterprise (2009): *Fifty Dresses that Changed the World: Design Museum Fifty* (London: Conran).

Dior, Christian (trans. Antonia Fraser) (2007 [1956]): *Dior by Dior: The Autobiography of Christian Dior* (London: V&A Publishing).

Dior, Christian (2008 [1954]): *The Little Dictionary of Fashion: A Guide to Dress Sense for Every Woman* (V&A Publishing).

Edelman, Amy Holman (1998): *The Little Black Dress* (London: Aurum).

Elkin, Lauren (2016): *Flâneuse: Women Walk the City in Paris, New York, Tokyo, Venice and London* (London: Chatto & Windus).

Erlich, Howard J (ed.) (1996): *Reinventing Anarchy, Again* (Edinburgh/San Francisco: AK Press).

Evans, Caroline and Alessandra Vaccari (eds) (2020): *Time in Fashion: Industrial, Antilinear and Uchronic Temporalities* (London: Bloomsbury Visual Arts).

Finnane, Antonia (2008): *Changing Clothes in China: Fashion, History, Nation* (London: C Hurst & Co.).

Fogarty, Anne (2011 [1959]). *Wife Dressing: The Art of Being a Well-Dressed Wife* (London: V&A Publishing).

Fox, Chloe (2018): *Vogue Essentials: Little Black Dress* (London: Conran Octopus).

Fraser, Kennedy (1985): *The Fashionable Mind: Reflections on Fashion 1970–1983* (Boston, MA: Nonpareil).

Friedan, Betty (2013 [1963]): *The Feminine Mystique*, Norton Critical Edition (New York: W W Norton & Co., Inc).

Fukai, Akiko (ed.) (2004): *Fashion in Colors: Viktor & Rolf & KCI* ('Viktor & Rolf: Self Portrait') (Kyoto: The Kyoto Costume Institute).

Fukai, Akiko (2010): 'Future Beauty 30 Years of Japanese Fashion', in Catherine Ince and Rie Nii (eds), *Future Beauty: 30 Years of Japanese Fashion* (London: Barbican Centre and Merrell Publishers Ltd).

Gamman, Lorraine and Merja Makinen (1994): *Female Fetishism: A new look* (London: Lawrence and Wishart).

Garfield, Simon (2011): *Mauve: How one man invented a colour that changed the world* (London: Faber & Faber).

Glenn, Susan A (2000): *Female Spectacle: The Theatrical Roots of Modern Feminism* (Cambridge, MA: Harvard Univ. Press).

Gorman, Paul (2001): *The Look: Adventures in Pop & Rock Fashion* (London: Sanctuary Publishing).

Harvey, John (2014): *Kuro no bunkashi* (trans. Yomi Tomioka, Tokyo: Toyoshorin), originally published as *The Story of Black* (2013) (London: Reaktion Books).

Haslam, Dave (2015): *Life After Dark: A History of British Nightclubs and Music Venues* (London: Simon & Schuster).

Hollander, Anne (2016 [1994]): *Sex & Suits: The Evolution of Modern Dress* (London: Bloomsbury Academic).

Howell, Georgina (1977 [1975: Allen Lane]): *In Vogue: Six Decades of Fashion* (London: Condé Nast Publications).

Hume, Lynne (2013): *The Religious Life of Dress: Global Fashion and Faith* (Dress, Body, Culture) (London/New York: Bloomsbury Academic).

Hume, Lynne and Nevill Drury (2013): *The Varieties of Magical Experience: Indigenous, Medieval, and Modern Magic* (Santa Barbara, CA: Praeger).

Huysmans, J K (2004 [1880]) (trans. Brendan King): *Parisian Sketches* (London: Dedalus).

Jarman, Derek (1995): 'Black Arts: O Mia Anima Nera', *Chroma: A Book of Colour – June '93* (London: Vintage Classics).

Jennings, Helen (2011): *New African Fashion* (London/Munich: Prestel).

Kaiser, Susan B (2019 [2011, Berg]): *Fashion and Cultural Studies* (London: Bloomsbury Visual Arts).

Keenan, W J F (2000): 'Clothed with Authority: The Rationalization of Marist Dress Culture', in Linda B Arthur (ed.), *Undressing Religion: Commitment and Conversion from a Cross-Cultural Perspective* (Oxford: Berg), pp. 83–100.

Kondo, Dorinne (1997): *About Face: Performing Race in Fashion and Theater* (New York: Routledge).

Kuchta, David (2002): *The Three-Piece Suit and Modern Masculinity: England, 1550–1850* (University of California Press).

Kuhns, Elizabeth (2003): *The Habit: A History of the Clothing of Catholic Nuns* (New York: Doubleday).

Lister, Jenny (2019): *Mary Quant* (London: V&A Publishing).

Lockman, Zachary (2004): *Contending Visions of the Middle East: The History and Politics of Orientalism* (Cambridge: Cambridge University Press).

Luke, Michael (1991): *David Tennant and the Gargoyle Years* (London: Weidenfeld & Nicolson).

Maeda, Ujo (1980): *Mono to ningen no bunka-shi 38 iro some to shikisai* (Tokyo: Hosei University Press).

Marcus, Greil (2011): *Lipstick Traces: A Secret History of the Twentieth Century* (London: Faber & Faber).

Melville, Herman [1851]: *Moby-Dick; or, The Whale* (New York: Harper & Bros): <https://melville.electroniclibrary.org/moby-dick-side-by-side> [accessed 6/3/2021]

Mendes, Valerie (1999): *Black in Fashion* (London: V&A Publishing).

Menkes, Suzy, Olivier Flaviano, Aurélie Samuel et al. (2019) : *Yves Saint Laurent Catwalk: The Complete Haute Couture Collections 1962–2002* (London: Thames & Hudson).

Mercer, Mick (1993): *Gothic Rock: All you ever wanted to know … but were too gormless to ask* (Los Angeles: Cleopatra).

Montgomery, Ann (2008): *Another Me: A Memoir* (iUniverse).

Nicol, Robert (1992): *The Ritual of Death in Colonial South Australia* (Adelaide: Cummins Society).

Niessen, Sandra A, Ann Marie Leshkowich and Carla Jones (eds) (2003): *Re-Orienting Fashion: The Globalization of Asian Dress* (Dress, Body, Culture, vol. 29) (Oxford: Berg).

North, Maurice (1970): *The Outer Fringe of Sex* (London: The Odyssey Press).

Palomo-Lovinski, Noël (2010): *The World's Most Influential Fashion Designers* (London, A&C Black).

Parkins, Ilya (2012): *Poiret, Dior and Schiaparelli: Fashion, Femininity and Modernity* (London: Bloomsbury).

Pastoureau, Michel (2008) (trans. Jody Gladding): *Black: The History of a Color* (Princeton, NJ: Princeton Univ. Press).

Picardie, Justine (2006 [2005]): *My Mother's Wedding Dress: The Life and Afterlife of Clothes* (New York: Bloomsbury).

Polhemus, Ted and Lynn Procter (1978): *Fashion and Anti-Fashion: An Anthropology of Clothing and Adornment* (London: Thames & Hudson).

Polhemus, Ted and Lynn Procter (1984): *Pop Styles* (London: Vermillion).

Proll, Astrid (ed.) (2010): *Goodbye to London: Radical Art and Politics in the 70's* (Ostfilfern: Hatje Cantz).

Quant, Mary (1984): *Colour by Quant* (Worthing: Littlehampton Book Services).

Raynor, Stephane (2018): *All About the Boy* (London: Carpet Bombing Culture).

Reinach, Simona Segre (2021 [2018]): 'Ethnicity', in Alexandra Palmer (ed.), *A Cultural History of Dress and Fashion in the Modern Age* (London/NY: Bloomsbury Academic), pp. 151–70.

Ribeiro, Aileen (2003 [1986]): *Dress and Morality* (Oxford: Berg).

Ross, Josephine (1992): *Society in Vogue: The International Set between the Wars* (London: Condé Nast Publications).

Rovine, Victoria L (2008): *Bogolan: Shaping Culture through Cloth in Contemporary Mali* (Bloomington: Indiana University Press).

Saint Laurent, Yves and Diana Vreeland (1984): *Yves Saint Laurent* (London: Thames and Hudson).

Savignon, Jéromine, Gilles de Bure with Pierre Bergé (foreword) (2012): *Saint Laurent Rive Gauche: Fashion Revolution* (New York: Abrams).

Schiaparelli, Elsa (2018 [1954]): *Shocking Life: The Autobiography of Elsa Schiaparelli* (London: V&A Publishing).

Secrest, Meryle (2014): *Elsa Schiaparelli* (New York: Knopf).

Silverman, Eric (2013): *A Cultural History of Jewish Dress* (Dress, Body, Culture) (London/NY: Bloomsbury Academic).

Selzer, Michael (1979): *Terrorist Chic: An Exploration of Violence in the Seventies* (New York: Hawthorn Books).

Steele, Valerie (1985): *Fashion and Eroticism: Ideals of Feminine Beauty from the Victorian Era to the Jazz Age* (New York: Oxford University Press Inc.).

Steele, Valerie (1991): *Women of Fashion: Twentieth Century Designers* (New York: Rizzoli International Publications).

Steele, Valerie (1992): 'Chanel in Context', in Juliet Ash and Elizabeth Wilson (eds): *Chic Thrills: A Fashion Reader* (London: Pandora).

Steele, Valerie (1995): *Fetish: Fashion, Sex & Power* (New York: Oxford University Press Inc.).

Steele, Valerie (2001): *The Red Dress* (New York: Rizzoli International Publications).

Steele, Valerie (ed.) (2005): *Encyclopaedia of Clothing and Fashion*, vol. 1 (Detroit: Thomson Gale).

Steele, Valerie (2007): *The Black Dress* (NY: Harper Design).

Steele, Valerie (2017 [1998]): *Paris Fashion: A Cultural History*, rev. edn (London: Bloomsbury Visual Arts).

Steele, Valerie and Jennifer Park (eds) (2008): *Gothic: Dark Glamour* (New Haven: Yale University Press).

Stemp, Sinty (2007): *Jean Muir: Beyond Fashion* (Suffolk: Antique Collectors Club Art Books).

Strong, Roy (1988): *Cecil Beaton: The Royal Portraits* (London: Thames & Hudson).

Sy, Hady and Beatrice Dupire (eds) (1998): *Yves Saint Laurent, 40 Years of Creation* (International Festival of Fashion Photography 1998).

Talley, André Leon (2012): *Little Black Dress* (NY: Skira Rizzoli).

Tester, Keith (ed.) (1994): *The Flaneur* (London/NY: Routledge).

Tolstoy, Leo (1999 [1877]) (trans. Louise and Aylmer Maude): *Anna Karenina* (London: Wordsworth Editions).

Troy, Nancy J (2003): *Couture Culture: A Study in Modern Art and Fashion* (Cambridge, MA: MIT Press).

Trunk, Jonny (2010): *Dressing for Pleasure in Rubber, Vinyl & Leather: The Best of AtomAge 1972–1980* (London: Fuel).

Walkowitz, Judith R (2012): *Nights Out: Life in Cosmopolitan London* (London: Yale University Press).

Watson, Linda (1999): *20th Century Fashion: 100 years of style by decade and designer, in association with Vogue* (vol. 1, Fashions 1900–1949) (London: Carlton).

Weiner, Annette B and Jane Schneider (eds) (1989): *Cloth and Human Experience* (Washington: Smithsonian Books).

Wharton, Edith (2008 [1920]): *The Age of Innocence* (London: Vintage Classics).

White, Emily (ed.) (1984): *The Fashion Year, Vol. 2* (London: Zomba Books).

Wilson, Elizabeth: *Adorned in Dreams: Fashion and Modernity* (rev. edn 2009, I B Taurus [1985, Virago Press]).

Wilson, Robert Forrest (1926 [1925]): *Paris on Parade* (Indianapolis: The Bobbs-Merrill Company).

Winterburn, Florence Hull (1914): *Principles of Correct Dress* (New York: Harper & Brothers).

Young, Caroline (2019): *Living with Coco Chanel: The homes & landscapes that shaped the designer* (London: White Lion).

Articles, periodicals, online

Ahmed, Osman (2020): 'What will the fashion industry look like post-Covid 19', *i-D*, 25 September [accessed 26/11/2020]: <https://i-d.vice.com/en_uk/article/z3eaz4/what-will-the-fashion-industry-look-like-post-covid-19>

Ahmed, Osman (2021): 'Marni AW21 appears via a fashion show on Zoom', *i-D*, 5 March [accessed 8/3/2021]: <https://i-d.vice.com/en_uk/article/k7avqm/marni-aw21-appears-via-a-fashion-show-on-zoom>

Allaire, Christian (2019): 'Billy Porter on Why He Wore a Gown, Not a Tuxedo, to the Oscars', *Vogue*, 24 February [accessed 25/2/2020]: <https://www.vogue.com/article/billy-porter-oscars-red-carpet-gown-christian-siriano>

al-Qasimi, Noor (2010): 'Immodest Modesty: Accommodating Dissent and the "Abaya-as-Fashion" in the Arab Gulf States', *Journal of Middle East Women's Studies* 6:1, pp. 46–74 [acc. 24/11/2022]: <https://doi.org/10.2979/MEW.2010.6.1.46>

Anjo, Hissako (2005): 'A Study of the Discourse on the early collection of Comme des Garçons: The distance between the image and position in the contemporary discourse and the recent discourse', *Journal of the Japan Society of Design*, vol. 47, pp. 3–17.

Anon. (1926): 'October 1926/The First *Vogue* introduces Coco Chanel's LBD', *Vogue*, 1 October.

Anon. (1979): *Sounds*, 10 November.

Anon. (1988): 'John Galliano Autumn/Winter 1988', *Evening Standard,* 15 March.

Anon. (2003): 'Autumn Winter 2003 couture: Chanel', *Vogue* [accessed 14/12/2022]: <https://www.vogue.co.uk/shows/autumn-winter-2003-couture/chanel>

Anon. (2015): 'Alexander McQueen: Savage Beauty – About the Exhibition', Victoria and Albert Museum [acc. Jan. 2020]: <http://www.vam.ac.uk/content/exhibitions/exhibition-alexander-mcqueen-savage-beauty/about-the-exhibition/>

Anon. (2019): 'Ying Gao unveils Robotic Clothing that reacts to the Chromatic Spectrum', *Visual Atelier 8* [acc. 17/2/2020]: <https://visualatelier8.com/2019/10/3/ying-gao-robotic-clothing/>

Arai, Toshiki (2018): 'Long Interview with Rei Kawakubo: *Koboreru shiroi tomeina shizuku* [A white transparent spilling drop]', *Switch* 36:6, pp. 30–31.

Augustin, Alice (2017): 'Dark Nights at Paris's La Main Bleue', *Red Bull*, 1 Sept. [acc. 14/2/2020]: <https://daily.redbullmusicacademy.com/2017/09/la-main-bleue-feature>

Bain, Marc (2018): 'Only black is the new black: a cultural history of fashion's favourite shade', *Quartz*, 4 Feb. [acc. 3/1/2020]: <https://qz.com/quartzy/1194798/only-black-is-the-new-black-a-cultural-history-of-fashions-favorite-shade/>

Baker, Lindsay (2015), 'Alexander McQueen: Fashion's dark fairytale', BBC online (2015): <http://www.bbc.com/culture/story/20150313-fashions-dark-fairytale>

Benaïm, Laurence (2005): 'Azzedine Alaïa & Yohji Yamamoto in conversation with Laurence Benaïm', in *A Magazine* #2, p. 47.

Binlot, Ann (2019): 'Yuima Nakazato introduces fermented microbes and digital fabrication to the guarded tradition of haute couture,' in *Document*, 18 July [accessed 17/2/2020]: <https://www.documentjournal.com/2019/07/what-is-biocouture-meet-the-japanese-designer-yuima-nakazato/>

Blanks, Tim (2015): 'Gareth Pugh Fall 2015 Ready-to-Wear', *Vogue*, 21 Feb. [acc. 24/5/2018]: <https://www.vogue.com/fashion-shows/fall-2015-ready-to-wear/gareth-pugh>

Blanks, Tim (2020a): 'Shiny Erotic Definitions at Saint Laurent', *Business of Fashion*, 26 February [accessed 26/2/2020]: <https://www.businessoffashion.com/reviews/fashion-week/shiny-erotic-definitions-at-saint-laurent/>

Blanks, Tim (2020b): 'Anthony Vaccarello Reveals Collaboration with Helmut Lang', *Business of Fashion*, 29 Sept. [acc. 12/12/2021]: <https://www.businessoffashion.com/

articles/luxury/anthony-vaccarello-saint-laurent-helmut-lang-collaboration/>

Blanks, Tim (2021): 'London's Creativity Lights Up Dark Times', *Business of Fashion*, 24 February [accessed 25/2/2021]: <https://www.businessoffashion.com/opinions/fashion-week/londons-creativity-lights-up-dark-times/>

Bowen, Kim (1990): in *BLITZ* magazine, January.

Buck, Joan Juliet (1979): 'Karl Lagerfeld: the private life of a public fantasy', in *Vogue*, 1 August, p. 222.

Chalcraft, Emilie (2013): 'Voltage by Iris van Herpen with Neri Oxman and Julia Koerner', *dezeen*, 22 January [accessed 17/2/2020]: <https://www.dezeen.com/2013/01/22/voltage-3d-printed-clothes-by-iris-van-herpen-with-neri-oxman-and-julia-koerne/>

Charpy, Manuel (2012): 'Craze and Shame: Rubber Clothing during the Nineteenth Century in Paris, London, and New York City', in *Fashion Theory: The Journal of Dress, Body & Culture* 16:4, pp. 433–60.

Chen, Vivian (2017), 'Alexander McQueen brings pagan legends to Paris Fashion Week', *South China Morning Post* online: <https://www.scmp.com/magazines/style/fashion-beauty/article/2077158/alexander-mcqueen-brings-pagan-legends-paris-fashion>

Chitrakorn, Kati (2021): 'Award-winner Nensi Dojaka on her future in the fashion business', *Vogue*, 29 Nov. [acc. 14/1/22]: <https://www.voguebusiness.com/fashion/award-winner-nensi-dojaka-on-her-future-in-the-fashion-business>

Clark, Meredith (2022): 'Meghan Markle's Oprah interview outfit named Fashion Museum's dress of the year', *The Independent*, 24 February [accessed 26/2/2022]: <https://www.independent.co.uk/life-style/oprah-meghan-markle-interview-outfit-b2022604.html>

Coburn, Theresa and Jonathan Melton (2019): 'London calling: subculture in the early 1980s', *Back to the Future: 1979–1989* [accessed 20/2/2020]: <https://digital.nls.uk/1980s/society/london-culture/?fbclid=IwAR3JcPmnVLDrttmGKnutqGEtw7xDK-wTGE4FiTniBxthimJ76vO7E20SAP0>

Cox, Adrienne (2019): 'The Qipao: Defining Modern Women in the First Half of the 20th Century' (University of Kansas: History honors thesis).

CuteCircuit: [accessed 31/3/21] <https://cutecircuit.com/>

Diderot, Denis and Jean le Rond d'Alembert (eds) [1751]: *Encyclopédie, Ou Dictionnaire Raisonné Des Sciences, Des Arts Et Des Métiers*: See <https://artflsrv03.uchicago.edu/philologic4/encyclopedie1117/navigate/16/74/>

De Loisne, Mariejo (1982). 'À l'est, du nouveau', *Gap*, May, pp. 118–19.

Dolan, Timothy Cardinal (2019), 'Heavenly Bodies: Fashion and the Catholic Imagination', comments from the press conference: <http://cardinaldolan.org/index.php/heavenly-bodies-fashion-and-the-catholic-imagination/>

Dorré, Gina Marlene (2002). 'Horses and Corsets: *Black Beauty*, Dress Reform, and the Fashioning of the Victorian Woman', *Victorian Literature and Culture*, vol. 30, no. 1, pp. 157–78.

Ealy, Aaron (2015) 'The Five Most Scandalous Fashion Shows in Recent History', *Paper* (2015) [accessed January 2020]: <https://www.papermag.com/the-5-most-scandalous-fashion-shows-in-recent-history-1427643470.html>

Edwards, Louise (2000): 'Policing the Modern Woman in Republican China', *Modern China* 26:2, pp. 115–47: <https://doi.org/10.1177/009770040002600201>

Entwistle, Joanne (2000): 'Fashion and the Fleshy Body: Dress as Embodied Practice', in *Fashion Theory: The Journal of Dress, Body & Culture* 4:3, pp. 323–47: <https://doi.org/10.2752/136270400778995471>

Evans, Jordan X (2018): 'Black Panther, Black Power, and the Black Nationalist Tradition', *African American Intellectual History Society*, 21 March [accessed 22/2/2020]: <https://www.aaihs.org/the-black-panther-black-power-and-the-black-nationalist-tradition/>

Farra, Emily (2018): 'This Under-the-Radar Designer in the New Met Exhibition Takes "Fashion Nun" to New Heights', *Vogue*, 9 May [acc. Jan. 2020]: <https://www.vogue.com/article/met-gala-2018-exhibit-designer-cimone>

Filip, Marius (2019): 'Wolves Amongst the Sheep: Looking Beyond the Aesthetics of Polish National Socialism', in *The Pomegranate: The International Journal of Pagan Studies* 21:2, pp. 210–36 (Equinox Publishing).

Flaccavento, Angelo (2020): 'At Paris Couture, History Over Hype', *Business of Fashion*, 23 January [acc. 23/1/2020]: <https://www.businessoffashion.com/reviews/fashion-week/at-paris-couture-history-over-hype/>

Givhan, Robin (2018): 'A layman's guide to understanding a fashion week runway show', *The Independent*, 11 February [accessed 14/2/2020]: <https://www.independent.co.uk/life-style/fashion/laymans-guide-understanding-fashion-week-runway-show-thom-browne-spring-summer-2018-giant-unicorn-a8201086.html>

Givhan, Robin (2020): 'Fashion was broken even before the pandemic. A reboot could be just what it needs', *The Washington Post*, 15 June [accessed 16/8/2020]: <https://www.washingtonpost.com/lifestyle/style/fashion-retail-business-bankrupt-stores/2020/06/12/463572b0-9c56-11ea-ac72-3841fcc9b35f_story.html>

Graham, Mhairi (2015): 'Iris Van Herpen: fashion's hi-tech priestess', *Dazed*, 5 June [accessed 11/10/2019]: <https://www.dazeddigital.com/fashion/article/24899/1/iris-van-herpen-fashion-s-hi-tech-priestess>

Henry King, Lorraine (2021), 'Black skin as costume in *Black Panther*', *Film, Fashion and Consumption* 10:1, 1 April, pp. 265–76: <https://doi.org/10.1386/ffc_00024_3>

Heroldová, Helena (2014): 'Allure of the Body: Chinese Qipao', *Annals of the Náprstek Museum* 35:1, pp. 23–38.

Hollander, Anne (1984): 'The Little Black Dress', December, published online [accessed 10/1/2020]: <http://www.anne-hollander.com/wp-content/uploads/2015/02/The-Little-Black-Dress-Connoisseur-1984.pdf>

Horwell, Veronica (2017): 'Azzedine Alaïa obituary', *The Guardian*, 20 November.

Horyn, Cathy (2021): 'At New York Fashion Week, Sex Is On Everyone's Minds', 11 September [accessed 14/1/2020]:

<https://www.thecut.com/2021/09/cathy-horyn-nyfw-spring-2022-review-eckhaus-latta.html>

Hume, Lynne (2019): 'Religious Dress', in *The International Encyclopedia of Anthropology* (Wiley Online Library: John Wiley & Sons) [entry: wbiea2406].

Jones, Jonathan (2006): 'Madame XXX', *The Guardian*, 1 Feb. [accessed 29/1/2020]: <https://www.theguardian.com/culture/2006/feb/01/3>

Kambasha, Michelle (2021): 'Colourism still bolsters anti-blackness in pop culture', *Indie*, 23 Feb. [acc. 30/3/2021]: <https://indie-mag.com/2021/02/colourism-pop-culture/>

Kane, Daniel (2011): 'Richard Hell, *Genesis: Grasp* and the Blank Generation: From Poetry to Punk in New York's Lower East Side', *Contemporary Literature* 52:2, pp. 330–69.

Kansara, Vikram Alexei (2021): 'From West to East: Recentering the Fashion World', *Business of Fashion*, 19 Feb. [acc. 14/1/2022]: <https://www.businessoffashion.com/briefings/retail/from-west-to-east-recentering-the-fashion-world/>

Kia, Kara (2020): 'Lace or Latex? London Fashion Week's 2 Biggest Trends Couldn't Be More Polarising', *Popsugar*, 24 February [acc. 10/3/2020]: <https://www.popsugar.co.uk/fashion/london-fashion-week-autumn-winter-2020-trends-47246582>

Leach, Alec (2020): 'Fashion week as we know it is dead. Or is it?', *i-D*, 18 August [acc. 20/8/2020]: <https://i-d.vice.com/en_uk/article/bv83qa/fashion-week-as-we-know-it-is-dead-or-is-it>

Leitch, Luke (2020): 'The end of modernity: what will fashion look like after the pandemic?', *The Economist*, 24 July [acc. 14/1/2022]: <https://www.economist.com/1843/2020/07/24/the-end-of-modernity>

McCormack, Fiona (2013): 'Apple's iPhone Marketing Strategy Exposed', *Business 2 Community* (2013): <https://www.business2community.com/marketing/apples-iphone-marketing-strategy-exposed-0661613>

Madsen, Anders Christian (2018): 'Christopher Kane Autumn/Winter 2018 Ready-to-Wear', *Vogue*, 19 Feb. [accessed 24/5/2018]: <http://www.vogue.co.uk/shows/autumn-winter-2018-ready-to-wear/christopher-kane>

Madsen, Anders Christian (2021): 'Christian Dior Fall 2021 Ready-to-Wear', *Vogue*, 8 March [accessed 21/5/2021]: <https://www.vogue.com/fashion-shows/fall-2021-ready-to-wear/christian-dior>

Madsen, Anders Christian (2022a): '"I Want to Embrace Different Proportions": Pierpaolo Piccioli's Body Diverse Valentino SS22 Haute Couture Show', *Vogue*, 26 January [accessed 26/1/2022]: <https://www.vogue.co.uk/fashion/article/valentino-haute-couture-ss22>

Madsen, Anders Christian (2022b): 'Raf Simons Spring 2022 Ready-to-Wear', *Vogue*, 30 Sept. [accessed 14/1/2022]: <https://www.vogue.com/fashion-shows/spring-2022-ready-to-wear/raf-simons>

Madsen, Anders Christian (2022c): 'Valentino Spring 2022 Couture', *Vogue*, 26 January [accessed 26/1/2022]: <https://www.vogue.com/fashion-shows/spring-2022-couture/valentino>

Marriott, Daniel (2012): 'Extremist Symbolism in Fashion – A Cultural Statement or Unacceptable? You Decide …', in *Huffington Post*, 2 October [accessed 20/2/2020]: <https://www.huffingtonpost.co.uk/daniel-marriott/extremist-symbolism-in-fashion_b_1930025.html>

Martin, Richard (1998): 'A Note: Gianni Versace's Anti-Bourgeois Little Black Dress (1994)', in *Fashion Theory: The Journal of Dress, Body & Culture* 2:1, pp. 95–100.

Meisenzahl, Mary (2019): 'The iPhone is available in 6 colours, including purple for the first time ever – here's how to decide', *Business Insider* [accessed 13/2/2020]: <https://www.businessinsider.com/apple-iphone-11-colors-purple-green-yellow-white-black-red-2019-9>

Menkes, Suzy (2013): 'The Colourful History of the Little Black Dress', *The New York Times*, 5 August [accessed 1/3/2020]: <https://www.nytimes.com/2013/08/06/fashion/06iht-fblack06.html>

Mitra, Amrita (2021): 'Unravelling the Story of the World's Cast-Off Capital', *Slow Fashion Movement*, 14 June [acc. 14/1/2022]: <https://www.slowfashion.global/blog/34/unravelling-the-story-of-the-worlds-cast-off-capital>

Miyachi, Izumi and Hiroyuki Kikuchi (1999): '20 seiki donna jidai dattaka, pari mōdo heno chōsen', *Yomiuri Shinbun*, 23 August, p. 11.

Mower, Sarah (2002): 'Saint Laurent Fall 2002 Ready-to-Wear', *Vogue*, 10 March [acc. 31/1/20]: <https://www.vogue.com/fashion-shows/fall-2002-ready-to-wear/saint-laurent>

Mower, Sarah (2008): 'Prada Spring 2009 Ready-to-Wear', *Vogue*, 22 Sept. [acc. 24/5/2018]: <https://www.vogue.com/fashion-shows/spring-2009-ready-to-wear/prada>

Mower, Sarah (2017): 'Alexander McQueen Fall 2017 Ready-to-Wear', *Vogue*, 6 March [accessed January 2020]: <https://www.vogue.com/fashion-shows/fall-2017-ready-to-wear/alexander-mcqueen>

Mower, Sarah (2022): 'Christopher Kane Fall 2022 Ready-to-Wear', *Vogue*, 21 February [accessed 21/2/2022]: <https://www.vogue.com/fashion-shows/fall-2022-ready-to-wear/christopher-kane>

Mull, Amanda (2020): 'Fashion's Racism and Classicism Are Finally Out of Style', *The Atlantic*, 7 July [acc. 13/1/2021]: <https://www.theatlantic.com/health/archive/2020/07/fashions-racism-and-classism-are-going-out-style/613906/>

Murphy, Anna (2020): 'Is this the end of fashion trends?', *The Times*, 5 Sept. [acc. 26/9/20]: <https://www.thetimes.co.uk/article/is-this-the-end-of-fashion-trends-c6c2j677q>

Nakazato, Yuima, 'Brand Philosophy', n.d. [acc. 17/2/2020]: <http://www.yuimanakazato.com/about.html>

Nervous System: <https://n-e-r-v-o-u-s.com/kinematicsCloth/>

Okwodu, Janelle (2021): 'Kim Kardashian's Met Gala Look Rewrote the Red Carpet's Rules', *Vogue*, 13 September [accessed 13/9/2021]: <https://www.vogue.com/article/kim-kardashian-balenciaga-met-gala-2021-look>

Ouchi, Junko (1983): '1983 Spring-Summer Paris Collection', in *Katei gaho*, p. 129.

Passadori, Paolo (2020): 'The streetwear trademark "BOY

London" declared invalid …', *Lexology*, 4 March [accessed 17/8/2020]: <https://www.lexology.com/library/detail.aspx?g=55e4343c-bb1f-46dd-b746-7c3a481dd614>

Phelps, Nicole (2018): 'Marc Jacobs Fall 2018 Ready-to-Wear', 14 February [accessed 24/5/18]: <https://www.vogue.com/fashion-shows/fall-2018-ready-to-wear/marc-jacobs>

Picardie, Justine (2005); 'The darkness', *The Observer: Fashion*, 28 Aug. [acc. 15/3/2021]: <https://www.the guardian.com/lifeandstyle/2005/aug/28/fashion.shopping1>

Provo, Leah M (2013): 'The Little Black Dress: The Essence of Femininity' (Univ. of Cincinnati: Master of Design thesis).

Quick, Harriet (2020): 'Why Black Is Back On The Style Agenda As AW20's Most Faultless and Seductive Shade', *Vogue*, 7 Nov. [acc. 12/12/2021]: <https://www.vogue.co.uk/fashion/article/ode-to-black>

Rabkin, Eugene (2021): 'Op-Ed: Sex Doesn't Sell. Voyeurism Does', *Business of Fashion*, 21 December [acc. 21/12/2021]: <https://www.businessoffashion.com/opinions/marketing-pr/op-ed-sex-doesnt-sell-voyeurism-does/>

Radin, Sara (2019): 'How Colour in Fashion Has Been Used Throughout History to Display Political Solidarity', 14 May, *Teen Vogue* [acc. 30/9/2020]: <https://www.teenvogue.com/story/color-fashion-history-political-solidarity>

Roberts, Mary Louise (1993): 'Samson and Delilah Revisited: The Politics of Women's Fashion in 1920s France', *The American Historical Review* 98:3, pp. 657–84.

Rodgers, Charlotte (2019): 'High Glamour: Magical Clothing and Talismanic Fashion', in *The Pomegranate: The International Journal of Pagan Studies* 21:2, pp. 172–85 (Equinox Publishing).

Rovine, Victoria L (2009): 'Viewing Africa through Fashion', in *Fashion Theory: The Journal of Dress, Body & Culture* 13:2, pp. 133–39.

Ryzik, Melena (2018): 'The Afrofuturistic Designs of "Black Panther"', *The New York Times*, 23 Feb. [acc. 20/2/2020]: <https://www.nytimes.com/2018/02/23/movies/black-panther-afrofuturism-costumes-ruth-carter.html>

Sainderichin, Ginette (1982): 'Le bonze et la kamikaze', *Jardin des Modes*, December 1982, p. 5.

Samet, Janie (1982): '6 jours de mode, 36 collections 4500 modèles', *Le Figaro*, 21 October, p. 2.

Sherman, Lauren (2022): 'What Happened to Fashion's Dream Factory', *Business of Fashion*, 28 January [acc. 28/1/2022]: <https://www.businessoffashion.com/briefings/luxury/what-happened-to-fashions-dream-factory/>

Shimek, Elizabeth D (2012): 'The Abaya: Fashion, Religion, and Identity in a Globalized World', *Lawrence University Honors Projects* 12: <https://lux.lawrence.edu/luhp/12>

Spencer, Hayley (2021): 'Dressing after times of crisis: What can we learn about post-pandemic fashion from the 1920s', *The Independent*, 19 March [acc. 1/5/2021]: <https://www. independent.co.uk/life-style/fashion/pandemic-fashion-roaring-twenties-trends-b1819559.html>

Tewari, Bandana (2020): 'Op-Ed. How Fashion Perpetuates Modern-Day Colonialism', *Business of Fashion*, 21 May [acc. 22/5/2020]: <https://www.businessoffashion.com/opinions/global-markets/op-ed-how-fashion-perpetuates-modern-day-colonialism/>

Thomas, Dana (2002): 'The Epoch of *A-POC*', *Newsweek*, 7 July. *Times, The*: 15 March 1993.

Tokiotours (2013): 'Viktor & Rolf designed a "living" Zen rock garden, inspired by Kyoto's Ryoanji temple' [acc. 12/1/2020]: <https://tokiotours.wordpress.com/2013/07/06/viktor-rolf-designed-a-living-zen-rock-garden-inspired-by-kyotos-ryoanji-temple/>

Tulloch, Carol (2010): 'Style–Fashion–Dress: From Black to Post-Black', in *Fashion Theory: The Journal of Dress, Body & Culture* 14:3, pp. 273–305.

Vail, H W (2018): 'Inside the Met's "Heavenly Bodies" Exhibit', *Vanity Fair* online, 7 May: <https://www.vanityfair.com/style/2018/05/met-exhibit-heavenly-bodies>

Van Herpen, Iris (2013): 'Voltage' [accessed 13/2/2020]: <https://www.irisvanherpen.com/haute-couture/voltage>

Voight, Rebecca (1983): 'East Meets West in Paris', in *Passion*, March, pp. 24–25.

Watson, Linda (2004): 'Geoffrey Beene: Godfather of minimalism in modern American fashion design', *The Independent*, 30 September.

Wolfe, Tom (1970): 'Radical Chic: That Party at Lenny's', *New York Magazine*, 8 June, pp. 26–56.

Yamada, Mio (2013): 'The future of fabrics woven with the past,' *The Japan Times*, 21 Feb. <https://www.japantimes.co.jp/culture/2013/02/21/arts/the-future-of-fabrics-woven-with-the-past/#.XkwVRtL7QdU24>

Selected films, television

Clisby, Ted (dir.) (1979): *Who is Poly Styrene?* (UK: BBC Arena).

Coogler, Ryan (dir.) (2018): *Black Panther* (USA: Marvel Studios).

Cutler, R J (dir.) (2009): *The September Issue* (USA: A+E Networks).

Edwards, Blake (dir.) (1961): *Breakfast at Tiffany's* (USA: Paramount Pictures Corporation).

Kershner, Irvin (dir.) (1978): *Eyes of Laura Mars* (USA: Columbia Pictures).

Kleiser, Randal (dir.) (1978): *Grease* (USA: Paramount Pictures Corporation/Actual Reality Pictures).

Lee, Spike (dir.) (1992): *Malcolm X* (USA: 40 Acres and a Mule Filmworks).

Morgan, Peter (2016–): *The Crown* (UK: Left Bank Pictures and Sony Pictures Television for Netflix).

Nichols, Mike (dir.) (1988): *Working Girl* (USA: Twentieth Century Fox).

Seidelman, Susan (dir.) 1985. *Desperately Seeking Susan* (USA: Orion Pictures).

Westwood, Vivienne (2012): 'Seditionaries. 430 King's Road', interview with Janet Street-Porter, 18 December [accessed 14/2/2020]: <https://www.youtube.com/watch?v=rp8M-fley0s>

ACKNOWLEDGEMENTS

This book and forthcoming exhibition have been made possible by the support of many. I am grateful to all the curators, conservators, exhibition & design colleagues, critical friends, photographers, exhibition lenders, fashion designers, industry practitioners, picture library and publishing staff, collections services and administrative colleagues involved in bringing the project to life.

Special thanks go to the contributors to the book: Lynne Hume, Iain R Webb, Makoto Ishizeki, Fiona Jardine and Pamela Parmal. I am greatly indebted to them for lending their expertise. I am especially grateful to project Assistant Curator, Carys Wilkins, whose exemplary research skills and expertise have been invaluable in developing the exhibition and publication. Likewise, I am indebted to Emily Taylor and Claire Blakey for assistance with editing the book's essays; and to Qin Cao, Margaret Maitland, Sally Tuckett and Sarah Worden for helping to shape the final chapter.

Thanks also go to Lisa Mason and Clare Hyatt for looking over early drafts, as well as to my wider Art & Design department colleagues for their continuing support, enthusiasm for, and patience with this project. Christopher Breward, Hamish Bowles, Sinéad Burke, Mal Burkinshaw, Chris Hunt and Iain R Webb have all helped generously along the way with their deep knowledge of fashion. I am especially grateful to Phoebe English and Carli Pearson for providing the designer's insight into the LBD; and to Vin + Omi, who created a bespoke black dress incorporating naturally dyed, waste nettles for our original exhibition planned for 2020.

Sincerest thanks also go to each of our lenders to the forthcoming exhibition, institutional and private, who have been exceptionally accommodating as the project timeline shifted in accordance with the restrictions of the Covid-19 pandemic. Colleagues in museums in the UK and internationally have helped generously with research, especially Rosemary Harden of Fashion Museum, Bath, and Miles Lambert of Manchester City Galleries.

Georgina Ripley

Author information

Lynne Hume is Associate Professor and Honorary Research Consultant at The University of Queensland. As an anthropologist, her interests include a diversity of topics: religion, alternative spiritualities, aboriginal cultures, consciousness studies, sensorial anthropology, and anthropology of dress and bodily adornment. She has had eight books published, book chapters in edited collections, academic journal articles and encyclopaedia entries. <https://uq.academia.edu/LynneHume>

Makoto Ishizeki is Curator at The Kyoto Costume Institute, specialising in contemporary as well as men's fashion. He has participated in curating several fashion exhibitions including *Fashion in Colors* in 2004, *Luxury in Fashion* in 2009 and *Future Beauty* in 2010–14, and co-curated the exhibition *Dress Code: Are You Playing Fashion?* in 2019–2020, which travelled to the Bundeskunsthalle, Bonn, in 2021.

Dr Fiona Jardine taught Critical and Contextual Studies in the School of Textiles and Design, Heriot-Watt University 2013–17, and now teaches Design History & Theory at The Glasgow School of Art. Her research focuses on contemporary and 20th-century Scottish art, design and culture, particularly on narratives of production and promotion in the fashion and textile industries. For several years, she has studied Muriel Spark's life in dress through archival, biographical and fictional sources. From 2017–20 she was a Trustee of the Bernat Klein Foundation and currently serves on the Arts & Heritage Committee at House for an Art Lover.

Pamela A Parmal was formerly Chair, and David and Roberta Logie Curator, of Textile and Fashion Arts at the Museum of Fine Arts, Boston, where she oversaw an encyclopaedic collection of textiles and dress. Given the global nature of the Boston museum's collection, her work has focused on technique, which crosses all boundaries, as well as the global interchange of technology and design. She has curated and co-curated exhibitions including *Fashion Show: Paris Collections 2006* in 2007, *Embroideries of Colonial Boston* (2010), and *#techstyle* (2016); her most recent work explored the role of dress in the portraits of John Singer Sargent for a show that was co-organised by the MFA, Boston and Tate Britain.

Georgina Ripley is Principal Curator of Modern & Contemporary Design at National Museums Scotland, where she is primarily responsible for the fashion and textile collections from 1850 to the present day. She has curated exhibitions including the forthcoming one to accompany this publication, and *Body Beautiful: Diversity on the Catwalk* (NMS 2023; NMS 2019, on tour until Dec. 2022), and was Lead Curator for the Museum's permanent Fashion & Style gallery (opened 2016). Most recent publications have focused on representations of intersectional masculinities in contemporary menswear and image-making; she is also conducting ongoing research into British fashion designer Jean Muir (fl.1962–1995), whose archive forms part of the National Museums Scotland's collection.

Iain R Webb is a writer, curator and academic. He is Professor of Fashion & Design at Kingston School of Art and associate lecturer at Central Saint Martins and Bath Spa University. During his career he has been fashion editor of *BLITZ*, the *Evening Standard, Harpers & Queen, The Times* and *Elle*. He is author of several titles, including *Bill Gibb – Fashion and Fantasy*; *Postcards From the Edge of the Catwalk*; *As Seen in BLITZ – Fashioning '80s Style*; *Vogue Colouring Book*; *John Galliano for Dior* and *Rebel Stylist*. Previous curatorial projects include exhibitions at ICA, RCA, Somerset House, Holburne Museum, Bowes Museum and Fashion Museum, Bath. Latest projects include *Colouring Fashion*, a colouring zine celebrating creativity and difference, produced in association with Graduate Fashion Foundation and the Fashion Minority Alliance, and *Drawing Fashion: sketchbooks from the edge of the catwalk*, an exhibition of his fashion show sketch books spanning four decades, at Drawing Projects UK (June–August 2022), and *The Fashion Show* at V&A Dundee (June 2023–January 2024). <Instagram: hopeandglitter>

Text acknowledgements

Every attempt has been made to ensure the copyright ownership of all text in this publication has been cleared. If any sources have been inadvertently missed, please advise the Publisher. Thanks are due for permission to reproduce extracts from the following sources:

Barbican Centre/Merrell Publishers Ltd

Ince, Catherine and Rie Nii (eds) (2010), *Future Beauty: 30 Years of Japanese Fashion.*

Bloomsbury Publishing Plc

Rebecca Arnold (2001), *Fashion, Desire and Anxiety: Image and Morality in the 20th Century.*
Elizabeth Wilson (revised edition 2009 [1985, Virago]), *Adorned in Dreams: Fashion and Modernity.*
(I B Tauris, an imprint of Bloomsbury Publishing Plc)

Anne Hollander (2016 [1994]), *Sex & Suits: The Evolution of Modern Dress.*
Susan B Kaiser (2019 [2011, Berg]), *Fashion and Cultural Studies.*
Alexandra Palmer (ed.) (2021 [2018]), *A Cultural History of Dress and Fashion in the Modern Age.*
Ilya Parkins (2012), *Poiret, Dior and Schiaparelli: Fashion, Femininity and Modernity.*
Eric Silverman (2013), *A Cultural History of Jewish Dress.*
(Bloomsbury Academic, an imprint of Bloomsbury Publishing Plc)

Noël Palomo-Lovinski (2010), *The World's Most Influential Fashion Designers.*
(A & C Black, an imprint of Bloomsbury Publishing Plc)

Aileen Ribeiro (2003 [1986]), *Dress and Morality.*
(Berg Publishers, an imprint of Bloomsbury Publishing Plc)

Lawrence and Wishart Limited

Lorraine Gamman and Merja Makinen (1994), *Female Fetishism: A new look*
(By permission of Lawrence and Wishart Limited. Reproduced with permission of the Licensor through PLSclear.)

Octopus Publishing Group

Design Museum (2009), *Fifty Dresses that Changed the World: Design Museum Fifty*.

Chloe Fox (2018), *Vogue Essentials: Little Black Dress* (Reproduced by permission of Octopus Publishing Group Limited)

Orion Publishing Group

Michael Luke (1991), *David Tennant and the Gargoyle*. (By permission of Orion Publishing Group. Reproduced with permission of the Licensor through PLSclear)

Penguin Random House

Georgina Howell: *In Vogue: Six Decades of Fashion* (© 1977 Condé Nast Publications Limited. Reprinted by permission of Penguin Books Limited)

Josephine Ross (1992): *Society In Vogue: The International Set between the Wars* (London: Condé Nast Publications Ltd)

Taylor & Francis Group

Richard Martin (1998): 'A Note: Gianni Versace's Anti-Bourgeois Little Black Dress' (1994), in *Fashion Theory* 2:1, pp. 95–100.

Carol Tulloch (2010): 'Style—Fashion—Dress: From Black to Post-Black', in *Fashion Theory* 14:3, 273–303. (Reprinted by permission of Taylor & Francis Ltd, <http://www.tandfonline.com>)

Jennifer Craik (1994): *The Face of Fashion: Cultural Studies in Fashion*, by permission of Informa UK Ltd.

Dorinne Kondo (1997), *About Face: Performing Race in Fashion and Theater,* by permission of Taylor and Francis Group LLC (Books) US. (Reproduced with permission of the Licensor through PLSclear)

Thames & Hudson Ltd

Fashion Since 1900, by Amy de la Haye and Valerie D Mendes © 1999, 2010 and 2021. (Reprinted by kind permission of Thames & Hudson Ltd, London)

Twentieth Century Fox

'WORKING GIRL' © 1988 written by Kevin Ward. Twentieth Century Fox. All rights reserved.

Individuals and organisations

The publisher would like to thank the following individuals and organisations who kindly granted reproduction rights:

Lucinda Alford, Antique Collectors Club, Hamish Bowles, Mal Burkinshaw, Carpet Bombing Culture, Jasper Conran, Fiona Dealey, Dominico Dolce, Phoebe English, Stefan Gabbana, John Galliano, Robin Givhan, Rosemary Harden, Hatje Cantz, Lorraine Henry King, The Kyoto Costume Institute, Harry Leuckert, Greil Marcus, Jonny Melton, Jean Muir, Omnibus Press, Carli Pearson, Penguin Random House, Mary Quant, Quarto, Reaktion Books, Jil Sander, Simon & Schuster, Valerie Steele, Philip Treacy, V&A Publishing, Linda Watson, Wellbeck Publishing, Wellesley College

With additional thanks to:

5 Continents Editions, Adam Anczyk, African American Intellectual History Society, AK Press, *The American Historical Review*, *Annals of the Náprstek Museum*, *BLITZ* magazine, Sarah Burton, *Business of Fashion* online, Collins Design, Condé Nast Publications, *Contemporary Magazine*, Adrienne Cox, Annette Day, Timothy Cardinal Dolan, *Evening Standard*, *Le Figaro*, John Paul Gaultier, *The Guardian* online, Harvard University Press, Anne Hollander, *i-D* online, *The Independent* online, Indiana University Press, International Festival of Fashion Photography, Stephen Jones, Lawrence University Honors Projects, Alexander McQueen, Metropolitan Museum of Art, *Modern China* online, Ann Montgomery, Yuima Nakazato, *The New York Times* online, *Newsweek*, Oxford University Press, Pierpaolo Piccioli, Ted Polhemus, *The Pomegranate* online, Billy Porter, Princeton University Press, Lynn Procter, *Quartz* online, Rizzoli New York, Sanctuary Publishing, *Switch* magazine, Poly Styrene, Diana Taylor, *Teen Vogue* online, *The Times* online, Tokiotours online, *Visual Atelier* online, *Vogue* online, *The Washington Post* online, Vivienne Westwood, Anna Wintour, W W Norton & Co. Inc, Yohji Yamamoto

INDEX